Dr. Z

Dr. Z

The Lost Memoirs of an
Irreverent Football Writer

Paul Zimmerman

TRIUMPH
BOOKS

Library of Congress Cataloging-in-Publication Data

Names: Zimmerman, Paul.
Title: Dr. Z : the lost memoirs of an irreverent football writer / Paul
    Zimmerman.
Description: Chicago, Illinois : Triumph Books, 2017.
Identifiers: LCCN 2017009840 | ISBN 9781629374642 (hardback)
Subjects: LCSH: Sportswriters—United States—Biography. | Football—
United States. | BISAC: SPORTS & RECREATION / Football. |
BIOGRAPHY & AUTOBIOGRAPHY / Sports.
Classification: LCC GV742.42.Z56 A3 2017 | DDC 070.4/49796092 [B] —
dc23 LC record available at https://lccn.loc.gov/2017009840

This book is available in quantity at special discounts for your group or organization. For further information, contact:

Triumph Books LLC
814 North Franklin Street
Chicago, Illinois 60610
(312) 337-0747
www.triumphbooks.com

Printed in U.S.A.
ISBN: 978-1-62937-464-2
Design by Patricia Frey

Contents

Foreword

My first encounter with Paul Zimmerman (I don't think he was in the "Dr. Z" realm then) happened in my first week as a pro football writer. This was in May 1984, after the NFL draft, when I was writing for the *Cincinnati Enquirer*, and the Bengals had three picks in the first round of the draft. Pretty good haul, everyone thought. The Bengals had turned the first pick in the draft that year into a linebacker (Ricky Hunley), a defensive end (Pete Koch) and a guard (Brian Blados). We can now look at that haul and say: meh. But as a rookie beat man looking for guidance and a strong opinion about the performance of the Bengals in the draft, I called around the league for press-friendly GMs and zeroed in on one other person: *Sports Illustrated* football maven Paul Zimmerman, whom I'd read for years, going back to when the magazine got rolled up and stuffed in my dorm mailbox at Ohio University.

I have no idea what Zimmerman told me when I reached him on the phone, but I do remember thinking he gave me a lot of time. Like 45 minutes. For some schmoe he'd never met, Zimmerman opened up his draft trove for me and just kept going and going. I was impressed. The guy who'd written brilliantly on the real Chuck Noll and the tortured genius of Al Davis and who explained the game better than anyone alive in *The Thinking Man's Guide to Pro Football* had that much time for a know-nothing rookie in Cincinnati.

That's sort of the foreword to this foreword. The reason why I'm bullish on this book, and on a man who has been silenced since a series of three strokes hit him in 2008, finally getting his words out is because Paul has so much to say. Sometimes I've liked it. Sometimes I've hated it. But Paul Zimmerman is the most genuine person I've met in 60 years of life. That's

Paul. One of the truly unfortunate parts of his affliction — he can hear and see and feel and taste, but he can't speak or read — is that he always was the life of the party, he always could talk about any subject in any walk of life and he could read anything from a tabloid to *Moby Dick*, happily.

But it is our great fortune that you get to read words about his life that he crafted in the last years before he was rendered speechless. When I read the manuscript a couple of years ago, I said to his wife, Linda, "We've got to get this published. We just have to." Fortunately, Triumph Books loved it the way we did, and so here you are, the book Paul so desperately wanted to get in your hands.

I worked with Paul at *Sports Illustrated* from 1989 to 2008 and I've got stories about him. Plenty. As I sat down and tried to figure what would give you the best sense of him, I had a very strange thought. *Mock drafts.* Every spring the magazine would have Paul do its mock NFL draft for the issue just before the real NFL draft. Near the turn of the century, I was doing a mock draft too … for the magazine's website, *SI.com*. A mock draft, if you don't know, is an exercise in futility. You try to predict, pick by pick, each one of the selections in the first round. It's the impossible dream. The smartest NFL beat men might get a quarter of the picks correct after

(Linda Bailey Zimmerman)

weeks of talking to the scouts and GMs and coaches about their plans for the first round.

This was a fairly fruitless exercise to me; I tried to be good, but I understood that a mistake on the second pick could have the kind of domino effect that would make the next 10 picks wrong. Just too many X factors that could mess you up. To Paul, it was a referendum on whether you knew your stuff. He would start working on it the week after the Super Bowl, and I'd always wonder why; most GMs wouldn't have seen all the players yet, so how could they know? But every little nugget helped. Paul would work the phones, then buttonhole the decision-makers at the league meetings in March, then work the phones through April. Sometimes it paid off hugely. In one of the great mock performances in NFL history, he got eight of the first nine picks in 2000 correct and hit on Ron Dayne (New York Giants) and Chris Hovan (Minnesota Vikings) later in the round. A-plus.

But in other years, we'd talk on the Sunday before the draft, the day his mock was always due, and I'd pass along a piece of information or two (such as: "Paul, Green Bay's not taking Koren Robinson; guarantee it"), and he'd lapse into an angry string of this-guy-with-the-Packers-screwed-me-and-now-what-am-I-gonna-dos and feverishly go about adjusting his draft, getting back on the phone. What Paul wrote *mattered* so much. He was so principled about it.

With that in mind, I will leave you with the five lessons I learned from Paul Zimmerman:

1. **Never go to the star with the mob around him in the locker room.** Everybody's going to have that stuff. Go get your own stuff, apart from the crowd.
2. **Always seek out the smart offensive linemen.** "They know everything," he once told me, "and nobody talks to them much because they don't touch the ball. And they love to talk."
3. **Make the extra phone call and do the extra interview.** Read his stuff. Paul lived for details. You're not doing your job if you file a story and think: *I should have talked to the tackle who made the important block on that play.* This wasn't work for him. It was as simple as knowing when you'd completed the job and, if you had 27 interviews to do for one story and two for the next one, so be it. He just knew.

4. **Don't be a slave to quotes.** Too often, stories read like quote-transition-quote-quote, etc. Tell a story. You're the writer. Write. His best stuff, far and away, is when he tells a tale about a play or a game or a person, written in his intelligently acerbic way.

5. **Compete.** He'd be shocked to hear me say this because I doubt he ever said a word to me about it over the years. But every time he covered a game, he was going to write a better story than *The New York Times* guy. Every time he talked to Joe Montana, he was going to get better stuff than the ESPN people. Every time he did the mock draft, he was going to beat the good writers in Dallas and Green Bay. He was driven to do that. It was not something he ever had to say to me; I could see it in him. And I think of it to this day.

Quite a mentor he was. In so many of us who do this work today, he's a part.

— Peter King

Introduction

I met Paul in March of 1995 when he came to Phoenix to cover the NFL meetings at the Arizona Biltmore. He was working out in the athletic center and cornered an employee, asking: "Who is *that*?"

Paul and I spent the next two years dating long distance. He was in New Jersey, and I was in Phoenix. We'd meet in California, Sedona, Jersey. He was the most intriguing person I had ever met. Crazy ... brilliant ... wild ... like two cats thrown into a pillowcase to fight it out.

When we were apart, he'd write detailed accounts of his days. His letters always smelled of cigars and were always addressed to "The Flaming Redhead."

In '97 we met in San Francisco for dinner at Masa's and an overnight stay in the city before heading up to our favorite getaway in Mendocino. I knew I was getting weary of the back-and-forth across the country and I wanted to know where we were headed.

The dreaded talk.

"So Paul ... what do you see happening with us?"

"Hmmm ... ah ... umm ... well, I could see you moving to New Jersey and getting an apartment."

"And how much time do you see me staying in that *apartment*?"

"Well, you could go and water your plants."

That's it. I jumped up and headed upstairs to pack. I was heading back to Phoenix. There was no need to head up the coast. This guy was clearly bonkers.

He followed me up the stairs and then sat on the bed.

"Would you marry me?"

"Well, I'm sure as hell not moving to New Jersey to water plants."

From that moment on he was totally onboard ... totally committed. He made all the arrangements for our wedding and reception. Paul was so involved that he wanted me to take part in every aspect of his life and career. I went to meetings, games, interviews. It was a fabulous ride ... with an amazing partner.

I remember the interview with Johnny Unitas. Paul was invited to Johnny's home outside of Baltimore. We were greeted by Johnny and his English bulldog, a big, laboring hulk of slobbering love. Johnny spent a few hours with us. He had me on the floor demonstrating plays. I kept thinking, *Don't ask me any football questions. God, I don't want him to know that I know next to nothing about what he's talking about.* So I kept asking him questions. I remember when Johnny shook my hand, thinking that his handshake was a little weak. Later in the conversation he showed us how he had to wrap his hand around a golf club to get a better grip because there was just too much football damage. (This interview, by the way, led to the *Sports Illustrated* article, which is included in the chapter on quarterbacks.)

Paul and I were together 24 hours a day. He'd work downstairs in his library, and I'd be upstairs working in my studio. If he hadn't talked to me in an hour, or he wanted "another word for ... ," he'd call me. I found it very endearing. He was such a bull and so obstinate to the rest of the world but so thoughtful toward me. He never gave me the bluster. Truth be told ... I think my red hair scared him.

Paul decided to take a sabbatical at the end of the 2006 football season. He wanted some time to begin writing his memoirs. There were so many aspects of Paul's life that many of his football fans knew little about — wine tasting, book and coin collecting, travel. He wrote and he didn't start with any outlined plan or order to his recollections. He just followed his memories, and memories have a way of coming out in an odd order. He figured that over time all of his life would be covered. He didn't realize that his time was limited. No one does.

On November 22nd, 2008, everything came to a halt.

A series of massive strokes will do that.

His light was snuffed ... his brilliance locked away inside of him.

Paul cannot read, write or speak. He has no alphabet so he can't type out words on a computer as Steven Hawking does. Not only is Paul physically disabled and in a wheelchair, but his world is also closed off.

He suffers from profound aphasia and apraxia. It is even difficult for him to point to his nose. He can clearly understand where his nose is located, but the signal from his brain to his hand to point to his nose becomes scrambled.

The toughest part of all of this? The brilliance is still there. He is still as sharp as a whip. He gets the joke before the rest of us do. He still suffers no fools.

Every single aspect of his life has changed. We can't even watch foreign films because Paul can't read the captions. I've tried reading them out loud, but that didn't work. His urge to collect is still strong, but now he's collecting cans of soda and rolls of paper towels instead of miniatures and rare books.

The best way for someone to communicate with Paul is to ask him questions that he can answer yes and no to. Even then he really has to concentrate, and sometimes concentrating so hard can lead to the wrong answer. We spend our days in an endless and confusing dance of pantomime.

There are no words to describe the heartbreak and anguish.

I went into action. Everything had to be adapted. I had to become Paul's voice ... Paul's advocate. In a sense I became Paul. I found that I became more aggressive. I had to be the bull.

It has taken years to find a balance.

Just when we thought that life had thrown us enough challenges, we faced another. The home that Paul had loved for over 50 years betrayed him. It became impossible to get Paul from one chairlift to another, impossible to get him in and out of the shower, impossible to keep him safe.

Paul ended up hospitalized — for the eighth time since his stroke — leaving him too weak to return home. He had to go back into Kessler Rehabilitation Center for three weeks. He has spent so much time at Kessler in both inpatient and outpatient facilities that he was featured in their annual calendar.

As his stint in Kessler neared an end, it became evident that Paul needed a safer environment than his beloved home could offer. My sister and I went to a dozen nursing facilities, asking dozens of questions ... and often leaving in tears.

I figured that after eight years I was cried out. I was wrong.

How many times can a heart break?

We now spend our days together at an assisted living/nursing facility ... and our nights separately. Life has its own cruel plan. But as Paul always said: "They're not going to break me."

No, damn it ... love will find a way.

— *Linda Bailey Zimmerman*

Editor's Note

Paul Zimmerman began writing his memoir in 2006 before suffering a series of debilitating strokes in 2008. *Dr. Z: The Lost Memoirs of an Irreverent Football Writer* is this unfinished manuscript in its entirety. When relevant, supplementary material from Paul's *SI.com* and *Sports Illustrated* work has been added.

Chapter 1

Mine Eyes Have Seen the Glory

I have covered sports for 48 years and have been primarily a football writer for many of them, I have an entire room full of charts and old programs and a lifetime full of memories. I close my eyes, and a panorama comes sweeping across my brain. I am what is known as a footballhead.

A few years ago, I had a dream. So vivid was that dream that I couldn't shake it for days, and at odd times, I would catch myself committing parts of it to paper, and they took the form of football plays. Yes, that's right. I dreamed about the X's and O's except that they didn't line up into patterns that would be recognizable by today's players. They were lined up in the single-wing formation.

The what? You know, the single-wing; the run and pass tailback lined up deep, behind the center in an abbreviated shotgun; the fullback set a step or two in front of him on either side; the wingback on the flank and the blocking back up near the line, cruising like an H-Back or second tight end of today, searching for the murderous blocking angles. What was different, though, was that I had lined up the current Michael Vick of the Atlanta Falcons in that formation that hadn't been regularly used in the league since 1951, and only by one team in those days, the Steelers.

Vick was my pass and run tailback star in that dream, 254-pound T.J. Duckett was my fullback, also known as the spinning fullback in the old days, because he'd often do a half turn and hand the ball off or fake a handoff; little Warrick Dunn would be my wingback. I could just see him slicing through the weak side on a short reverse, behind the blocking of

250-pound Brian Kozlowski, my blocking back. And wouldn't Koz have fun, leveling all those pigeons from the blind side?

I couldn't get the idea out of my head. The single-wing still was used by some successful college teams when I was in school. It was a thing of beauty when mighty Michigan ran it with Charlie Ortmann and Wally Teninga and Killer Kempthorn, formful and flashy when used by UCLA and at times USC — with a dazzling tailback named Frank Gifford — and downright nasty when you had to line up against it. Nope, no fun at all if you were a tackle, which I was, and you were playing in front of the imbalanced strong side. It felt like half a dozen different people were either double-teaming or trapping you. Playing against the short side meant lining up over the weakside end ... what a racket! It was like stealing. But that was another thing about facing the single-wing. The unfairness of it made you want to cry.

After a few days, that strange dream became a reality in my poor, tormented brain. I've seen quite a few guys who would have been brilliant as run-pass stars, working out of a deep tailback set — Randall Cunningham, the two Youngs, Vince and Steve, and, of course, Vick. I remember once asking Vince Lombardi what would happen if a team all of a sudden surprised everyone by coming out in a single-wing.

"It would embarrass the hell out of us," he said.

I put the same question to Bill Walsh.

"Oh my goodness," he said, "I've never thought of that. You could double-team right down the line, you could trap at almost every hole. My God, it would just chew up those three and four-man lines."

Then I took my looniness one step further. I called Dan Reeves, the Falcons coach, and laid out my entire single-wing scenario for him: Vick as the run and pass tailback, Duckett as the spinning fullback, etc. There was a pause.

"What's a spinning fullback?" he said.

I knew that at that point, it was time to get a grip on things. I had gone over the line. I'd shed my writer's garb and injected myself into the role of strategist, playmaker, God knows what. It had happened before but never to this extent. Usually it just consisted of material that appeared in print, observations that I'd made from the perspective of a former player, things that just were natural to me. My experience certainly had not been all-encompassing — the usual high school run, 3,000-mile trip to Stanford, thrust into the meat-grinder as a 16-year-old child and grimly hanging on for three seasons, never fully understanding the thrashing world of major college football that raged around me, a non-entity but still the possessor of knowledge that only can be gained by hours on the practice field. Then a transfer and the long trip back to Columbia, where I should have been in the first place.

"Possible use as a reserve lineman." The press book said about me, but we never had a full season to find out. The Ivy League Presidents Committee stepped in first and ruled me ineligible for the rest of my senior year for reasons I was too stupid to foresee, but Lou Little, the famous old coach, believed in getting fair value for the dollar, and I was occupying a place at the training table and eating shockingly more than my allotted three squares, so to cover it, I was appointed co-coach, actually line coach, of the 150-pound team. John Wagner and I coached the lightweights to a 2-3 record, finest record in CU lightweight history, you could look it up. And what valuable experience this provided me as a future writer, the ability to see things from the standpoint of an actual coach ... a coach who would spend Friday night drinking with the same classmates he'd have to coach the following day, a fringe lunatic who would occasionally get down and personally show his troops the beauties of the cross body and crab block, executing flawless technique against guys he outweighed by 75 pounds, a coach who would occasionally suit up old buddies who'd been thrown out of Columbia up to two years previously, some of whom weighed up to 190 pounds. Oh yeah, meet the coach, shouting incoherent gibberish at the referees from the sidelines, threatening the hotshots on the opposing team. Oh yeah, he's gonna win a Pulitzer some day.

The magic of the gridiron all came together in a blinding flash for one season, 1956, when I played for a league championship army team in Germany and was selected Honorable Mention All-Europe, and then there were four seasons in the $25-a-game semipro leagues around New York and finally a one-game comeback at age 36 in a league one level down, and that was it. Jim Thorpe was asked to step off the field and take his cleats with him.

What this did was to inject a kind of "I was there" style into my writing that some people find enlightening, but others feel is merely a show of arrogance. There are things you *do* learn, though. Trash talking, which gets such play in the daily chronicles, is meaningless, actually less than meaningless.

And at the NFL level, so are inspirational talks by coaches, unless they happen to be, "That's gonna cost you." Or "Don't forget to drop off your playbook before you leave." If you need to be inspired by a coach, you're in the wrong business. "Leadership ability," always is regarded as a big part of a quarterback's dossier, but quarterbacks seldom lead anybody; the teammates, who sweat alongside you, do. In fact, a lot of quarterbacks are disliked by the people who have to block for them or catch their passes. These are the things you just know from experience.

The first pro football locker room I ever saw was in 1960, the Eagles-Packers NFL Championship in Franklin Field, Philadelphia. I had been with the *New York World-Telegram & Sun* for about six months. I had been covering high school sports and I'd worked on the night desk in the summer, before the schools started, with the Little League World Series as my only bylined piece during that period. But they wanted to see how I would handle myself in the big arena, so they sent me down to do loser's dressing room quotes for our regular pro football writer, Joe King. It was a disaster.

The problem was that I was spending my Saturday nights playing guard for the Paterson (N.J.) Pioneers of the Eastern Football Conference, which billed itself as either Minor League Football or the NFL's farm system. Take your pick, but in reality it was one of the many outposts of semipro football. The Packers had lost to the Eagles, but I couldn't get over the way the Green Bay middle three of Jim Ringo, Fuzzy Thurston and Jerry Kramer had crushed the center of the Eagles' defense, including the great Chuck Bednarik. The first guy I saw in the Packer locker was Thurston.

"Hey, great job against Eddie Khayat," I blurted out. His eyes narrowed. He had just lost the biggest game of his life. Was this some kind of con job?

"Thanks," he said. I'd been knocked out by the smoothness with which they called their in-line audibles among themselves, their change-ups. I complimented him on it. By now Kramer had joined our little group.

"You're a writer?" he said.

I brushed it off. I told him that we were having trouble calling our audibles on the Paterson Pioneers. I asked them how they called them.

"Hey, Jim!" he called over to Ringo in the next locker. "I want you to meet this guy." So for 10 minutes or so, they laid it out for me, who made the call in each situation, how they handled the dummy calls ... and the Eagle tackles, Khayat and Jess Richardson, which they most definitely had done. The Packers ran for 223 that day. It was a nice friendly little group, and I was thinking, *Wow, it sure is great covering an NFL locker room.*

Then I noticed that the room was emptying. My page of quotes for Joe King was blank. Oh oh. I excused myself. I looked for Bart Starr. He was gone. They were helping Paul Hornung into his sportcoat; he had suffered a pinched nerve in his shoulder.

"How's the shoulder?" I asked him. "It hurts," he said. And he was gone. I searched for Vince Lombardi. He was on his way out the door, wrapping a muffler around his neck, for the cold.

"Uh, coach," I said.

"I said everything I had to say to all the writers," he said. "We needed more time, OK?" And he was gone. Everybody was gone except for a few stragglers, some equipment men loading stuff into bags. I made my way up to the press box, which was on an odd angle. It looked as if a strong wind might blow it, plop, right onto midfield of the venerable stadium. It matched my own feeling of impending doom.

Put a little pencil mustache on Humphrey Bogart, and I'd hire him to play Joe King in the movie version. Cigarette hanging out of the side of his mouth, a bottle of Heineken's close by his left hand, grey fedora pushed back on his head, with his press ticket in the band, Joe was everyone's idea of what an old-time sportswriter should look like. I stood behind him and watched him type.

"OK, waddya got?" he said.

"What do you want?"

"Gimme Lombardi."

"He was on the way out. He said they needed more time."

"And ... AND?"

"And that's what he said."

"OK, gimme Hornung. How about the shoulder?"

"He said it hurt." By now Joe had stopped typing. He was as fascinated by the horror of this as I was.

"What did Starr say?" he said so softly that I could barely hear it.

"Nope, I missed Starr," I mumbled.

Joe took his hat off and laid it on the desk. He turned in his seat and stared at me. "Son, what DID you get?"

"Well, I talked to Kramer and Thurston and Ringo about how they called their audibles, and ..."

He waved me away, as one would dispel a bitter memory. "Out, son. OUT! GET OUT!

"Jack ... Nat ... catch me up on Lombardi ... can you give me a little Starr ... Just a graf or two ... I SAID OUT OF HERE, KID! OUT!"

It took me two years before I saw the inside of a professional locker room again.

People have asked me what Lombardi was really like. My answer always is the same, "Tough to cover, but I'd have given five years of my life." Of the great mass of literature his life has produced, I can usually tell within a few pages whether the author of the latest Lombardi book ever met him, and if he did, if he knew him fairly well. The monuments to Lombardi, many of which are carefully researched and meticulously written, are worthy achievements, but they're missing an element. The people who really knew him mixed in the quirks and oddities, the little snappers, the times when he played the angles.

Once I covered a Green Bay practice when Marvin Fleming, the tight end, was a 21-year-old rookie, youngest player in the league. In the locker room, Lombardi passed his locker and stared at him. Then he did it again. Then he leaned over and said something to him that I couldn't hear. When the coach left, I asked Fleming what he had said. He smiled and shook his head.

"He said, 'Marvin, your eyes look dull. Have you been abusing yourself?'"

One of the first games the *New York Post* sent me out to cover, all by myself, was Green Bay at Chicago in 1966. I set up my audience with Lombardi well in advance for a Tuesday actually. That's how nervous I was. I took a cab from the airport and got there at lunchtime, an hour and a half before my appointment with the coach. It was raining heavily. I told the Packer receptionist who I was and what I was there for. She said, "You must be hungry." Coming from New York, I wasn't familiar with Midwestern hospitality. Yes, I certainly was hungry.

"There's a German restaurant down the street," she said. "They have a luncheon buffet, dumplings, sauerbraten, all you can eat. Do you like that?" I practically fainted. I couldn't talk. I was staggering. I nodded my head.

"It's only a few blocks, but it's raining," she said. "Here, you'd better take my car." And she handed me the keys.

I got back, well stuffed, in time for my audience with Lombardi. He was cordial. He asked me where I grew up and where I had played. I told him, adding that in high school we had scrimmaged against the team he was coaching, St. Cecilia's in Englewood, N.J., and that I had very fond memories of his power sweep. He threw back his head and laughed. Then he called in his line coach, Phil Bengtson, who'd had the same position at Stanford when I was there, just to check me out. Bengtson, God bless him, if it would have been England, he'd have been knighted. I'm sure he didn't remember a thing about me, but just to be a mensch, he gave it the, "Hey, nice to see ya ... how ya been ... I see that you've picked up a little weight," and so forth. Whew. I had passed muster.

So we chatted for a while, and then Lombardi got real serious and said, "You're a young writer, you're from New York, I'm going to give you a good story for your paper." Thump, went my heart, thump thump. "This is the game where I find out about my million dollar rookies, Grabowski and Anderson. All that money we paid them (combined contract a cool million, record numbers in those days) ... I've got to know whether they can play."

And on and on in that vein, until I am so feverish to call my paper and tell them to hold the back page because I've got a scoop from Lombardi, that I can hardly bear it. And I gave them the message, and they held the back page and next day's streamer, in red, blared, LOMBARDI TO UNVEIL MILLION DOLLAR ROOKIES.

P.S: Neither one played a down.

And as I sat there in the press box, watching the backs of those two players, their numbers boring holes in my brain, Jim Grabowski, fullback, No. 33, Donny Anderson, halfback, No. 44, watching their asses flattening on the bench as I prayed, implored whatever football Gods that lived high above Chicago's Wrigley Field to please, please, just send them in for a series or two. Nope, zero and zero. Finally, I mentioned it to one of the Packer beat guys, Bud Lea of the *Milwaukee Sentinel*. He started laughing.

"Welcome to the club," he said.

"Easy," he said. "He knows that Halas gets everything clipped from the out of town papers. So he might as well plant something, just to give him another thing to worry about."

You're a young writer, you're from New York, step this way, kid, this here's a pea, and it's gonna be under one of these three shells ...

Just as a follow, the Pack beat the Bears, 17-0, and held Gale Sayers to 29 yards rushing.

Obviously, it would be a defensive story for me. In the Green Bay locker room, Lombardi was sitting on a little counter in front of the cage where they handed out equipment, in the center of a cluster of writers in overcoats and hats. Steam was rising. They were interviewing the coach, but it looked like they were cooking him. I waited my turn and then asked, "What was your theory in defending Sayers?"

"Force him back into the flow of traffic,'" Lombardi said, "cut off his escape. It's a theory as old as football itself."

Fine. I had my Lombardi quote. It was time to talk to the players. The Packers locker was next to the equipment alcove, through an open door. Dave Robinson, the strongside linebacker who had had a good day, was about 10 feet in. I introduced myself and asked him, "What was your theory in defending Sayers?"

"Wait a minute! Wait a minute!" Lombardi shouted from the next room. Both rooms fell silent. I looked through the door, and he had popped up from the center of his steam table and was pointing a finger in my direction. Everyone was staring at me.

"The same thing," he said. "You asked me the same thing, in exactly the same words. What's the matter, didn't you believe me?"

A few of the players were hiding their faces, so the coach wouldn't see them chuckling. Robinson had a big smile on his face. He waved me to follow him around the corner. As I went, I heard Lombardi telling the writers, "The exact same thing ... see that guy there ... first he asks me about Sayers, then he goes in and asks them the same thing..."

A few days later, I was having dinner with someone who worked with gifted and talented kids. I told him the story.

"One mark of genius is to be completely aware of everything taking place in your immediate environment," he said.

Maybe so, but to me it was just a case of rabbit ears.

I interviewed Lombardi for the last time in May, 1970, slightly more than three months before he died. We were in the latter stages of the counterculture movement, campus unrest, hippies, flower people. Woodstock was less than a year old. I was curious to hear Lombardi's take on all this and I fully expected some diatribe about people who were too lazy or selfish to work, etc. His answer made me ashamed of myself for trying to stereotype one of the most unusual and perceptive thinkers I had ever encountered.

"They're showing an awareness of things; they're making themselves heard," he said. "They have a right to say what they want, and it behooves us to listen. I don't know … my own lack of awareness … in my own little sphere, maybe I didn't see the things I should have. My kids tell me things, and sometimes I have trouble understanding them. Well, I've got to learn."

He never had the chance.

I wish I could have sat down and talked real football with Lombardi, about how he originally came up with his greatest technical innovation, the "run to daylight" approach that swept through the league like a cleansing wind, bringing option blocking, option running, Freedom! He probably fooled around with it as a line coach at West Point and then gradually introduced it into the NFL in pieces. That's what I've never read in any of the multitude of Lombardi bios, the working of the mind behind the plan. Would he have opened up to me, a writer, as alien to the club as police reporters are to precinct cops? Who knows?

In 2006 the Jets beat the Dolphins by three points in the Meadowlands. The key moment in the game came when Miami, after having driven to the New York's 32, against a defense that rushed only four and brought no pressure, had a third and two with 38 seconds left. *Now, he's going to bring it now!* I thought. Eric Mangini, the Jets' 35-year-old coach, learned defense as a young assistant at Bill Belichick U, and his game was defensive innovation. Oh, he brought pressure, all right, two DBs coming outside the same flank, but he didn't bring it from the blind side, as I thought he would. They came from the left wing, entering into the widest field of vision of right handed Joey Harrington. His rushed pass was incomplete, the field goal was missed, the Jets won the game.

My brain was on fire. The front side! Of course. He wanted Harrington to see the blitz.

I called Mangini that night. I laid out my scenario. "You wanted to show him the blitz. You wanted to spook him, right?" Most coaches would give you a cliché answer to a half-assed technical question, but Eric and I go back a long way. I can talk to him.

"Right," he said. "That's what I did."

This wasn't what you'd call a scoop, not even something you could build a story around, if you were doing a first-day piece. And there weren't any fancy or controversial quotes to dress it up. But it's something that stays with me and makes me feel good every time I think of it.

"Simple pleasure for poor *bhisti*," to quote Sam Jaffe, playing Gunga Din in the movie of the same name.

Sometimes it doesn't work so well, and that's when the ego gets inflated, and you are firmly put in your place. Bill Walsh, the 49ers' Hall of Fame coach, liked to talk football theory or life itself, actually. I enjoyed listening to the way he phrased things, using the analogies of war ... Attacking in "quick lethal strikes ..." or descriptions that bordered on the poetic, such as his picture of Joe Montana as a "lithe, almost sensuous athlete." So on this one particular evening we were talking about personnel, and the makeup of the ideal squad, and I got a bit carried away and started voicing some theories about desire and the power of the will. And the more Walsh tended to agree, the more into it I got, and finally, in an absolute explosion of ego, I asked him, "Do you think I could ever have gotten a job in some team's personnel department?"

There was an embarrassing pause, and Walsh contorted his face into a pained expression. *How to explain it to this boob ... ?* Finally he said, "The problem is," and he paused to find the right words. "The problem is that you would fill a squad with players who would look very determined, chasing opponents across the goal line."

Disappointment is always part of the business. If you can't handle being put in your place from time to time, don't be a sportswriter. In the mid-1990s I was in the Colts' camp, doing my interviews for my scouting reports for *Sports Illustrated*'s pro football issue. I was almost through for the day when Tony Siragusa, their right defensive tackle, asked if he could speak to me for a moment. He took me down to the deserted weight room and talked for 40 minutes; I guess he didn't want his teammates to see him spending that much time with a writer. I always enjoyed the way Goose played, a little over 300 pounds, technically correct against the run (I had been arguing for years that the Vikings' great interior pass rusher, John Randle, never would make my All-Pro team because he was such a liability facing the running game), seldom out of position, almost impossible to trap.

So we talked about why the things he did were held in such low regard, why the pass rushers got the big contracts and all the publicity, how coaches always stressed a firm run defense but then gave all their praise to the sackers. I agreed. I hated it almost as much as he did. He was passionate on the subject, and I liked that about him. The place was practically locked up by the time I got out of there.

Move ahead a few years to the Wednesday press interview day before the 2001 Super Bowl, Ravens vs. Giants. The Baltimore players were being interviewed at their special tables in the ballroom of the Hyatt Westshore Hotel. The two tables that commanded the biggest collection of writers belonged to Ray Lewis and Siragusa, a full-blown 350 pounds now, raconteur, storyteller, future color commentator for Fox. He read a newspaper during the Q&A session, establishing obvious unconcern. His answers drew quick laughs, but I noticed that his eyes never seemed to move downward from the one area on which they were focused. Ah, well, if that's his shtick.

"Is this Ravens defense the best in history?" someone asked him.

"Name a better one," he said.

"Steel Curtain Steelers," I said.

"What are you, from Pittsburgh?" he said, looking up from his paper.

"No, from Jersey, same as you," I said. A few writers laughed.

When the meeting broke up, the Goose came over to me, plainly annoyed.

"What did you want to do that for, break up my act like that?" he said. I waited a moment, just to see if there was any recognition at all.

"You don't remember me, do you?" I said.

"No," he said. "Should I?"

Strangely enough, I liked that exchange. I liked what it did for my ego, or against it. It helped keep things in perspective. Some writers like to present themselves as characters in the drama. Newspapers discourage it, magazines encourage it to a certain extent (subject to review), but books, ah, you'll get encouragement on that level, if, truly you have something to say, presenting a point that cannot be made without your presence. When you have covered sports for 48 years, though, you can step aside for long periods and let the panorama present itself through your memories, and Lord knows, I can close my eyes, and those memories and visions will come flooding back: Al Oerter's primal scream in the little room under the Olympic Stadium in Tokyo, after he had ripped the tape off his torn rib cage and thrown the discus far enough to win his third straight Olympic championship; Muhammad Ali taking some of the most awful, the most devastating shots from Earnie Shavers, a fearsome puncher, the sweat bouncing off his head 10 feet as he shook his head, no, no, no, you can't hurt me; the Dallas Cowboys' running back, Duane Thomas, silent, totally incommunicative, trapped in his own private hell as the centerpiece of a weird, silent press conference with no words being spoken. The memories rise in a flood, and yes, I see myself in there, too.

Getting into the Olympic Village in Munich meant running a gauntlet of a double line of German security guards and taking a rifle butt to the head that knocked me to my knees, but I got in and was witness to the drama of the Israeli hostage crises, the single most terrifying event of the history of the game. To interview Igor Ter-Ovanesyan, Russia's assistant track coach whom I had known for many years, I had to join him in the middle of a deserted field. This was during the 1980 Moscow Olympics. "Never stand near metal when you are interviewing anyone here," he said. "Everything is bugged."

There were moments of high hilarity, a raucous chorus from an era now dead. An 11-year stint as a beat man for a metropolitan New York daily, covering the Jets for the *Post*, gave me the closest thing the sports beat had to war reporting. The trips to Oakland and the Weeb-Ewbank-Al Davis conflicts were like forays into a battle zone. I can see Weeb, his jowls trembling in fury, as he had the driver stop the team bus on Highway 17 outside the Oakland Coliseum to eject a guy Davis had planted on the vehicle, big fat former linebacker Maury Schleicher, "Schleicher ... Schleicher," Weeb was growling, barely able to get the words out.

And then there was the time I tried to see how many Raider venues I could be ejected from. First I was thrown out of Davis' office when I called attention to a framed photo of Ben Davidson breaking Joe Namath's cheekbone that had been taken down from the wall and stashed behind a desk. Then I was thrown out of the Raider locker room, bodily, by the two biggest assistant coaches, Tom Dahms and Ollie Spencer, one grabbing each elbow. This was too rich to pass up. I had to find out where they were practicing that day, show up and collect my hat trick. I found out, Cal State Hayward, the bowl. I lasted about 15 minutes inside until Al spotted me, pointed a finger and mouthed the words that I knew meant heave ho. The guy assigned to do the job was Bugsy Engelberg, the kicking coach. The piece I wrote that night was headed, "Kicked Out by the Kicking Coach," and my last vision of the scene was Bugsy, standing in the middle of the road, the wind flapping the towel around his neck, making sure that my car was departing.

Early in my career on *The Sacramento Bee*, I wrote one of the first pieces ever done on Rosemary Casals, who became one of the world's top-ranked women tennis players. I wrote about her in the Central Cal Juniors at the Sutter Lawn Tennis Club in Sacramento, a tiny 10-year-old, who could barely see over the net, battling a 13-year-old girl named Leslie Abrahams on a blistering 110-degree day. It was the greatest tennis match I've ever seen, two children racing around the court, tears streaming down their faces, clawing, scratching, the match finally won by Rosie in almost three hours. She traveled to the tournaments with her father, a tiny Mexican girl and her elderly Mexican parent denied access to all areas of the clubs except the court or the stands, spending their nights sleeping in their car to save money. I remember her telling me in a squeaky little voice how tough it was trying to get a full night's rest.

I wrote my first serious mood piece, poured my heart and soul into it, wrote about the "vicious 110-degree heat." One of the desk men tossed me a style guide. It had been written 50 years previously by Old Man McClatchy, the owner of the paper, and hardly changed. One of the rules was that you could never say it was hot in Sacramento. "Warm" was as far as you could go. I read, in my piece, the edited line, "110-degree warmth."

I had the last interview with Sid Luckman, the great old Bears quarterback, before he died. He was one of my earliest sports heroes. Seemed like every Fox Movietone Newsreel you saw in a theater had a clip of Sid throwing a long touchdown pass. Years later I did a film study of some of my old heroes and what I saw from Sid was a complete package of every route that's on the book today with absolute mastery of two of them, the timed up-and-under fade pattern and the deep go route, thrown with incredible softness and touch.

"I feel fine, except for my balance," Sid said that afternoon in Miami. He was 81. When he would stand up, a personal attendant would position himself alongside him. "I just keep falling down, can't stay on my feet."

My wife, Linda Bailey Zimmerman, and I drove down to Maryland to interview John Unitas a few years before his death. *(Editor's note: This article appears in Chapter 10.)* We sat on the covered porch of his house and relived old memories. I mentioned the winning drive against the

Giants in overtime in the '58 championship game, and he stiffened, and an irritation that must have been bugging him for more than 40 years jumped up because he only mentioned one play, the six-yard pass to Jim Mutscheller that carried down to the Giants' one, in overtime.

"A gamble," he said, sniffing. "They said it was gamble. No damn gamble when you know what you're doing" He glared at me. *Hey, John, I didn't write it. Honestly, I didn't.* He turned to Linda. "Look," he said. "This is how you move the strong safety over when you're running a diagonal and you want him inside." He set it up, he gave her the look he employed to look the safety off, the head fake. He got her out of position. No way she could have covered Mutscheller on that play.

At a family gathering, I heard her tell two of her brothers about getting down on the floor in the porch area of John Unitas' house and having him look her off the coverage on Mutscheller on one of history's most famous drives. They didn't believe her. Yeah, right, just you and Johnny U., the most famous quarterback in history.

I've been blessed with a wife who not only enjoys sports but understands them. No, not the technical aspects, the playbook element, but the heart of the competition, the emotion, the soul. We are at the 2003 Super Bowl in San Diego. We have dinner set up with Mike Giddings, former linebacker coach for the 49ers and the private personnel consultant for 13 NFL teams. He asks me if we minded if he brought a few people. Sure, why not? These are the people he brought: Curly Morrison, former Bears' and Browns' fullback; Billy Wilson, the 49ers' finest receiver of the 1950s, and San Francisco's Hugh McElhenny, "The King," one of pro football's great broken field runners of all the time. How many Sundays did I sit in the sunny side end zone in Kezar, shirt off, swilling my beer and screaming my head off for The King? *Oh no, we don't mind.*

A memorable dinner, my God, the stories. "Every time someone mentions George Halas, I have to laugh," McElhenny said. "He kicked me once, right in the side of the head. I was tackled near the Bears' sideline. Next thing I knew this wingtip, Thom McAn, is clunking me on the helmet. There's Halas, in his suit, kicking me in the head. I yelled at him, 'What the hell are you doing?' He just turned away."

That night Linda said to me, with just a bit of a catch in her voice, "I wish my father could have been with us tonight." He had died a few years before I met her. He had been a high school coach at one time. "He would have loved that dinner."

You live through the magnificent moments of sports as a spectator. Most of the time you are presenting a second view to a large mass of people who already have seen what you have. Writers with great narrative and descriptive talent can use their words as a paint brush and provide an artist's or a poet's rendition of what they have seen. It's called "writing the scene." It is also a technique used by people who don't really understand what has taken place, often ridiculing those who would try to solve the puzzle and venture into technical writing.

Technical writing is rare nowadays. I am still waiting to hear how America defeated the Soviet Union in that great Olympic hockey upset, but oh my God, how many stories have I had to endure about the magnificence of the human spirit or Old Glory or The Stars and Stripes or the will to win? Please, just tell me how we did it! But that kind of writing never really has been fashionable. I always thought the answer to the problem is to combine the intellect, in the form of technical writing, with the artistic, which means writing the piece as well and as colorfully and meaningfully as you can. Sometimes you can make it work; often you can't, but too often one or the other is neglected, for convenience sake.

But once you have locked a great event into your memory, what you are left with, and this is something that always remains fresh and meaningful, is the face-to-face presentation of the individual or individuals most vitally involved in the drama. This can be in the form of an interview, one on one if you're lucky, or in a mass setting, if you can see through the artificiality of the scene. What can become special, though, is the ability to approach a certain event or way of life or philosophy with one of the elegant spokesmen of the world of sports; it need not be a superstar, or even a regular, just someone who through words or deeds has achieved a certain elegance of spirit and, when approached through the luxury of reflection, can present it in a meaningful way.

There are some people I knew well enough to interview at length, and sometimes, during the course of that interview, the gate would open, if only for an instant, and I'd realize that I had just been allowed a rare look down a secret path. And then it would be gone. Sometimes it would come back, as a quick flash. Sometimes it would remain open, and those are the times during which I have developed friendships among the people I cover. It's not really a healthy route for a writer to follow. What happens if honesty demands the harshness of criticism?

In the early stages of Frank Gifford's career as a TV analyst, he was very sharp in his criticism, surprisingly acute. Then he just seemed to flatten out. One day I mentioned it to him.

"It just wasn't worth it," he said. "A lot of people I was criticizing were guys who'd been my teammates, or I'd played against. I knew a lot of them socially. Our wives were friends. And I'd say something, and it would change the relationship. No, it just wasn't worth it."

My best friend in all the years I covered the Jets was Winston Hill, the big tackle from Texas Southern. We'd work out together. Our wives would play tennis, our two infant daughters would play together in the playpen. One day he said to me, "There's going to come a time when I won't be playing as well. You're going to have to write it. I don't want our friendship to have anything to do with it … I want you to write it."

I shook my head. I couldn't talk. Tears were streaming down my face. "I'll never write it," I finally blurted out. "I'll write about something else."

I never wrote it. I wrote about other things. Besides, he never really slipped that much.

There were some scenes that just stood out in such sharp relief. One was an interview with Joe Namath on the dock behind his home in Tequesta, Florida. In 1969, my fourth year of covering the Jets, with Namath as the quarterback, something came up, and he stopped talking to me. Just like that, *bang*! I thought it had something to do with the league office forcing him to get out of his nightclub, Bachelors III. I was writing from training camp; a city-side reporter on the *Post* was covering the gossip stuff, the city angle. The paper combines our bylines. I guessed that had something to do with it, but I never found out.

"Hey Jimmy, what's the story?" I asked Jimmy Walsh, his agent. It's a scary thing to be a beat writer and not have access to the biggest name on your beat.

"He's just in a tough situation now," Walsh said. "He'll get over it."

It lasted for 24 years. It got ugly. A few others were in the same boat, Larry Fox, the beat writer for the *New York Daily News*, Dick Young, the *News'* lead columnist. He wouldn't even address a mass press conference if he spotted us in the crowd. He would tell other players to avoid us. You try to pretend you can shrug it off. It stayed with me like a lingering disease. I used to have nightmares about it.

Sometimes I'd dream that everything was fixed, and then I'd wake up to, *Oh, God, it's still going on.*

Twenty-five years after the Super Bowl season, *Sports Illustrated* did a quarter-century retrospective, and they told me I'd be going down to Florida to interview Namath. I said good try, but he doesn't talk to me. They said his secretary told them it was okay. I said his secretary didn't know who the writer was. They said, go anyway, so I did, knowing exactly what would happen. I'd fly in, rent a car, drive to his house and hear, "I'm not talking to you." I was ready for it.

What I wasn't ready for was one of the best and warmest sessions with an athlete that I'd ever experienced. He talked about his life, his disappointment in trying and failing in an acting career, how the game had affected his life. We swapped old stories about people we knew. I told him that with a few minutes to go in the Super Bowl game, I made my way down to the field, as writers always do, so I could get position on the dressing room and I was standing next to John Sample on the sidelines, behind the Jets' bench and I said, "Great game, John." And we shook hands. And Gerry Philbin, the notoriously violent defensive end, saw us and screamed at me, "The game's not over! Get the hell out of here!"

"My arm, feel my arm," Namath said. "Goose bumps. That's what I get when I hear stories about Philbin and those guys, goose bumps." And that was the way it went for an afternoon. And finally, when I was getting back in my car, I asked him what I wanted to know for 24 years, obviously waiting until the interview was over, "What did I write 24 years ago that bothered you so much?"

"I don't know," he said. "I don't remember."

"You don't remember? You don't remember?" I said, unable to hide the anguish. "You just about ruined my life and you don't remember?"

"Well, I was different then," he said. "I was more aggressive."

If someone were to ask me which were the sports figures I got along with best, I'd have to say the funny ones, the ones with a developed sense of humor. I mean, are we all really finding a cure for cancer out here? I fell in love with Katie Schmidt, the Olympic javelin thrower and American record holder because of her sense of humor. First press conference she gave at the Montreal Olympics, she was asked how she ever got started in the sport and she said she was from Vermont, a departure of a long line of whalers from whom she was descended, and they had taught her to throw the javelin as they had thrown their harpoons. The only problem is that Vermont is a land-locked state.

"Well, some of them bought it," she said. "I liked the headline the *L.A. Times* put on their story, 'Something Fishy with This Tale.'" I remember very clearly strolling down one of the streets in the Olympic Village with Katie, and we passed Ruth Fuchs, the world record holder from East Germany who'd been rumored to have been feuding with Schmidt, which was strongly denied by all parties, especially the political ones, and they smiled sweetly at each other, and Katie said, "Oh, hi, Ruth," and then sotto voce, "you bitch." I burst out laughing. She grinned. Fuchs looked puzzled. The cavalcade of sports. Why can't it all be like that?

One year the editors at *Sports Illustrated* asked me, "Who would you most like to do an off-season piece about?" and off the top of my head I said, "Jack Rudnay." Huh? Blank looks all around. "The center for the Chiefs," I said, the information, doing nothing to disperse the fog. Then I told them one story, and when it was over, they said, "Go and write him." This is the story: The season was 1974, NFL veterans were on strike in training camp. Rudnay was the leader of the Chiefs' strike faction, picketing the camp. David Jaynes was a quarterback from Kansas, the third-round draft choice. OK, rookies walked through the picket line, but when he issued the quote, "I feel that I can lead this team to victory," Rudnay noted it and said, "Oh yeah, we'll see about that."

Now the strike is over. Veterans and rookies are together in the first 11-on-11 practice. Jaynes, who has been the QB in camp, gets first shot under center, which is Rudnay. Hank Stram, the coach, is up in the tower, running the show. Before practice Rudnay had taken a pair of scissors and cut the crotch out of his football pants. When he got down to snap the ball, everything was hanging out. Jaynes began his call, "Brown right, red 34, ready ..." he reached down ... "Hut-hut ... whoooo!" And the ball went flying out of his hands.

"What the hell's going on down there?" Stram yelled.

"He won't take the snap, coach," Rudnay said.

"Well, get another quarterback in there."

And that was the beginning of the end for David Jaynes.

So there I was out in Lee's Summit, Missouri, and since I came from a strong labor family, Rudnay and I hit it off just fine. The interview started light and frothy, hey, you remember when? … but then it got serious, real serious, and we were into the hypocrisy of the NFL, not from a corporate standpoint but from the players themselves. Rudnay sponsored a group of terminally ill children whom he would bring to each home game. "My special people," he called them. He would gather with them outside the locker room and introduce them to his teammates, coming out. This has a fine ring to it, but pretty soon he noticed that after a few weeks of this, he and his group were being avoided. It was, "Oh, hi, how are ya," and they'd keep walking. His bitterness was deep. And almost as a companion piece, so was his feeling about, ssshhh, the Fellowship of Christian Athletes. He, well, he ripped them.

Now no one, repeat no one, ever had the guts to take on this organization, which equates football with the virtues of Christian life. Tom Keating, the old Raider defensive tackle who spent the '74 season with the Chiefs, told me that in one game against the Chargers, Coy Bacon, the right defensive end, collected two sacks and a lot of pressures off tackle Charlie Getty, the leader of the Chiefs' branch of the FCA.

"His locker was next to mine, and all the writers were over there after the game, asking what happened," Keating said. "I leaned over to listen, I wanted to hear, too. Charlie said, 'Well, I guess God didn't intend for me to block Coy Bacon today.' I mean, how would you like it if you were the quarterback, and you went into a game knowing that God didn't intend your left tackle to block his man?"

I mentioned this story to Rudnay. We were sitting in a restaurant near his home in Lee's Summit, where there were still active Jesse James fan clubs. He stared down at his plate and then launched into his tirade. "Typical," he said. "Emotional cripples, that's what the FCA breeds. Guys who can't handle it themselves, so they lay it all off on God."

His wife, Polly, was looking very nervous. I'd been writing everything down. "Are you sure you want to see this in a national magazine?" She said. He thought it over for a moment.

"Yeah. I guess I might as well be controversial in my old age," he said and continued his diatribe.

When it came time to write my story, I looked at the quotes again. I was very fond of Rudnay, both as a player and a person. I also felt that he had absolutely no idea what his life would be like if those sentiments ever saw the light of day. It was a hell of a flashy angle, but I took my pen and drew a line through all the FCA quotes. I just couldn't do it.

Sometimes you don't even realize it, but you run into a player you never really knew that well but trusts you well enough to raise the curtain, if only for brief moment. I sat with Lawrence Taylor one night when he just decided to sweep away the cliché quotes and break down the game from a purely analytical level. LT, who loved the joy of competition, who would regularly star in the contest the Giants players would hold before practice, setting a garbage can 50 yards away and seeing who could throw the most footballs into it. It was almost an impossible task, but when LT would let fly, they'd be banging off the can, with more of them dropping in than anyone else could manage, even the quarterbacks.

In the 1980s Jim Anderson, the L.A. Rams' trainer, adopted a mongrel dog from a local shelter. It became the club's mascot. They named it Ofer, standing for 0-for-6. It had been given seven days to live before it would be killed. Anderson got it on the seventh day. It had gone 0-for-6. Ofer's great joy was to guard an open locker, as a cocker goalie would, while various players tried to kick a tennis ball past him. It was practically impossible. He had lightning reflexes. He wouldn't swallow any fakes. When the Giants practiced in L.A. for the '87 Super Bowl against the Broncos, they used the Rams' training facilities. Everyone immediately took up the Ofer challenge. One day LT was unusually bubbly and animated for the opening of the press interview sessions. Someone asked him how come.

"I beat Ofer two out of 10 this morning," he said.

But on this night half a decade or so later, we sat at a table, late at night, in his ill-fated restaurant, one of the many business ventures that failed, and he tried to explain what really went on out there. Maybe he was just tired of making headlines with those standard macho quotes ... how he hit 'em so hard he could see the ... you can fill in the rest yourself. Maybe he just wanted to take it to a different level, what actually went on out there.

"Look, there just comes a moment in a game," he said, "when you know that's it. If you make the play, the game's over. It's very hard to explain. It's just something you feel. Maybe you're up by 10 points and you know if you score once more, just once, on anything, they'll quit. You can see it. You can feel it, maybe before even they know it. It could be when you're on defense, and you can see how desperate they are, and you make the stop, you get the sack and — ahhhh — the air just goes out of them. And the game's over. It's not a macho thing, it's not me against you or any of that crap and it's deeper. But you just know it."

I've felt that way sometimes, covering a game. And sometimes I was wrong. But then again, I wasn't down in the pit. LT was, and I appreciated the way he tried to get me to understand it.

I've been asked what was the greatest play I've ever seen. Steve Young's broken field 49-yard gallop that left Viking tacklers all over the field in 1988 comes to mind, but emotionally, I can't get away from a play I saw Taylor make in 1983, his third year in the league, in a game against the Super Bowl Redskins. In the context of the game, it was almost meaningless; the Giants were down by 10 points at the time, and on the chart, it went down as a 15-yard run by Joe Theismann. Taylor, rushing from the right wing, gripped 300-pound All-Pro left tackle Joe Jacoby by the shoulder pads and threw him, flushing Theismann out of the pocket, and the quarterback was off and running, with LT in pursuit. George Starke, the right tackle, peeled back to pick up Taylor, who knocked him to the ground without breaking stride. Fifteen yards down field, Taylor caught up to Theismann and brought him down. He had disposed of 560 pounds worth of offensive linemen and run down a 4.6 quarterback. Nowhere was the play ever mentioned. A superhuman defensive play.

I close my eyes and see Taylor, bent over in pain, by his locker after he had recorded three sacks against the Saints and forced two fumbles, single-handedly turning the game for the Giants, playing under the extreme agony of a torn pectoral muscle in his chest. Bill Parcells knelt in front of Taylor and leaned over, and they touched foreheads.

"I didn't think you'd make it," he said.

"I didn't either," Taylor said.

The NFL become my personal province and naturally the source for my richest store of memories. Pete Rozelle spoiled me for the commissioners who followed. I could talk to him as I would to a fan. I felt that I could ask him anything. He never ducked a question, and I also never heard him say to me, "This is off the record." He just trusted my good sense. I remember when the USFL sued the NFL in 1986 and won a settlement of $3. I rode back to the league office with Rozelle.

"I'm really proud of the way our owners handled themselves in court," he said. I asked him about the young owner who had enthusiastically endorsed the Porter report, a loony plan by a Harvard professor advising the NFL in the use of dirty tricks. It became a major arguing point for the USFL in court. Rozelle made a face when I mentioned the owner's name.

"A freakin airhead," he said.

"Let me get it right … a dickhead, was that the quote?" I asked him, faking some heavy note-taking. "An airhead, same as you," he said smiling.

I could always get a rise out of him one way. I'd say "Fifty-five to seven," and he'd go off. I was a sophomore at Stanford in 1950; he was the 24-year-old PR man for the University of San Francisco. A year later the great Dons team with Ollie Matson and Gino Marchetti and Burl Toler would go unbeaten — one of the great teams in history — but in '50 they were juniors and we beat them, 55-7. Ed Brown, the quarterback who would later play for the Bears, was hurt that day, and a guy named Lefty Gene Sweeters, who couldn't throw the ball in the ocean, threw twice as many interceptions as completions.

"Jesus Christ, out quarterback was out, and Sweeters wasn't even supposed to play that day," and he'd be off and running. Every time. I could get him every time.

The league always came down hard on gambling or the hint of it, and point spreads and the like. But Rozelle grew up where people liked to make an occasional wagers, and you know how some stuff dies hard. Once I asked him what he thought of a 49er-Viking game coming up. Just by instinct, without really worrying about the implications, he said, "Geez, you've got to like the Niners getting seven. I mean, they can run the ball."

When I did his obit for *Sports Illustrated*, I wrote about that incident, and one of the prissy editors killed the part about the betting line, which, of course, destroyed the whole point of the story.

Even before Rozelle announced his retirement, he didn't seem right, but I never wrote it and didn't even want to know for sure what a lot of us suspected.

"What's wrong with him?" I finally asked Browns owner Art Modell at one of the league meetings.

"No one's saying, but it's got to be some kind of a minor stroke," Modell said. "What we're seeing just isn't like him, is it?" No, it wasn't. It was a sad final memory.

Maybe it's because the sporting arena is such a vivid, explosive place, but it's very hard to accept the death of its dynamic performers. I just can't picture Walter Payton dead. I keep remembering the time I sat with him in the lobby of the Bears' dorm at their training camp in Lake Forest, Ill. He had brought his motorcycle in there and placed it next to a wall, and as I talked to him he just couldn't sit still. He'd sit, jump up, bounce a few times on the balls of his feet, jump on the seat of his cycle, bounce up and down, hop off, go back to the seat, bounce again, as he made a point, his words coming as fast as his movements, a dizzying capsule of energy itself. It was getting dark outside, and seen in the dim light of the lobby, Payton actually seemed to glow; it was as if an aura was emanating from him. Fascinating, a little scary, unforgettable ... how could he have died so young?

I wrote a book with Lyle Alzado. After I got to know him, he didn't hold back, talking about the fear and insecurity that gripped him throughout his whole career. He was the only player who ever told me he was using anabolic steroids while he was an active player. Six seasons after I did the book, he played in the '84 Super Bowl for the Raiders against the Redskins. The Raiders won big. He'd been a consistent force, exerting pressure on Theismann. The locker facilities in Tampa Stadium were cramped. Maneuvering was tough, as it normally is in a post-Super Bowl locker room, and I was struggling to get my quotes, inching through the mass of bodies. All of a sudden, someone was gripping my arm. It was Alzado. His eyes looked wild.

"I've got to talk to you," he said.

"Jesus, Lyle," I said. "Now? Right now?"

"Yeah, now. Let's go in back."

I didn't know that had happened, a major felony, someone busted for drugs, what? We went into a back area, behind the trainers' rooms and the washing machines and the piles of dirty uniforms, into almost pitch darkness.

"What? What is it?" I asked him. He stared at me for a moment.

"How'd I play?" He said. *Phew, what a relief.*

"Great, you played great, Lyle."

"Really, you're not shittin' me?"

"Really."

"Thanks," he said.

I know it's wrong, but I think of O.J. Simpson the same way I think of players who have died. Once I was on a talk show toward the end of his career and I was asked who were the nicest of the superstars, in any sport, to be around. It didn't take a lot of thought to answer it. The first guy who came to mind was Pele, the great soccer player, one of the most decent, humble people I've ever met. The second one was O.J. Simpson.

The answer didn't draw much of a reaction at the time. If you would have asked any of the beat guys covering the Bills, or even the 49ers during his two years there, they'd have told you the same thing. A few years ago, I was on another show and I was asked the same question. Before I answered it, I had to ask myself: *How much courage do you have?* Pele, over and out, would have been the easy answer, the coward's way out. I had gotten in trouble on a lot of these kinds of shows, popping some top of the head observation out quickly without time for reflection, and what always happens is that these talk show people cut you off in a hurry without giving you time to fully develop your answer.

They're like prosecuting attorneys. I could hear the guys now: "Are you totally aware of what he did, of the civil suit he lost in the death of Nicole Brown? Have you been asleep all this time? How could you be so blind and think only of your own relationship?" And so forth and so on. I could avoid all this. Better avoid it.

"Pele, the soccer player," I said, "and O.J. Simpson." And, of course, the storm came.

I just let the blows fall. I could have mentioned all the little kindnesses he showed during a 13-year professional relationship that began in his junior year at USC, all the little things he didn't have to do but did anyway, the times he'd call me late at night, just to clarify a story, to make sure I had things right, the kindness he'd shown to my teenage son. I could have mentioned the piece I did on him in his last year in football, with the Niners, when he and Al Cowlings — that's right — the same guy who drove the white car in that notorious TV episode, spent their day off driving me around their old neighborhood on Portero Hill acting as tour guides, almost … "This is where Joey T. backed his Camero into the grocery store window, this is where we used to play football on the street." And then the evening I spent with O.J. and Nicole in their penthouse apartment, looking down on the twinkling lights of the city, the softness of it, gripping her hand as he told me about his child who had drowned in a swimming pool, the tears, the silences, the reflective moments. *My God, this is a nice couple*, I thought. *I hope they find some joy in their lives.*

And then gone, smashed, shattered in a horrible explosion of deadly violence and infidelity. Yeah, I could have mentioned all the nice stuff, and then the talk show guy would really have laced into me, lumping me with one of those idiots who says, "Well, Saddam Hussein was always nice to me when I dealt with him." No, better keeping it buttoned up.

I saw O.J. on TV during the trial and afterward, and it wasn't the same person. I guess it could have been the drugs that did it to him, perhaps a heavier dose over a longer period than people imagined. His voice had thickened and coarsened, and there was violence in it that he'd never shown in the old days ... I'd never even heard of him being involved in anything ugly or violent on the field. And he looked different, thicker, darker, as silly as that might sound. It was a different person, a kind of monster, and that's why I thought of him as a member of the roster of the dead. The old O.J. Simpson was dead.

When I was in high school, my bible was Paul Gallico's *Farewell to Sport*, and the title for this chapter duplicates his opener ... out of respect. He touched on such a wide spectrum, but I have narrowed my focus to the sports I knew best. He saw the rise of big-time sports and its superheroes during his tour of duty, which lasted from 1923 to 1936. But my gosh, he lasted only 13 years until he wrote his signoff, his *Farewell to Sport*, which became my bible as a teenager. My question was what was his rush? He left to become a fiction writer, and for a while, I read everything he wrote, but aside from one magnificent and famous story, *The Snow Goose*, nothing from what I thought was a rather superficial output ever came near the depth and profundity of his sports writing.

He wrote about leaving the arena as a gradual closing of the door. Well, I'm not leaving it, not yet anyway. I'll say goodbye when the time comes, but right now I'll take what's there, even if it isn't the way it used to be. Reminds me of the old saying about New Orleans: "It ain't what it used to be and never was." OK, forgive me, an old man's memories. Maybe it's more of never-was, but to me they're still alive. All of them.

Chapter 2

Centrique To Freaque

I am looking in the mirror. I don't like what is looking back at me. I see 74 years of strange living. What I see is old, yes, but not *old* old, if you know what I mean.

The eyes, thank God, have not gone vacant yet. Henry Fonda in *On Golden Pond*, my father when he was nearing 80, you would occasionally see a reflected kind of light in his eyes, but very little from within. Unless you got him annoyed or angry. Then the stokers would report for their shift, and you'd see the start of a small flame. I would deliberately provoke him at times, just to see those flickers, unable to face the fact that there really wasn't much left.

No, I haven't gone blank yet. But the other one is tougher, that startled look you see in old people when someone comes into the room, without warning, or somehow their perspective has been even slightly altered. Their eyes flash, almost in pure terror, and then the look subsides. That's the one that scares me. I say to my redheaded wife, "You'll tell me, won't you, if my eyes get crazy and scared for no reason?" Yes. I'll tell you, she says, but I wonder. The thought terrifies me, the dimming of the flame, the eyes that gradually pick up that glaze.

So far they're just the eyes of someone looking for an excuse. To get angry or to tap a never-ending vein of hilarity, which, really, is the way to keep the party going, isn't it? As the immediacy of old age reaches out and takes hold, it seems like the middle ground between anger and hilarity keeps shrinking. Some say that it didn't occupy much space to begin with.

Nothing especially pleasant is revealed by the mirror, but nothing really startling, either. Hair and mustache in correct formation, ears appearing slightly larger, but doesn't that always happen as you get older? Teeth reasonably in place, except for a front one that was evicted many an autumn ago on some gridiron I don't even recall … kicked, punched, otherwise forcibly removed, who can remember? Usual scars reflecting many years in self-destructive sports, a long one straddling the left cheekbone that becomes more apparent during summer tanning. Occasionally I'm asked about it.

"A dueling scar," I say, repeating a line that has yet to draw a laugh. Actually it was the gift of a fat-assed lummox of a guard named Tom Burbank, who tripped over me and fell, his football shoe catching me under the eye, in a 1957 scrimmage on the WACOM (Western Area Command) Rhinos' field in Vogelweh, Germany. I remember the German doctors having an awful time getting the contact lens out. I haven't been able to wear one in that eye since.

Pencil scar running across the center of my nose. It's in an odd place. Usually your helmet gouges a permanent one higher up, but this was the result of the last break, which for some reason occurred in a more southerly region. The best picture ever taken of me was on the day after, showing both eyes blackened and the nose squashed flat against my face, which accurately reflected my outlook on life at the time.

Finally the chin, and the region beneath it, which can wreak such havoc among old people, which can produce such grotesqueries as the swollen orb of flesh, the fat bloop euphemistically called a double chin, or the horrible, stringy, cock a doddle doo of the emaciated throat. Long ago I recognized the fact that the neck was sacred, at first in deference to a Jack Dempsey quote I once read in *Boys Life* magazine that he always made sure he had a strong neck, so he could take a punch, and then, carrying through on an exercise I had begun at 15 to keep the muscles toned. Later it was designed to forestall the fat bloop or the Red Rooster Come Over Syndrome.

It was the same exercise through the years. Lie on a bench, first on my back, then my stomach, with my head hanging over the edge, put a towel on the back of my head, or my forehead, hold a weight on it — 30 pounds when I first started, gradually increasing to 50 — and do three sets of 15 raises each way. It only began to draw notice in my 60s, when I was going through my health club phase, and was managing to keep the underchin atrocities at bay. Invariably some Samaritan would wait till I was finished and then politely inform me that I was risking permanent infirmity.

"Look, I'm an orthopedist (or a neurologist, or chiropractor or psychopath) and I can tell you that what you're doing is extremely dangerous, extremely so," and so forth. Recognizing his kind intentions, I wouldn't inform him that I'd been doing the exercise for, roughly, 50 years.

But a woman, whom I found out was French, evidently had been watching me for a few weeks because one day she came over and said, "You know, in France we have a name for a person like you. We call him a *centrique*." Centrique, eccentric, I'd presume. That's been the path, all right, from centrique to freaque. My life story.

Have I really reached 74, or is it some kind of terrifying joke? In my head, it's all the same. Will I wake up tomorrow and find myself back in high school, waiting for the lunch hour break so I can play bottle cap hockey with Arnie Weinberg or Larry Van in the schoolyard?

When you're 74 you look for edges. Look at what I have and you don't! At least 50 more times in your lifetime, you will get something in your eye and you won't be able to remove it for hours, even days. That will happen to me only three or four more times. There will be at least 200 times when you will lose something you "just had a minute ago." You will be delayed; you will be late to where you're going. On at least 20 of those occasions, you will never find it. Never. For me? Ten more. Fifteen, tops. I could go on. The hundreds and hundreds of little indignities, all the busted straights and flushes God will deal you. Not me, folks. I've seen them already. I know when they're coming, when to fold my hand. Well, most of the time.

I am a chart freak. Everything must be charted and counted. Number of steps from ticket counter to plane in various airports, number of single shots fired in a movie, before the advent of automatic weapons, time it takes to sing or play the national anthem in various venues, top 10 football games seen, top 20 linebackers, 40 running backs. Top 10 incidents of pain encountered. (Makes it hurt less at the time. Try it, you'll see.) And I have charted the decades of my life, with a capsule on each.

When I was nine I looked upon my 10th birthday as a gateway to what people kept calling the "teenage years." I didn't really understand what made them so special, but I was always seeing features labeled "Teen Topics," "Tips for Teens," etc. In my mind I would shoot through ages 10 and 11 without even thinking about them. A teenager, gosh. Someday.

No big deal about my 20th birthday. It came and went. The goal was 21. Legal drinking age in many states, not New York, where I grew up, but in other places where it was kind of a big deal. Voting age. Plus lots of, uh, other things that somehow got you out of the class of "minor," and into major ... or maybe that was 18. Not really sure. College dropout at the time, going to work, then back to school. Too many issues whirling around to worry.

Thirty was a big one. The worst. Goodbye youth. I checked major league and NFL rosters to see how many 30-year-olds they had. The more the team had, the harder I'd root for it. I despised those with only a handful. "Well, he's 30 now. Don't know how much longer he can carry the ball and keep taking those hits." Words that would fill me with anger, and terror.

"What the hell, 30 isn't old," I'd say, and people would stare at me. Oh, God.

Forty was a breeze because for the last two years I had adopted the simple expedient of telling people I was 40, when my age was requested. I wasn't going to be caught again, as I was a decade earlier. I had braced myself for the fateful day, and when it finally came, it slipped by unnoticed.

The lying started at 50. It was just too nasty a thing to admit to. What the hell, I was still physically active. I could beat my son at tennis, at one-on-one hoops. OK, so he was only 11, but I could still move around all right. Except for that one time he challenged me to a sprint at 50 yards, and early on I realized that if I were to take one more aggressive step, the left hamstring was going to go. Kaboing! I just knew it. Well, sprinting's out, but the other stuff is still OK. So who needs to know I'm 50, right? RIGHT? Why are you turning away? They'll believe it if I tell them I'm 43 or 45. I mean I don't *feel* 50.

At 60 I sat down to write a piece called "Life at 60." But my finger hit a typo, and it came out 50. The number 60 was so terrible I just couldn't type it. Sixty years old, 60. I shook my head to clear away the idea of it. It wouldn't go away. The definitive break between middle and old age. People retired at 60. Not me. I had been divorced for a couple of years, I was paying off four assorted loans. Stop working? Not today, friends.

At the class reunions, I'd look at my schoolmates to see who looked older than me, younger. I wasn't sure because I didn't want to imagine what I looked like. Howard Slusher, the sports agent, had told me that his wife had "just run away with her 60-year-old golf instructor." We both shuddered.

I thought the same way I did when I was in college. I mean I still do, but I evaluated people the same way, hated the phonies, liked the same foods, the same movies. OK, so sometimes when I got up in the morning, I encountered strange aches that never existed, but that's not old age, is it? IS IT? And most of them eventually went away anyway. Sixty was an assassin that had hidden behind the door in a dark room. It was an outlaw that had ambushed me on a rocky trail. A blindsider. I never saw the hit coming, maybe because it had been such a gradual thing.

And then there was the matter of sex. For the most part, sex at 60 was a Three Stooges movie. I wouldn't have minded watching it. I just don't want to be in it. The cliché of old roue with young tootsie? Please. How about women my own age? I quote the words the famous winemaker, Andre Tchelistcheff, once said, and, of course, he was talking about women a bit older, but I still recalled his statement: "Tasting an old wine is like making love to an old woman. It's possible. It might even be enjoyable. But it requires a great deal of imagination."

Seventy was odd and indescribable. At the reunions I no longer sought comparison with my classmates. I rooted for them. God, look how youthful he looks. Isn't it wonderful? Joe Kutchukian, the tennis player, for instance. Hair still dark, a real bounce to his walk. Then he died suddenly. News of it buckled my knees. Who had ever thought about the hand of death? But all of the sudden they started dying. And then you felt the breeze of it yourself … angina pectoris, a procedure followed by a staph infection that blew my femoral artery, ruptured it clean. What was it that Manolete, the bullfighter, died of? Horn wound to the femoral, right? He went into shock. Memo to self. Do not, repeat, not go into shock. Jammed a towel over it, tight, held it down with my elbow and drove my Honda with the other hand, eight miles to Morristown Memorial and the emergency room. Should I run this red light? Would be just like one of those Jersey cops: "I don't care *what's* wrong with you."

Next day I asked the intern, Charlie Willekes, who'd played basketball at Iowa, or maybe it was Iowa State, "How much longer did I have?"

"About eight minutes," he said.

When my daughter heard about it, she asked me, "Were you scared?" I had to think it through very carefully. Scared? Not really. Annoyed, actually. Annoyed that I'd get blood on the rug downstairs, that the towel would slip off in the car. A logistic problem more than anything. I don't think she believed me.

That's what you do when you're 70. You tell people about your ailments, just the things no one wants to hear, and which I'd sworn I'd never mention. And I won't. No more … except for that one.

But by the time I was 70, sunshine had entered my life — in the form of a flaming redhead from Arizona 20 years my junior, Linda Bailey. Up there in his office, God had opened his file cabinet and found my folder and said, "What do you say? Let's give the old turtle a break." And there she was. The Flaming Redhead is how she appears in my regular column on the *Sports Illustrated* website, a constant governor on the engine that wants to take me to pretense and hypocrisy and high blown invention, a welcome voice of sanity. I get mail from those who say they enjoy our relationship that finds its way into print, our obvious affection, especially when it involves a cranky old dog such as myself, and the cynic in me says that if I were reading this in another context, I'd call for an all aboard the Hallmark Express. But at this stage in life, what it has done has been to rub the edges off the bitterness, that at one time I felt would cripple me, and replace it with someone with whom to share the annoyances, and yes, the high hilarity, of life's looniness.

And the craziness keeps growing doesn't it, gathering steam? Language has become crazy. When did they start calling short people height deprived, and poor people financially deprived? When did nouns invade the stronghold of verbs and shell them into submission? Obsoleting, texting, liaising, impacting. When did airline personnel numb you with their linguistic bludgeoning?

"Why don't you talk right?" I ask the stewardess, excuse me, the flight attendant.

Make that the air comfort coordinator.

"What do you mean?"

"Why do flights terminate instead of end? Why do people de-plane? Do they plane? Why are lights always illuminated instead of lighted? Or just lit?"

"Because it sounds better."

"Do you go home and tell your husband, 'Honey, please illuminate the light?'"

"I'm not married."

The Flaming Redhead whispers to me, "See that, you can't win."

When the flight has landed, I tell the stewardess, "You know something? I didn't put my tray table up for the landing." The look is a look of abject horror.

"You DIDN'T?"

"No, I ensured that it was in an upright position."

She looks toward the cockpit for help, make that for assistance, for anyone who can assist her in dealing with this obvious freak, uh, freaque. It is too late. People are already starting to file out.

The Redhead helps me get through "the world's madness," to quote the words of poor Kid McCoy, the former middleweight champ, who killed himself with a bullet to the head. She is a sounding board for its hilarity. Then the men with the wrecking ball came and destroyed some of the most beautiful things in my particular province, which happens to be language. The beauty and grace of the King James version of the Bible, for instance, some of the most memorable phrases in the English tongue, have been edited down, dumbed down actually, by these tin-eared butchers. The late author, Isaac Bashevis Singer, put it best.

"I received a wonderful gift the other day. *The Complete Works of William Shakespeare, Edited and Improved Upon by a Man Named Horowitz.*"

Ah, but I'm running far afield, way off the track, which is what I'm afraid this memoir has in store for you. It is constructed roughly along the lines of my favorite sports memoir, *Farewell to Sport* by Paul Gallico, beginning with a chapter bearing the same title, out of respect: Mine Eyes Have Seen the Glory. I will bring you into my world, of course, through almost 50 years of covering the vast spectrum of sports at every level, from the rock strewn high school fields of metropolitan New Jersey to five summer Olympics and 40 Super Bowls, and I'll go back further, to my own days as a competitor.

Chapter 3

Boxing Ernest Hemingway

They used to put me in the ring with Ernest Hemingway because we were roughly the same size, even though I was 15, and then 16, at the time. He was a little shorter than me. I stood 6-1 1/2, which was as tall as I'd ever get, and weighed 220, which, unfortunately, is only a streamlined memory now. I was the heaviest kid on my high school football team by 30 pounds (you have to remember this was 1948-49) and I had about five pounds on Hemingway. I think this was one of the reasons he liked to get in the ring with me; you'd have thought he'd have been annoyed at the idea of George Brown, who owned the gym, sticking him in there with a young punk, but once I heard him tell Brown, "I like to get in there with that kid. He's big and he can take a punch and he doesn't complain."

I wanted to be a fighter. Other kids read about famous aviators and ballplayers, I read about Sullivan and Jake Kilrain and the famous bare-knuckle fighters, Bendigo and Mendoza and the great Heenan-Sayers match and how the British gentry would wager on first blood, "first to show the scarlet." My best friend in high school, Paul Lansky, shared my passion. Paulie was a lightweight with great savvy and ring awareness, "generalship," they used to call it. Actually he did quite well in the ring, captain of the West Point team, when boxing was a collegiate sport. Then he had the sense to quit. I hung around for a while, putting together an unimpressive record in amateur and collegiate bouts and a final one in the army, never really getting myself in good enough shape but always able to take a punch — too many of them, actually.

"You want to go to my gym downtown to train?" He said one day in school. Oh my God, training in a real gym in downtown New York. It was a long subway ride away … our high school was in the upper reaches of the Bronx, where street numbers ran in the 240s. Hilltoppers from the Horace Mann, that was us. But who cared about a long ride after school? A gym, man, with actual fighters and everything.

I don't know how Paulie got connected with George Brown's. It was most likely through his father, who was part of the Manhattan celebrity whirl … yes, you've heard of his father, whose first name was Meyer. Once in a while, we'd catch a ride in his car down to the gym. He was friendly, he and Paulie had a loose, easy relationship. The kids in school talked about the fact that he was somehow connected with gambling, and there was mention of him hopping back and forth from Miami to Havana to a place in Nevada called Las Vegas. That's all I knew. I don't remember seeing anything about him in the papers in those days. Once I asked Paulie if his father really was into some kind of gambling, and he mentioned that he was involved with the Wurlitzer Company that made jukeboxes. It didn't seem very interesting to me. His dad once seemed interested when he asked me what my father did and I told him he was a union leader.

"What union?" he said. "ILGWU, the Garment Workers," I said. He nodded and smiled. "A fine union," he said. "They really look after their workers there."

I told my father what Meyer Lansky had said. His face stiffened. He didn't say anything, which I thought was strange.

The thing I liked about Brown's was that Brown himself liked to throw everyone into the ring. Hemingway enjoyed that, too, because that was his only form of exercise up there and he liked to check out the unlikely-looking-clientele and see how they handled themselves with the gloves on, if, indeed, Brown could get them to give it a try. Hemingway also enjoyed creating odd boxing scenarios. Boxing with Ezra Pound when they were young writers in Paris was something he always liked telling.

"He was a tall, skinny guy; it was like fighting Ichabod Crane," Hemingway said. It's a very vivid memory. He was sitting on a rubbing table, encased in those rubber wraps people used to wear in those days to make them perspire, with a sweatsuit on top of it. It was his favorite place to relax, and his favorite garb. He'd even box with that stuff on, which made body punching a waste of time.

"You didn't want to hit Ezra too hard because he'd quit. But just tap him hard enough to get him mad. Then he'd start flailing, and the real fun would begin."

For Brown the formula was simple. As a renowned trainer, boxing was the best form of exercise he knew, and with the big, 16-ounce pillows he had for gloves, it was tough really to get hurt. So he encouraged everyone to box. Once, when I had started writing sports and covering boxing, I asked Cus D'Amato, Mike Tyson's first manager, if he knew Brown. Cus paused for emphasis, as he used to do before he delivered one of his lectures about sport, and said, "One of the great purists of the ring."

Tall and aristocratic looking with thinning hair and an aquiline profile, Brown was rumored to have been the oldest enlisted man in the service during World War II. No one ever really knew his age. He looked like mid-50s. Occasionally he'd step into the ring to demonstrate some teaching point, and everyone would stop to watch. He was graceful for a big man; he'd glide. You weren't aware of him actually taking steps. His prime emphasis was the avoidance of getting hit; he liked fighters whose faces resembled the ones with which they began their career. The sluggers, the take-two-to-land-one guys, disgusted him. When he was in the ring himself, it was rare when anyone snuck a punch in on him. His attitude toward the sport was surprising, since the most famous fighter he ever trained, middleweight champ Harry Greb, was a nonstop brawler.

George Plimpton once quoted Hemingway, talking about Brown's own ring days: "He could have been champion if he had been able to accept the idea that he was going to be hit once in a while."

I mentioned to Cus D'Amato that I had been there on a few afternoons when he brought his young protege, Floyd Patterson, up to Brown's to work with the master. He nodded.

"Brown was a purist as far as defensive fighting was concerned. That's what I wanted Floyd to understand before he started facing the big boys."

The implication was obvious. When you have a fighter with a glass jaw, you try to keep him from getting hit. Most of the time it worked for the future heavyweight champ.

Not all of Brown's clients, especially the celebrity variety, would climb in the ring. I never saw Quentin Reynolds, a big-name journalist and author in those days, put the gloves on. Nobody ever wanted to see Champ Segal in the ring or get in there with him personally. Champ was one of those legendary Broadway characters everyone seemed to know. He was probably in his early 50s … big, bigger than me, and brawly with a coarse haw-haw-haw laugh and a habit of shouting when he talked. Once, on the four-wall racquetball, which we called paddleball, court, I was playing some doctor from Long Island, and he cut me off and set up a block and I ran him over, getting to the ball. He hollered, "You young son of a bitch," and came at me, slashing with the paddle. I backed up and tried to fend him off.

From the little spectator perch next to the court, I heard this big guffaw where Champ had been watching the match, and then he was on the court. "You guys don't wanna FIGHT!" he yelled between heehaws and then held us apart, firmly, one hand on each of us. I couldn't move. I mean, the guy was strong.

He'd had few professional bouts in his youth, but mostly he'd been a street brawler. When he stripped down in the locker room, I could see two neat white bullet scars on his belly. There had been at least one book written about him, *They Called Him Champ*, and when I knew him, he was the owner of a bar and restaurant on Broadway, House of Champs. At Brown's one of the favorite stories they told was about the time two young gunmen tried to stick up Champ, while he was behind the bar. He reached across and flattened the first one. The second one fired wildly and ran out onto the street. Champ followed him out and shot him dead. No, the patrons at Brown's weren't sad that Champ wasn't inclined to step into the ring.

The Gimbel boys, who were on the boxing team at Yale, always would drop in when they were in town. One afternoon I saw Dan Bucceroni, a light heavyweight main-eventer, working out. Another time the big Swedish heavy, Olle Tandberg, was there. Normal customers who attended strictly for the workout usually would be matched against Norm Barth, the equipment man, a short, chunky weightlifter, and later Jimmy Devlin, who had just come over from Ireland and eventually would become a leading New York-area referee. Jimmy had been a promising lightweight in the old country and he'd merely run them through some speedwork, but anyone foolish enough to get him annoyed would get smacked.

One afternoon, as I was dressing, I heard this whap-whap-whap from the ring and I rushed out to see what had happened. A concert violinist named Kovacs, whose action mainly centered on Carnegie Hall catty-corner across the street (Brown's was at 225 W. 57th St., 11th floor) had been trading whacks with Norm Barth and he'd gotten the worst of it. He was sitting on a training table, next to the one on which Hemingway was trying to take a post-steam room nap, rubbing his nose, looking very red in the face.

"What's up, Mr. Kovacs?" I asked him. "Ees not fair," he said. "Ees a sport, not where you keel each other. He hit me the keeser and the smeller." I could see Hemingway shaking with laughter. Later he enjoyed relating incident. "Oh, that was good," he said. "In the keesaire and smellaire. Perfect."

Boxing with Hemingway tested your brute strength. It was literally push comes to shove. Very few lethal punches were exchanged. Brown's final word, before I stepped into the ring, always was the same. "No right hands." He didn't want some wild-assed 16-year-old getting all caught up in the magic of the moment and trying to chase away his most famous customer. It put me at a disadvantage, naturally, but in a strange way it accomplished an interesting thing. In time, I developed a better left hand than right, although I'm normally right-handed. Hemingway wasn't comfortable sparring at long range, and neither was I. God had burdened me with 220 pounds at age 16, even 15, for a reason, and that wasn't about to escape my notice. It seemed that Hemingway might have felt the same way because he liked to jack you up in the clinches and muscle you into the ropes and punish you in close. If you allowed yourself to relax, you could get bumped up a bit, so you didn't relax, especially when his punches would go south and come dangerously near your groin. You had to stay alert.

But it was fun. I enjoyed it immensely, bulldogging and grappling with one of the great authors of our time. I can't remember anyone ever getting hurt. Tired yes, extremely so. I didn't tell anyone about it. For one thing, no one would have believed me. For another, it would have sounded like bragging. I remember reading on a few occasions what an accomplished boxer Hemingway was. I don't think the people who wrote that ever saw him in the ring. He was a big, burly guy who could rough you up a bit, but a skilled boxer? Naah, sorry. I heard people quoted about Hemingway's supposed mean streak, that he could be nasty when he was drunk, that he'd started his share of fights. Perhaps it was true, but at Brown's we never saw that side. He was relaxed and happy in that atmosphere, a friendly guy who liked to tell stories, who liked to laugh.

In reading other accounts of Hemingway's life, I realized this wasn't a good period for him. *For Whom the Bell Tolls* had been a success, both artistically and financially, but that was almost a decade before I knew him up at Brown's. Since then he had marked time with magazine work and non-fiction pieces, and every once in a while, there would be something in the paper asking when he was going to get it together for a major novel. Someone told me he was drinking a lot in those days, then coming up to Brown's to sweat out the alcohol. I must admit that, up to that point, I had not ready any of his novels, although I had seen the movie, *For Whom the Bell Tolls*, with Gary Cooper and Ingrid Bergman and Akim Tamiroff. But I was well aware of his short stories even before we studied them in my senior year at HM.

I was often tempted to tell him how much I loved his boxing stories, especially "Fifty Grand" and "The Battler" and then "My Old Man," about the crooked jockey and his adoring son. That was me, Joe Butler, watching his dad work the horses out in the early morning, on the misty tracks around Paris. I could feel the dampness coming through the sweater that I'd pulled up around my neck. And I wanted to tell him my favorite story was one they never mentioned in school, *The Light of the World*, about two whores, each of whom claimed they had known Stanley Ketchel, the middleweight champ. But I couldn't do it; it just wasn't something you wanted to talk about in the loose, relaxed atmosphere of Brown's, where Hemingway felt so much at ease, talking about things such as what was best for sweating out a hangover or whether or not the rubber wraps could really burn the weight off. It was a place where people could kid him interminably about his weight ... his nickname was "Broadsides" up at Brown's ... but instinctively I knew that it would be poor form to introduce anything that had a literary smell to it. Wasn't it the hunter-guide, Wilson, who had told Macomber in Hemingway's story, "The Short Happy Life of Francis Macomber," that you could talk something out if you talked about it too much? And now, looking back on the period, it might not have been the right note to strike, praising him about things he had written a quarter of a century before then.

Maybe I was wrong, or perhaps just shy, but I felt that even an honest admission of how much his stories had moved me would somehow be off-line ... in that atmosphere, near one of those rubbing tables next to the window, under Hemingway's inscribed picture to Brown. It was almost 60 years ago that I saw that picture, Hemingway in some sort of winter hunting outfit, holding a brace of pheasants or partridges in his hands, with his inscription, "To George Brown and his two educated hands." And then his inverted triangle, signaling the left out word, "good," before "educated." I often wondered why he had gone back and added that word. More than 50 years later, the picture came up at a Sotheby's sale, probably from Brown's heirs. Brown had been with Hemingway in his home in Ketchum, Idaho, when he had killed himself. He had been a pallbearer at his funeral.

At Brown's, Hemingway would get great pleasure from scanning the sports pages, stopping at any reference to boxing to let you know what idiots covered the sport. One magazine piece in particular drew a huge laugh from him.

"You've got to listen to this," he said to whomever was within hearing distance. "Here's this guy writing that Joe Louis was the greatest fighter of all time. He says that Louis had such great reflexes and punching power that he could probably even fight a wild animal and win."

Now he was a radio announcer, broadcasting the regular Madison Square Garden Friday Night Fights from Gillette.

"We're bringing you, direct from ringside, Joe Louis vs the bear. The bell ... Don Dunphy ..." and now Hemingway's voice took on the slightly nasal twang of the famous radio announcer of the '40s: "Louis jabs, the bear backs off. Louis jabs, the bear backs off. They move into a clinch ... And we cut to the next scene."

Chapter 4

Journalism

The first time I read Tom Wolfe proclaiming that the New Journalism and Personal Journalism were something of a modern phenomenon, I felt like asking him, "Did you ever hear of Rudyard Kipling?" When I read, not too long ago, about the revolution in sportswriting that introduced the freshness of penetrating, iconoclastic observations and in-depth quotes and probing interviews, my only reaction was that the people who actually believed this stuff didn't understand much about the history of the profession.

There were real phrasemakers in the old days, and when I was a kid, I used to cut out their snappers and one-liners and keep them in a big notebook. There was paunchiness and wit and sparkle that we don't see too often nowadays. Not that the old-time sportswriters were that much better, day in, day out, but when one of them connected on something, it went out of the park.

Have you ever heard of Frank Graham? Columnist for *The New York Sun.* Nobody ever put it better, referring to the athlete on the verge of retirement who all of a sudden feels the need to talk to you about "an exciting new project I'm involved in."

"They learn to say hello," Graham wrote, "just when they should be saying goodbye."

I grew up with this kind of stuff. It was my English Lit seminar, my exploration into the classics.

Graham, again, covering the Max Baer-Tony Galento fight in Jersey City in 1940, and I would have to call this my favorite lead:

"They rolled the clock back last night and two cuckoos jumped out."

I can quote you parts of that story. The fight ended when Galento couldn't come out of his corner for the eighth round.

"I can't breed," was Graham's quote for Two Ton Tony.

And post-fight, Baer, who was known as The Clown Prince, did a little waltz around the ring with a dwarf who was part of his ringside entourage.

"Three cuckoos," was Graham's closing line.

The lead columnist on the paper for whom I worked, the *New York World-Telegram & Sun*, was Joe Williams. I never met him. He was a remote figure, imperious, often quoted. One of his one-liners I never forgot was, "Fame is as fleeting as a ferryboat shine," Anyone who ever had ridden the Staten Island ferry knew what that meant. A shoeshine cost a nickel. The kid would run a rag across your shoes, and when you took five steps or so after you got off the boat, they were just as dusty as they'd been before the rag. As fleeting as a ferryboat shine.

My own career? Well, I wish I could put a definite beginning on it, and tell you, yes, this is where my 51-year run as a sportswriter got its definite start and paint one of those misty, moody pictures for you — racehorses in the early dawn, the slap and crack of pads during a miserable, sweaty scrimmage, the piercing shouts of high school kids during a local wrestling tournament. But no, it began with a series of catch-can assignments for *The Sacramento Bee*, the high schools, naturally ... you always began a career with high school sports in those days ... but there was also the hustle of carving a beat out for myself when one didn't exist, a local hockey league played on an undersized rink among teams with names like the Rexalls; junior tennis, watching a pair of stern-faced 12-year-olds staring each other down. Mostly, though it started with 64 personal letters and a 1957 Volkswagen making its way down the West Coast from town to town as I searched for a job.

I talk to kids two years out of school nowadays, who tell me they're desperate to write sports, and then they lay out their agenda; well, the NFL would be nice, and of course, Major League Baseball, and if they have to cover the fights, well, they'll do it as an accommodation. A few times when I've offered advice about a certain word called humility, I've been told, "I'm sure it was easier when you broke in."

Easier, yeah. A few weeks short of graduation from journalism school, the chilling realization struck me that no one wanted to hire me, despite the fact that the Columbia J-School was supposed to be my ticket anywhere. I found a copy of *Editor & Publisher* and looked up newspaper addresses. Then I wrote 64 individual letters to sports editors around the country explaining why I was especially suited to cover sports in his area. Eventually I got four replies, no, there's nothing available. Sixty stiffs. Then I visited every newspaper office in the New York area, seeking an audience with the sports editor. Two saw me, a guy named Zellner at *Newsday* in Long Island, and Bob Stewart at the *New York World-Telegram & Sun*. Actually he remembered me as a football player, at Columbia, and he pulled out a five-year-old squad picture that I was on. He told me to keep him posted.

Then I packed up my '57 VW that I'd bought in the army in Germany, drove out to Seattle, where I had a friend to stay with for a few days, and headed down the coast, town by town, coming in cold asking for work. I made it as far as Sacramento and *The Bee*. Someone had quit the day before I showed up.

"How'd you find out so quickly?" Bill Collins, the sports editor, asked me.

"The Columbia Journalism School keeps us informed," I told him. I think that's what swung the job for me, the lurking suspicion that I was backed by some kind of mysterious information network. Things seem to come in streaks. A month later Bob Stewart wrote me to come back to New York and cover schoolboy sports for the *World-Telegram*, the *Telly*. This was a tough one. *The Bee* had hired me when no one else would. I felt that I owed them at least a year. That's what I wrote Stewart; under the hanging dread that in so doing I had banished myself for all eternity to greater Metropolitan Sacramento and the northern wilds called SupCal, Superior California. Actually I made it back to NYC and the Telly after 14 months, and that leads us to an interesting story of payback for all those rejection slips.

It's five years later after I started with *The Bee*. I'm covering the 1964 Summer Olympics in Tokyo. We've been given assigned seats in the press room, where we write our stories. The reporter sitting next to me is not totally tuned in. He keeps asking me questions such as, "Was it the heats or the quarters that Bob Hayes ran today?" Basic stuff. Finally came the moment I was waiting for. He stared hard at me and asked, "Didn't I meet you somewhere?"

"You turned me down for a job five years ago," I said. Georg Myers, sports editor of *The Seattle Times*. He quickly changed the subject, talking about the basketball team's chances or something. I changed it right back.

"You told me not to try to get in the business because it was too crowded."

Next day he had his seat changed.

Seventeen and a half years later he got even. This was at the 49ers-Bengals Super Bowl in Detroit after the 1981 season. It was my brush with serious fame, the kind enjoyed by Al Capone and John Gotti. I had ripped the idea of a Super Bowl in Detroit. The worst thing about it was that I had ripped it on national TV, *Good Morning America*. The city rose up in a frenzy. Editorial writers outdid each other in eloquence, basically proclaiming that New York writers had no business crossing the Hudson and invading the territory where decent people lived. None was more animated than Georg Myers, who launched his tirade on a personal level, "The whale that walks like a man," was one of his phrases about me that I remember. My wife, now my ex-wife, thought his description was fairly accurate.

My first newspaper job, on *The Bee*, was, in retrospect, a dream job for a young writer just starting out. The paper was scrupulously honest. You were held strictly accountable for every quote, every fact.

There was an odd, old fashioned, conservative strain to the paper, too. The saying around the city room was that the style guide was written by someone who had been dead for 50 years, old C.K. McClatchy, the founder and owner. There were some weird rules it was necessary to remember. The high school, for instance, always has to be referred to as The C.K. McClatchy High School, never just McClatchy. So, in writing out stories, we would use the full designation the first time, to get it out of the way, and from then on, it was The Lions in every reference.

You weren't allowed to use contractions. The old man just hadn't liked them, make that had not liked them. This was a stunner, the idea of filling your story with "had not," and "can not," and "did not," but that was the rule. You could never write that it was hot in Sacramento, and that included all derivatives. It was "warm," even though people were dropping from the heat, which could get up to 110 degrees.

When you were on the road, covering something up in Sup Cal, for instance, you always had to dateline your story with the name of the county attached, after a comma. The standing joke was that a gunman jumps into a cab in downtown Sacramento, sticks his gun in the driver's ribs and says, "Roseville, comma, Placer County."

High schools would be my major beat, but since I came there in the summer, school was out, and I worked the night desk. A couple of days after I started, city-side was running short so they asked to borrow me from sports. I was given a story on which to put a headline. The story involved a guy named Marelli, the Human Fly, who would scale building walls with suction cups on his feet. Well, one day he was scaling a wall in Quebec and a cup broke and down went Marelli. Morto. My job was to write a one-column, three-line head for the story, very tricky, very cramped character count, something impossible, like five or six. This is the head I came up with:

"'Fly'
Flies,
Dies"

No indeed, that style of smart-alecky Columbia J-School stuff did not go over on the city desk of *The Bee*, and the piece was given to someone else to work on. My next one, though, was my last. Elizabeth Taylor, whose husband, Mike Todd, had recently died, had announced her engagement to Eddie Fisher. This time I had more room to work with, a 24 head, two lines, two columns. At the J-School we got applause for wittiness. Old habits die hard, and my deucedly clever head was:

"Philadelphia Singer
To Wed Widow Todd"

I was sent back to Bill Collins and the sports desk. Here, you take him. *The Bee*'s city desk fascinated me, though, because of the collection of characters who manned the slots. My favorite was a real old timer named Wayne Slick Selleck, who actually wore one of those green eyeshades that were known as the trademark of ancient newspaper men. Slick had some great stories about the old days, but the best thing he had was a scrapbook he had compiled of the bizarre and outlandish, much of which was of a smutty nature. On the few occasions that he'd bring it to the office, I used to pass up my dinner break to find a corner and go through it. I'd beg him to let me take it up to the library where I could be alone with it, in peace, but he wouldn't let it out of his sight, and I didn't blame him.

My favorite item, out of a spectacular collection, involved a large photo that led the features page of *The Bee*, mid-1920s. It showed a movie actress who was passing through Sacramento by train. She was posing at the station, posing very prettily, with a stylish dress and hat and veil, in front of a background that was bleak desert, which I guess was much of the area in those days. And in that barren background, two dogs were humping. I laughed every time I looked at that thing.

I was single and caught up in the excitement of actually doing newspaper work. I was making $85 a week, and it seemed that I always had money in my pocket. My little duplex in North Sac cost $61 a month, later lowered to $60 by my Polish landlady because I was quiet and paid on time. My big meal of the week was the $2.99 All You Can Eat, Roast Beef and Shrimp Newburg special at Sam's Rancho Villa in Carmichael. It would hold me for 24 hours.

On Sunday during the football season I'd drive up to The City, to San Francisco, and root for the 49ers in Kezar. On Tuesday, I'd either go up to The City again and visit my buddy, Al Ginepra, my former teammate at Columbia who worked there, or I'd drive up to Amador County and check out the old gold country towns. Arthur Robinson, a former writer for the *New York Journal-American*, lived there, in the little town of Volcano. He'd do occasional guest pieces for *The Bee*, "This was old New York," type of stuff, and I was fond of visiting him and hearing stories of the old days.

It was 88 miles from my house to San Francisco, on 1-80, and I'd enjoy the Tuesday trip, going, but the return was brutal, mainly because it was late at night and I was fighting sleep. I had a whole bag of tricks designed for staying awake. Some worked, some didn't. I'd pick up any and all hitchhikers. Hell, I'd welcome them. They usually hung out around the Oakland side of the Bay Bridge, except when it was too late. Then I was on my own. I felt like making a sign, "Conversation is required."

One night I was heading back in the wee hours, and I'd just about given up on the idea of having any companionship, when I spotted an air force sergeant with a duffel bag. He was going to McClellan Air Force Base, near Sacramento. Perfect. I tried some conversation, and the guy was just about a mute. He'd offer a one-word answer here and there, but basically he just stared out the window. Approaching Martinez, I felt sleep overcoming me. I pulled the car over and tried the surest prescription, push-ups, which supposedly lowered the head and got the blood rushing there and gave you some measure of wakefulness. I did all this without a word to the sergeant. When I got back in my '57 VW, he was checking me very carefully. Yes, quite carefully indeed.

I made it as far as Vacaville, where you'd smell the onion from the fields. I went through the same drills, this time grunting a bit as I did it. Might as well put on a show for this guy. Now there was a bit of panic in his face. Everyone knew about weirdos who hitchhiked and picked up hitchhikers, I started up. He reached a decision.

"You can let me out here," he said.

"Oh noooo," I said, doing my best Vincent Price imitation. "You've got to go to Sacramento."

"I'm getting out here!" He said and tried to open the door while the car was moving.

"OK, OK already," I said and let him out.

Another time I had almost given up when I saw a guy in one of those collegiate jackets with the leather sleeves, thumbing it. Great, we'd talk about sports or something. We had gone about a mile when he said, "Have you thought about your relationship with Christ?" Then I noticed that his jacket was from some bible college. Well, what the heck, conversation is conversation. He kept it going, with an occasional interjection from me, for almost the entire ride.

When we arrived, he said, "I can see that you're certainly interested." I assured him that I was.

"Do you mind if I send you some information?"

I forgot to mention that my day off usually would start in the early afternoon because they had in Sacramento something that plugged right into my gaming instincts, and that was house poker, the card rooms. These were days long before the Texas Hold 'em craze, in fact Hi-Lo was just coming into vogue. But the downtown parlors featured three games: five-card draw, lowball and something called pangani that I never understood. Every New York kid knows poker especially if he's worked summers as a busboy or waiter in the Catskills or Poconos. Man, this was for me.

I limited myself to two nights a week, the nights before my day off. I played only draw, table stakes, which sounds rougher than it was because no one really had much money. Two hands are imbedded in my mind. They'd play with a bug in the deck, the joker, which was wild for use in straights and flushes; otherwise it was an ace. I got to know the players after a while, and one element to avoid were the fruit pickers. Old men mostly. They'd work in the fields all day and they'd come into the card room, seeking to score just heavily enough to buy a good meal and a bottle. They were the most conservative players in the game. They'd wait forever for that one hand that would put them over the top, then they'd push their chair back and leave. Two of them at your table would just about kill a game. Three and you'd be better off waiting for a seat to open up somewhere else.

Well, I was in a game with one old picker who'd been quiet for almost an hour, I was sitting under the gun, to the left of the dealer. I looked at my hand and I had aces over 10s, two pair. So I opened for a few dollars. Everyone folded, except for the old guy about three seats down. He raised a few dollars. I knew exactly what he was doing. He'd caught a pat straight or flush and he was only raising moderately, so as not to scare away any fish — such as me. I was tired of the game. I wanted to leave anyway, so I called a stupid play. An 11-1 shot to fill up, one chance out of 12.

I drew my one card. He stayed pat, as I knew he would. I sweated in that card, opened the corner a tiny amount, then a little more, and more. I didn't see anything. Still blank. Then I opened it all the way. It was the bug. I'd filled up aces. I gave it the schoolboy Hollywood bit, the light grimace of disgust, then I looked up to see if he saw me flinch, etc. I checked, he bet moderately, maybe $5 or so. I pushed in all I had in front of me, which was maybe another $20.

He stared at me for a good 30 seconds. "You young son of a bitch!" he yelled and flung his cards on the table and stalled out of there. What was revealed was a bust. Nothing. He was trying to steal one. Poor old guy. Must have gotten hungry and impatient, and if I didn't hit, I wasn't going to call him, no way.

I did all right in games in downtown Sacramento. Then I'd always make the same mistake, I'd be standing out on the corner of 2nd and A Street at 3 a.m., when the city card rooms closed with my modest winning, maybe $30 or so, and I'd be faced with the same decision. Do I go home with my loot or do I go across the river into West Sacramento, West Sac, where the all night card rooms were, where the big boys hung out? I'd always think it through and make the wrong choice. Over the river I'd go, and very few times would I emerge with what I came in with.

Second memorable hand. My first hand in West, Sac, which served to define the whole thing. I was dealt trips. I drew one card, kept trips and a kicker, trying to fool 'em, checked and raised, did my kiddie magic, took home a small pot. Across the table a beady-eyed little guy with a toothpick in his mouth removed the toothpick and muttered, "Big fuggin play." He'd read me all the way. It took him about 40 minutes to clean me. That's the way it went in West Sac.

I'd bounce back from those nights. I'd put a limit on my losses and I'd just cut the food intake until I caught up, and, of course, there was always the monumental foodfest at Sam's to look forward to on the weekends. The cafeteria at *The Bee* was dirt cheap, and I'd cook my own dinners during the week.

Someone sent me an Adelle Davis book about eating healthy. I became not exactly addicted but interested in health foods. I'd make my own yogurt, I'd buy abalone — that's right, you could buy it fresh in those days in any fish store for less than $3 a pound — and bread it with wheat germ and deep fry it in safflower oil.

It was a nice life. One night someone abandoned a black kitten on my doorstep. I called the local SPCA. Do you take in stray kittens? Yes we do. What do you do with them? We try to find homes for them. What if you don't? Then they're put to sleep. Pause.

"You mean you KILL THEM?" Intake of breath on the other end, followed by "Goodbye, sir."

Not supposed to say that. It's got to be a euphemism, put 'em to sleep, lay 'em to rest, something like that. Well, I didn't want that on my conscience, so R.C. and I became roommates. That's the name I gave her. She was a fantastic leaper, and that's when the Niners' R.C. Owens was making all those leaping end zone catches they called the Alley-Oop.

We had an interesting relationship, and I use the term "roommate" advisedly. I'd never had a cat before. I grew up with dogs. But life with R.C. couldn't have been easier. I'd let her out in the morning. I didn't know what she did with her day; she didn't know what I did with mine. When I'd return in the evening, I'd whistle and I'd hear pat-pat-pat, and she'd pitty-pat across the low roof, jump down and wait for the door to open. Have a meal, take a dump, go to sleep, that was it. Minimal affection, but tolerance. That was the key to it.

Once I came back early and checked to see if I could find out how R.C. spent her time. She was up on the roof ... she seemed to like the way the sunlight reflected off it ... hanging out with a small cat group, her social set, just enjoying each other's company.

When it was time to go home, I had to find a home for R.C. I wound up giving her to my best friend out there, Nick, the tennis pro at the Arden Hills Club. He had three daughters, 12-year-old twins, plus nine-year old Denise, who later was ranked the No. 4 woman player in the U.S. A lot of, "Oh please, daddy," and then he and his wife finally consented after I swore that R.C. was a male. I got a letter from him a few months later.

It ended, "R.C. is fine. By the way, HE's pregnant." I had occasion to visit them a few years later. The girls had changed R.C.'s name to Mandy. She was lying in a fluffy cat bed when I looked in on her. She didn't know me. She had gained weight and she had that dopey, sleepy, fat-faced look that house cats get sometimes. The girls talked baby talk to her. I thought of the old R.C., the tough, self-sufficient street cat, the fantastic leaper. Ah well, as long as she was happy.

I covered tennis, which was how I got to know Nick. I got to love the sport. I did a serious mood piece on Rosie Casals, aged 10, outlasting Leslie Abrahams, 13, in a three-hour marathon. In the Central Cal juniors, the blistering heat, uh, warmth, sand flying, getting in their hair, their eyes, the two kids racing around the court, tears streaming. The best match I ever saw. I remember interviewing little Rosie afterward, a tough Mexican-American kid, going around to the tournaments with her white-haired father, the two of them shunned by the fancy clubs, which wouldn't put them up overnight, having to sleep in their old jalopy of a car.

"It was the gear shift that killed me," she said.

I covered stuff other people didn't want to cover. Sammy Weiss, a high-level midget race car driver, was a story. I knew nothing about auto racing. Sammy led me through it, fed me vital information, checked my copy to make sure I hadn't screwed anything up. A few weeks later, he was killed in a practice run. I had written the last story on him. I was getting calls from all over, from both wire services, from car magazines for technical information. I could tell them nothing more than what they'd already read. They must have thought *The Bee* had some real idiots on its staff.

Every once in a while, I'd get on a crusade. The McClellan Air Force Base football team was one of them. In 1959 they went unbeaten in the regular season. They were an active, overachieving bunch of guys who hadn't played anybody. Their record looked impressive with victories over teams such as Santa Clara and San Jose State. The problem was that it was the jayvees, not the varsities of those schools, that they had beaten. But their PR releases never mentioned that part of it.

I got on the directors of the armed forces sports programs for ignoring this eager bunch of hardworking guys. "They're unbeaten … they deserve to play in the Shrimp Bowl," I wrote in many different ways. The Shrimp Bowl in Galveston was for the service championship. Someone must have listened because, all of a sudden, McClellan was invited. The opponent was Quantico, typically the Notre Dame of the armed forces. It was rumored that Billy Vessels, the former Oklahoma All-American, was on that team. There were other college stars, a lot of officers who'd been in ROTC programs in school. Quantico was loaded.

The final score was 90-0. You could look it up, Shrimp Bowl 1959 season. Oh my God, had I done that? I was at the airport to meet the McClellan team on its return from the game. It looked like a troop transport bringing back the wounded. Guys were coming out in casts, on crutches, all bandaged up. I talked to one poor guy who had his arm in a sling.

"When we came out for the warm-ups, they had so many guys that they circled the entire field," he said. "I thought, 'Oh oh, we're in trouble.'"

I led a healthy life. My work shift during the week, when there wasn't an event to cover, was 6:30 a.m. to 2:30 p.m. I loved those hours. It meant I had the whole afternoon off. So I'd go down to the Y and go through a workout routine (we got free admission) and maybe play a little half-court hoops if there were enough people there and then I'd go over to Arden Hills and play tennis all afternoon, courtesy of Nick, even though I wasn't a member. I weighed around 250 when my VW first had rolled into town. In a few months, I had lost 35 pounds and was right around my old college playing weight. One workout day particularly stands out.

This was on my day off, and it was raining, and I decided not to drive to The City. I went to the Y early in the morning, had a long workout. I was getting ready to leave, but a full-court basketball game was being organized. They were short one person, me. So I got into it. The game got heated. We lost, just barely. Hey, let's have another. It was one of those lunatic things that catches you in its vortex and doesn't let go. Tennis would be out. It was a marathon basketball session, group insanity. Finally it ended, but I couldn't let go. I did some more exercises, had a swim. Don't ask me why. Then I stepped on the scale. I had weighed in at 209 that day, I weighed out at 199, first time I'd been below 200 since I was 14. Oh my God. This deserves a reward.

I called Buscaglia's in Jackson, one of the gold country towns. They had a family-style lunch, seven days a week. Meatballs, lasagna, veal chops, just load up.

"How late do you serve the lunch?"

"You come, we'll stay open for you," Mrs. Buscaglia said. Oh boy.

I ate from about 3 p.m. until 7. Next day when I checked into the Y, the scale registered 212.

Nick and his wife and his friends became my social set. I've never been a clubby type, but that didn't seem to matter. Everything was fairly loose and relaxed, California style. Except for something that happened one night, and I've puzzled over it for many years.

There was a man named Mike with whom I'd play tennis occasionally. I'd heard that he'd played football at Cal, and he certainly was big enough, naturally big before the days of heavy weight training, massive through the chest and shoulders. He was dark complexioned and glowering and he looked like the kind of person you didn't want to get mad at you. His tennis game was big, crushing forehand, big serve, net game, etc. But the interesting thing was that if you managed to hang with him and return his shots, and maybe do some fluky stuff, spins and drops and whatever, he could be beaten. He'd fold. It was curious.

When he first heard that I'd gone to Columbia he asked me what years, and when I told him, he said his brother had been a baseball player there. I asked him for the name, and he brushed it off. "Never mind, you wouldn't have known him," he said. Again, curious.

One night we were at Nick's house for a small party. Mike had had a bit to drink, and all of a sudden, my ears caught the unmistakable sound of anti-Semitic mumblings from him, Jew this and Jew that. Not particularly vicious, but present. I ignored it, and it got worse. Was I the target of this? I was about to say something. I mean, I had to react in some way, but I also had to plan my strategy.

I went into the kitchen and sat down. How to handle it? I didn't think a conversation would do it. Things had gone beyond that. But, and this was a definite part of it, he was big, real big, and he looked as if he could handle himself, and me, too. I had to get him quickly, preferably while he was seated, and I had to get him more than once, and then, hopefully, people would jump in and break it up. All this was going through my head as I sat there in Nick's kitchen. I must have looked a bit weird because Nick came in and immediately said to me, "You're upset about Mike, aren't you?" And I said yes.

"Before you go nuts," he said, "let me explain a few things to you."

First of all, Nick explained, his last name wasn't the one he gave me, but something a lot longer and more ethnic. Second of all … well, I wasn't the only Jew in the room. I was stunned. And then it hit me. It all fell into place, the way he would fold when you put it to him on the tennis court, the reason why he wouldn't identify his brother. And I felt this tremendous wave of sadness. All this trouble to hide it, to live a lie, the anguish he must have gone through every day. All the aggression was gone. I just felt very sorry for Mike. I made my excuses and left. I've often wondered what ever happened to him.

Nick and his family, his wife Gerry, whom he'd coached well enough for her to win the Central Cal women's tournament one year, his three girls, all of whom were ranked at one time, remained friends for many years, even after I left Sacramento. He was an unusual person. When he played the circuit, he was called the Bad Boy of Tennis. He worked as a cab driver in San Francisco and learned how to play on the public courts and wasn't above a friendly wager or two on his efforts. He had all the psych routines down, taking off the sweater and then putting it on, changing racquets when an opponent was on a streak, changing shoes.

When I knew him, he was a terrific coach of junior players, and he had a unique trick that always worked.

"When they're in a group lesson, and it's toward the end of the hour and their concentration is flagging," he told me, "the way you can always bring them back is with money. It doesn't have to be much. A dime or a quarter will do it. You just tell them, 'OK, you're getting 10 backhands to hit, and whoever hits the most on the court gets the quarter.' And all of a sudden, their concentration's back."

Every time I pass through Vacaville on my trip from Sacramento to San Francisco, I think of a story Nick told me about growing up there. There was a bridge, he said, called The Lion's Paw Bridge. It got its name from an incident that happened when he was a child. A circus had been going through via railroad. Somehow something jolted the car carrying a lion and the door opened. A male lion escaped and ran into the hills of Vacaville, which was pretty primitive in those days. He established himself with the mountain lions in those hills. He was rarely seen, Nick said, but on warm nights you could hear him roaring.

One day they were building a bridge over a stream where the lions would come to drink in the evening. The cement was still wet when the male lion stepped in it, leaving a paw print that remained. Hence, The Lion's Paw Bridge. I never met anyone who verified that story, but I don't care ... l loved it so much. The second story of Nick's is even better.

When he was very young and working in San Francisco, he married a flaming redhead, just as I did many years later, only she had the temper to go with her hair. He said the fights they had were explosive.

"Once she came after me with a kitchen knife," he said. Finally they split up. They'd had a son. She remarried a businessman named McCarthy who wanted to do the right thing for the family, the right thing being giving the boy a decent upbringing and education — provided Nick relinquish the rights to him.

"I was struggling to make a living," Nick said. "I did it."

He didn't see him again, for maybe 15 years.

"Then one day," Nick said, "when I was a teaching pro, I came into the pro shop after a lesson, and this tall young guy is sitting there. He'd been waiting for me. He just stared at me when I came in. I stared at him.

"'You're Neil,' I said. He nodded. He'd left home, left McCarthy and his mother.

"'I've come to stay with you,' he said. I called his mother, my ex-wife.

"'He wouldn't give me any peace,' she said. 'He kept saying, 'I know this isn't my father. I'm nothing like him. You've got to tell me who my real father is.' I couldn't stand it anymore, so finally I told him. And he just left.'

"So I brought him home," Nick said. "The girls got all excited. 'We've got a brother! We've got a brother!' After dinner I took him down to the basement to play him a little ping pong. I let him win one, let him win another, came from behind and beat him. We put some money on it. He got all excited, wouldn't let me leave, just the way I used to be. Then I really beat him. I kept saying, 'You can't be my son. It's not possible. How could I have a pigeon for a son?'"

So Neil McCarthy enrolled at Sacramento State, played basketball and eventually wound up head coach at New Mexico State. Once I told the story to my mother, who loved tales like that. She always used to tell me stories of the old country and gypsies who put curses on people and that kind of thing.

"Look at my hand," she said. "It's shaking. That story makes me shake."

I had a lovely way of life in Sacramento. The living was easy, so easy that it scared me. I can work here and grow old here and die here, and nobody ever would have heard of me. I had reverted to a New York way of thinking. Then Bob Stewart of the *New York World-Telegram* told me to come back and write schoolboy sports for them. My co-workers on the sports staff gave me a Duncan Hines *Guide to Dining Out in the U.S.* as a going away present, and I planned my trip accordingly in an attempt to gain back all the weight I had lost.

I found a two-room apartment on West 106th St. for $75 a month, a step up from my North Sacramento duplex, but then again, I was making more money, too, something like $98 a week. What killed me about living in the city was not being able to find a parking spot for my Volkswagen, at least not a legitimate one. Not being able to park near your home would have been unheard of in Sacramento.

But in New York, it was a way of life: the endless circling, block after block, finally parking a little too close to a hydrant or just shading into the bus stop area. It just struck me as so unfair. So as a protest, I let the parking tickets pile up (they weren't serious into towing in those days). The payoff came years later, when I wound up in the court on Centre St., with a massive fine on the books. If you pay by check, you go into a little room, while they call the bank. If they're told it'll clear, you can go home. If not, you don't get out of that room on your own. I made it — just barely.

The Telly was on Barclay St. in lower Manhattan. My first day in the office, I was introduced around, and we had lunch in the telephone building across the street, myself and the desk guys, including an old timer named Eddie Murphy, who was close to 80 and nearly blind. It was cafeteria-style, and I was still in my Sacramento health foods mode, so loaded my plate with fresh fruit and yogurt and some raw vegetables. Eddie stared at it. He sniffed. He moved for a closer look.

"What did you do, lose a bet?" He said.

It was summer, so I worked the night desk until the high schools began. I'd write headlines, read copy, write cut lines, the same stuff I'd done, off and on. The best overline for a picture that I ever wrote was not used. I'm still bitter about it. Del Webb, co-owner of the Yankees, had just gotten married, and we ran a picture of him and his wife stepping off the plane. My kicker line was: "Newlywebbs."

Marty O'Shea, the assistant night editor, killed it. Demeaning, he said. I begged, pleaded. No dice.

Around midnight every shift, a welcome figure would arrive, John Condon, the publicist from Madison Square Garden. He'd arrive with his regular bribes for the night-side guys, the real power elite who could get stuff into the paper. Sandwiches from the Stage Deli, big ones, huge, just the things you dream of. A big cheer would go up when John arrived. Talk about smart PR men. He got just about anything he wanted in the paper.

The night sports editor was Sal Gerage, a young guy who had gone to Seward Park High School with Bernie Schwartz, a.k.a Tony Curtis, the actor. A brilliant desk man, that was Sal, with a real flair for nicknames. Phil Pepe, who'd been the schoolboy writer before me, was Bugs Bunny, for his prominent front teeth. Bill Bloom, the tiny little man who wrote horse racing, was The Japanese Admiral. I was Tarzan. I think I was the only one who actually liked my nickname.

I was the new guy, so I would get the clunkier stuff to copyread. Keeping awake was a problem. I figured that working at night, sleeping during the day would be an open invitation to spend my days at Jones Beach, snoozing under the sun. It didn't quite work out. Sleeping on the beach is fine in theory but not for real. It takes about three hours to get 40 minutes sleep. The slightest noise will wake you, and you were always edgy about not getting caught in traffic, going or coming.

I'd be tired coming in to work, even more so when my parade of clunkers would start. First there was Larry Robinson on golf. Not really too bad, but if you'd be eating a piece of toast while you were reading it, you might choke to death. Then came Lou Miller on the trotters, and my head would start nodding. Zander Hollander on yachting would almost finish me; my eyes would barely focus on the copy. And the coup de grace was always George Coleman on the horse shows. Clunk! My head would hit the desk.

"Hey, wake up, Zim. You've got copy to move."

I'd been there about two weeks when I discovered a wonderful thing. Night clubs were very big in New York, back then in 1960. *The Telly* covered hundreds of them, thousands. There were always a couple of night club reviews in the paper every day. Midtown New York, little joints in the Village, in Brooklyn, Queens, yes, there was something to say about each one. A curious thing was that the pieces carried bylines of many different people. How big was the staff, anyway?

Then I found out that anyone could cover a nightclub. Just had to ask. You got no pay for it, but you were comped on food and drink for you and a companion. You could praise the show, rip it, whatever. They didn't care. Just mentioning it was the thing. Wow! Talk about planning a sensational date. I mean, you could interview any of the performers. "My date, the night club reviewer."

I became a regular. Never in my life had I had such an assortment of dates ... budding actresses, a Jantzen swimsuit model, you name it. Then one day Robin Terkel, our guild rep, talked to the entertainment department and demanded that we get paid for our reviews. Now I'm a strong union man, always have been, but ... "Jesus, Robin, just leave it alone, OK? We're doing fine." Nope, fair's fair, he said. No overtime, no night club coverage. Fine, said management. Goodbye and good luck to the sweetest deal anyone ever had.

You've never seen so many dates abandon a human being in your life. They were like rats leaving the sinking ship. "Uh, can I speak to Laura, please?" "Well. Laura isn't here right now ... no, I don't know when she'll be back ... I'll tell her you called."

I decided to concentrate on what was at hand. There was a young lady who wrote for the society page who was just as sweet looking as her name. Lilla Lyon. A blonde, not exactly willowy, in fact slightly on the robust side, but that was fine. She was a society girl herself, I was told. I didn't get very far there, I'm afraid. Not that she wasn't always pleasant.

I remember one night, Joe King, our pro football writer, was in the office late, writing his story. Case of Heineken's on one side, pack of cigarettes on the other, that was Joe, banging out his piece on the Giants. I was in there doing some high school wrap up or something, and Lilla had been covering a society ball, and she walked by our little sports alcove. Joe looked up.

"Wanna beer?" he asked her.

"I'd love one," she said. He started opening a Heineken.

"Oh, a beer?" she said. "I thought you said a pear."

"A pear?" Joe said, looking confused. "A pear?"

He left the office. A couple of blocks away, the Washington Market, one of the great produce centers in New York, was just swinging into life. Fifteen minutes later, Joe came back, followed by a young, sweating produce worker in an undershirt. He carried on his shoulder a case of pears.

"Right over there," Joe said, pointing to Lilla's desk. The guy put down the case and left. Lilla was dumbfounded. Joe tipped his hat and came back to his typewriter to finish his story.

"You see that?" He said to me. "That's the way you do it."

I started dating one of the copygirls named Barbara. One weekend she invited me up to her parents' house in Westport, Conn. When we arrived her mother suggested we go for a swim in the ocean. Fine with me. I gave it the old Burt Lancaster in *From Here to Eternity*, charging into the waves. Smush! The first one hit me in the face. And knocked out my front tooth. Not a real tooth, you understand, a fake one that you could take out and put in again. It was called a flipper. The real one had been knocked out years ago.

I tried diving for it. The water was murky. I dove and dove.

"What are you doing over there?" Barbara yelled at me. "Oh, nothing, nothing."

I never found it. And now it was time to go in for dinner. I was introduced to her father.

"You work in sports, huh?" he said. I said yes, careful to keep my lips tightly drawn. "I like to read Joe Val," he said. Joe Val was our racing handicapper.

"Joe's a real nice guy," I said.

"No, you don't understand," he said. "Joe Val isn't a real person. It's a pseudonym."

"Well, maybe he's not a real person, but I had lunch with him yesterday."

He repeated his same litany, almost word for word. "You don't understand ... Joe Val isn't a real person," etc. I mean, could somebody really be this dumb?

"Look," I said, "you might not believe this, but Joe Val ..." I was getting a little hot, and then I noticed that they were all staring at the gap where my tooth should have been, father, mother, Barbara, her brother. I had gotten carried away.

Barbara told me that later, her mother had said to her, "Please, dear, don't ever bring that young man here again." That was the beginning of the end of that romance.

I had a great time covering schoolboy sports. I had to pick an All-Met football team every year, encompassing the city and the huge surrounding area of Westchester County, metropolitan New Jersey and Long Island. I was always on the road, seeing games live, watching films with the coaches, scouting practices. I had huge books of charts. In short, I was doing what I later did in my NFL coverage for all those years and I was in dog heaven.

After the season we threw a dinner at Mamma Leone's on 48th St. for our All-Mets. Larry Robinson, who covered college football as well as golf, got college players to attend and sit with the kids, Joe King got Giants, Larry Fox got Titans from the AFL. The entertainment section got a comic to come and entertain every year. The best was Bill Cosby. The kids loved him, but when we tried to tell him afterward how much we appreciated his coming there, he turned his back and told his agent, "Let's get out of here." Ah, well.

When Richie Kotite became coach of the Jets in 1995 and I was out at their camp one day, he fished in his wallet and pulled out a little, laminated newspaper clipping. It was something from my All-Met piece in 1960, the capsule comment I had written on him. "Headed for the big time," I had written.

I remember driving down to Poly Prep in Brooklyn in the rain and watching him against Horace Mann, my alma mater.

"I never forgot that," he said, "and I never forgot that dinner at Mamma Leone's."

Nostalgia means magnification by many degrees, but we had an awfully good staff on the *Telly*. Willard Mullin was and remains to this day the greatest sports cartoonist who ever lived. The Brooklyn Dodger Bum was his creation. He would hand in his cartoons on huge, white poster boards, and they would just lie around the office afterward, to be thrown out by the cleaning crew. One night I decided that it was a shame to see them trashed, so I took a bunch home. It was one of the few smart things I ever did in my life because they sell for about $500 apiece now in the Leland's sports auctions, and anything with the Brooklyn Dodger Bum on it is pushing four figures.

Joe Williams was the imperious column figure, Lester Bromberg ranked with the *Mirror*'s Dan Parker as the country's greatest boxing writer, Joe King was a respected veteran pro football reporter, and Larry Robinson? Well, few people looked more like a big-time sportswriter than he did.

In 1954, my senior football season at Columbia, we traveled to Penn to scrimmage the Quakers before the season began. Larry Robinson was the only sportswriter who made the trip. He was tight with our coach, Lou Little. On the way back, the team stopped in some fancy pizzeria for a meal, and we ate in a banquet room that had a kind of raised dais in front. Coach Little sat there, next to Robinson, whose elaborate cravat, topped off by a big, round, florid face and huge mop of white hair gave him the look of a person who would be not out of place covering the Crimean War or the League of Nations … certainly someone who might stop your heart stone dead if he decided to interview you. So during the meal, we would get up from time to time and stroll past the dais, displaying ourselves before this legend of a sportswriter, who was deep in conversation with the coach, as they ate their spaghetti. Chest out, heads tucked down into our necks … please, God, let this man interview us. Finally Coach Little looked up and noticed this passing parade.

"All right, you matinee idols," he growled in that raspy voice of his. "Back to your seats."

Our baseball writer was Dan Daniel, the first president of the Baseball Writers Association, winner of every award obtainable and generally conceded to be the most authoritative figure in the sport. He'd been the official scorer for 20 of the 56 games in Joe DiMaggio's consecutive hitting streak in 1941. When Lester Bromberg was covering a fight in Havana in the 1950s he ran into Ernest Hemingway, who asked him, "How's Dan Daniel … that great writer?"

Nobody could remember when Dan started writing for the *Telly*, but he once told me he wrote his first bylined story, for the *New York Herald*, five years before Babe Ruth broke into the major leagues, which was 1914. When I first got to know Dan, he was 70, a loud, funny guy with a great sense of humor, a wonderful master of ceremonies who'd always take charge of our All-Met dinners. He wrote a wildly popular Tuesday feature called

"Ask Daniel," one of the first of the Mailbag columns that later became so fashionable. Dan had a temper, too, and nothing would set him off as much as the repeated question: "Didn't one of Babe Ruth's 60 home runs go into the stands on one bounce and shouldn't it have been ruled a ground rule double?"

Like someone who couldn't leave a sore tooth alone, he would always answer that particular query, his fury mounting with every response. "No! No! No! How many times will it take before your peanut brain can accept the fact that this never happened?" and so forth. And so naturally, the young guys on the staff, the bad boys such as me and Phil Pepe and a whacked out copy boy known as The Bomber, would pipe the question and slip it into his mailbox.

"Mr. Daniel, I certainly respect your knowledge, but my grandfather told me for a fact that one of Babe Ruth's 60 home runs ..." etc. And Dan would storm like King Lear. "What is wrong with these people?"

So I gradually moved up the ladder, from schoolboys to college sports, with an occasional look-see into the professional arena, a fairly smooth progression with one glitch. Sal Gerage, our night editor, had been enamored with an old Tim Cohane column of the early 1940s called Frothy Facts. He wanted to see it revived and he decided I was the guy to revive it. I was told to be bright and sparkling and lively.

Well, the urge to be clever is one that will destroy you; the straining will blow you apart. I look back on those columns now through fingers spread over my eyes. The less said the better. Occasionally a laugh or two, but clearly, I was not ready for that kind of action. The worst thing was what it did to my ego. Listen, everybody, I'm a columnist now! But there was one good element involved with the venture. At the bottom of each column, which appeared three times a week, was a little feature called: "10 Years Ago Today, and then 25 Years Ago Today."

I got the items from our morgue, which had, in addition to old *World-Telegrams*, other papers as well. I had my own desk set up back there in the library. I'd get interested in murder trials of the 1930s, Korean War news, the pennant race of 1938. I'd start following old comic strips day after day ... Terry and the Pirates, Dick Tracy, etc. I'd go in after lunch, and before I knew it, the night crew was coming into work. I was lost in a time warp. That's where I found those great Frank Graham one-liners, the Joe Williams observation. I collected them, put them in a notebook.

In an old *New York Daily News*, I discovered an absolute gem, my all-time favorite one-liner from the editorial page. It was during the Cold War era, and the USSR and Communist China were showing signs of aggression toward each other. They were having a stare-down across the Yalu River, and the news was ecstatic that these two enemies of our country might actually come to blows. The editorial proclaimed how wonderful this all was, and then it ended: "Go to it, bums!"

After a while I started going back even further, into the 1920s, even though the research wouldn't serve my column. I wanted to see what Paul Gallico was like before he quit in 1936 and wrote *Farewell To Sport*, which had been my bible. I wanted to read Grantland Rice day to day. I discovered an interesting thing, which I've mentioned before. The old timers were streak hitters, some stuff great, but occasionally they'd take a pass during a lull and concoct a whole piece about, say, the release of the weekly football statistics.

Rice was a hell of a yarn-spinner, though, and how many of today's sportswriters, forgive me, media (God, how I hate that word) would pepper their stuff with verse. I particularly liked Rice's story about when they were at the Yale Bowl, covering a football game, and afterward, as they were sitting in the press box, banging out their stories, a young writer, working hard to capture the mood, pointed at the setting sun and asked, "Is that the west over there?"

"Son," Rice said, "if it ain't, you've got yourself a hell of a story."

Pretty good capsule on the sillier aspects of our profession, huh? I've only heard it put better two times. The first time was by Sonny Liston. Someone asked him why he didn't like sportswriters, and he said, "A sportswriter looks up in the sky and asks you, 'Is the sun shining?'" The second one, concerning writers in general, came from an Eskimo hunter north of Hudson Bay, a subject of frequent journalistc essays about life in the Far North.

"One day, newspaper," he said, "Two day, magazine. One week, book."

The king of the one-liners, in fact he would do periodic columns that would be nothing but them, was Jimmy Cannon of the *New York Post*. Everyone read them and quoted them. His column was called "Nobody Asked Me, But ..."

"I don't like Boston because every man looks like me."

"If Howard Cosell were a sport, it would be Roller Derby."

"Chances are the lady's miserable if she wears a heart-shaped locket she bought herself."

"Men who eat a lot of candy don't do much boasting."

High school columnists tried to copy him, magazine writers, talk show hosts. Nobody could do it as Jimmy could. His regular columns were terrific, too, at least to my way of thinking. He had been influenced by Hemingway, an old drinking buddy, and he favored short, punchy sentences, bullet style at times. And then he'd go long and wrap it all up. He got a lot of emotion into his pieces, still in that hard style. It rubbed off on a lot of us. Toward the end of his life — he died in 1973 — he reaped a bit of scorn from the younger writers because of his unabashed appeal to the heart, at times. He was also not comfortable to be around. He had a way of complaining about things. I see a lot of him in myself.

Gallico's *Farewell to Sport* might have been the single most influential sports book I read as a youngster, but Cannon became my journalistic idol and remained so. I started reading him in high school and seldom missed one of his columns. One of them, a piece on the 1948 Notre Dame-Northwestern game, I cut out and pasted to mirror. In it he described a kid who had suffered a head injury in the game and had a near-seizure in the locker room, a nasty contrast to the drunks still celebrating in the stadium. It made me almost quit football, repeat, almost.

In 1960, when I was leaving, in disgrace, from the Franklin Field press box after the Packers-Eagles championship game — disgrace because I had failed to provide the needed losing locker room quotes for Joe King — Cannon asked, "Anyone driving back to New York?" I offered a tentative, "Me."

I had been in the business a year and a half. I kept my mouth shut for the most part, but l did offer one item for his Nobody Asked Me column, something I was meaning to send him.

"Let's hear it," he said.

I said that it always struck me funny that guys drinking at the bar in western movies always had the right change. The following week, when his next Nobody Asked Me column came out, I practically tore the paper open to get to it. It was the lead item. And five down from it was this one: "Guys who wear white socks look like they have sore feet." I'd been wearing white socks.

He invited me up to his apartment on the West Side, and I had a couple of drinks and looked through a lot of memorabilia — Jimmy with

Hemingway and Toots Shor and Jackie Gleason, Jimmy with his longtime girlfriend, the actress Ann Sothern, or maybe it was Joan Blondell. I always got the two confused. I heard a lot of stories.

In later years we became road compadres. I always liked to be on a football trip with him. I remember going up to a Jets game in Buffalo, and the day before, the Bills' PR man, Jack Horrigan, took the Jets writers to that old battle wagon, War Memorial Stadium, to show us its new paint job.

"What do you think, Jimmy?" He asked afterward.

"Rouge on corpse," Cannon said.

On the Jets bus from the airport to the hotel, Jimmy was sitting in the back, and for some reason, the conversation switched to great eaters of the past. He mentioned fat Jack Lavelle, always billed as the Giants' super-scout, and Herman Hickman, the 300-pound Yale coach, and some skinny Englishman who'd had part of his stomach shot away in the war and couldn't get filled up. Pretty soon the players started drifting back in twos and threes. By the time we got there, the front of the bus was empty, and back of it, around Jimmy's seat, was packed. Some writer asked him how pudgy Leonard Koppett of *The Times* would have compared to the big boys.

"Kopett? Kopett?" Jimmy said, spitting it out as if it were a bad word. "He's the kind of guy who starts every meal with a pound of Crisco."

The two writers who were closest to Jimmy at the end were Dave Anderson of *The Times* and myself. We'd go everywhere, we'd always ask him to join us if we were going out to dinner. "We worship at the shrine, don't we?" Dave once said. I agreed.

Chapter 5

Super Bowl Memories

This column appeared on SI.com *on Jan. 28, 2005.*

The personal memories of covering 37 Super Bowls pile onto each other. Sometimes it's hard to separate them. Action on the field fades, plays tend to blend into one another and, besides, the memories of the games involve only watching, not doing, or being part of. So what I will give you are little bonbons from the great feast of Super Bowls through the years, tiny tastes, and, of course, all of them purely personal. So here they are:

Fear and Loathing in Houston

Some years ago I used to run a writers' handicapping pool. A buck a man, closest to the actual score takes it all. In 1974, Dolphins vs. Vikings in Houston, I was in the press room early, putting up my pool sheets on the bulletin board and I saw this bald-headed guy squinting at the rules of the contest in a not-too-focused fashion.

"I'm not a regular sports writer. You gonna let me in your pool?" he said. I recognized him as Hunter Thompson, whom I had read was covering that Super Bowl for *Rolling Stone.*

"Only if you've got a buck," I told him. He assured me he had, so I told him to record his entry on the board.

"How about more than one pick, under different names?" he said. All of a sudden, it dawned on me that this was a guy who was going out of his way to seek rejection from authority figures, and that's what I, of all people, must have represented to him.

"A buck a pick," I told him. "Make 'em good names."

He liked that. A fellow outlaw. None of his picks came close, and when his piece came out, he had done a real hatchet job on the writers, "Rozelle's hand maidens," he called them, except for yours truly. "Paul Zimmerman of the *New York Post* handled the writers' handicapping pool in a professional manner," he wrote. Yaaay!

"You feel like going out tonight?" he said that day in the press room. Sure, why not? Well, he took me to the toughest bar I'd ever been to in my life. Nothing but 250-pound street guys with ponytails. It was the kind of place where you drink your drink and stare straight ahead and speak when spoken to.

So we're sitting there, and Hunter has been quiet and all of a sudden he says, out of the blue, "This place ain't so tough." Oh oh. There's a general stirring around. See, the thing with him was that when he was stoned he got real quiet. I only learned that too late. The bartender leaned over and said to me, "You'd better get your buddy out of here." Hunter overheard.

"No one's running me out of here, I don't care how tough he is."

"Hunter, I'm leaving," I told him. "You can either come with me or stay. I've got two small ones at home, and they'd like to see their daddy again."

"Go on, I don't give a damn," he said and continued ranting in similar fashion. And yours truly showed the white feather and scrammed. Next day he showed up in the press room with bumps on his head and a few bruises. I never did find out what happened, and he didn't mention it in his *Rolling Stone* piece either.

My Favorite Line

My favorite Super Bowl line came in the 1985 contest between the 49ers and Dolphins, the only one held in the San Francisco Bay Area. It is the big Wednesday interview session in the Amfac Hotel in Burlingame, and the ballroom doors have just opened, spilling forth a huge mass of writers with their notebooks and little carry-bags and stuff. A gigantic, lowing, mooing herd.

Two young women in Amfac uniforms are standing across the hall, and I hear one of them saying, "This is incredible … incredible … simply incredible."

"What's incredible?" I ask her.

"I've never seen so many straight guys in my life," she says.

Mo$t Valuable Interview

Favorite Super Bowl interview — 1977 in Pasadena, Raiders vs. Vikings. Make that most *valuable* interview. I'm in Phil Villapiano's room one afternoon. Those were the days when you could interview players anywhere at all. My Jersey buddy and all his paisans are there, sitting around, eating hero sandwiches, drinking sodas and beer.

"Hey, you ever bet on games?" says Phil, the Raiders' outside linebacker.

"I can't ... it wouldn't be professional," I told him.

"C'mon ... you work for the *New York Post*, and I know the guys on that paper bet their asses off." Which, of course, was true. Our sports editor, for instance, was a huge investor. So I told him, yeah, there was action in that office.

"Well, do 'em all a favor and tell 'em to put the house on us," Phil said. "No way we won't cover 6 1/2."

I thanked him and so did the guys on the *Post*. Final score: Raiders 32, Vikes 14. Valuable interview, huh?

Cashing in on the Jets

Want to hear another wagering story? Sure. Jets vs. Colts, Super Bowl III. I'm covering it for the *Post*, as the Jets beat writer. Our columnist is Larry Merchant, whom you might see on TV, doing the fights on HBO from Vegas. I'm sure he moved out there to get closer to the action, because Larry liked to make a wager or two.

The opening line on the game is Colts minus 17. Larry bet the Jets with the points. He was coming off a good season and he had written a book telling people all about the secret of betting on NFL games. Its title was *The National Football Lottery*.

We're staying in the Jets' hotel, the Galt Ocean Mile in Fort Lauderdale, and the place is a zoo. Wives, kids, madness by the swimming pool, players being pestered, non-stop. There was a team revolt over what the players perceived as a plan to give them watches instead of Super Bowl rings, if they should win, and a near fight between Joe Namath and the Colts' Lou Michaels, and all sorts of lunacy.

"This team is gonna get murdered," Larry said to me during the week, very nervous about his bet. I agreed with him. So did the bettors because by kickoff on Sunday the price had risen to 19 1/2, an almost unheard of one-week swing during Super Bowl week.

Larry panicked and bailed out, taking the Colts and laying the 19 1/2. In other words he could have caught a reverse middle. If Baltimore would have won by 18 or 19, he'd have lost both ends. The prospect had him in a sweat as the game began.

Well, it was soon obvious that it wasn't going to happen that way, and Larry breathed a huge sigh of relief and settled down to enjoy the contest. Afterward, as we were heading down to the locker room, someone asked him, "How'd you do, Larry?" He put on his cool-as-a-cucumber, *National Football Lottery* face and said, "I had the right team."

Yeah, he had the right team and he had the wrong team. He had both teams. I almost blurted it out. Even now, thinking about it brings a smile to my face.

Punked

The whole scene surrounding Super Bowl III ranks among the great memories, but the best part of it was watching those tight, steel-jawed faces of the NFL writers, as it became obvious that the Jets were going to win. The AFL was a punk league in their eyes, and AFL writers such as me were treated as punks — trash, actually.

So did I act with grace and dignity in the press box as those guys suffered in their profound silence? I did not. "Hey, Tex, what was that score again that you predicted?" I shouted over to *Sports Illustrated*'s Tex Maule, who had forecast some ungodly Colt victory. "Hey, Arthur," I yelled over to *The New York Times*' Arthur Daley. "How much you have the Colts winning by?" Yeah, I know, crude and vulgar, but you have to remember we'd been taking a lot of crap from them through the years. A very happy memory of that Orange Bowl press box.

'It's Absurd'

Two good ones from Super Bowl IV, Kansas City vs. Minnesota. On Tuesday a story broke that K.C. quarterback Len Dawson was involved with a Detroit gambler named Dice Dawson (no relation). Ken Denlinger of *The Washington Post* and I hopped into my car and shot over to the Chiefs' hotel so we could talk to Dawson before they put him in quarantine. As we were heading out of the press hotel, we passed Daley and Gene Ward, the *New York Daily News*' lead columnist, going to dinner.

"It was just a rumor," I heard Ward say. "No substantiation."

Yeah, right. It was still a good Tuesday story. So we got to Dawson's hotel room, and he talked to us for a while, and the quote we focused on was, "There is absolutely nothing to that story. I've done absolutely nothing wrong."

Kenny went back to the press HQ to file his story. I was writing for an evening paper so I could stay later, which I did. When I got back to the press room, Ken was dictating, and Ward, sitting one row behind him, was straining to hear what he was saying. He heard it, but he screwed it up. Instead of "absolutely," he registered it as "absurd."

A few minutes later, as I was starting to write, I saw Ward tip his chair back, light his pipe, and begin to dictate to his desk. "Slug it 'New Orleans, Ward, confidential to the *Daily News*,'" he said. "'It's absurd,' Len Dawson told this writer in confidence last night."

That one goes under the heading of great journalistic moments.

Presidential Postgame

Postgame locker scene, again from Super Bowl IV, in decrepit Tulane Stadium. The Chiefs won, and Dawson was the game's MVP. President Nixon called. Dawson took the call in a little shack adjoining the locker area. As you squeezed your way in, an overstuffed armchair, of all things, was right in the pathway, and in the armchair was K.C. end coach Darrell (Pete) Brewster, snarling at the writers who were tripping over his outstretched legs, and we were snarling at him. A real jerk.

So Dawson took the call, and from outside, the guys who couldn't fit inside were yelling, "Who's he talking to?"

"President Roosevelt!" I yelled out at them. Brewster sat up with a jolt.

"Not Roosevelt, dummy," he said, with absolute hatred. "Nixon!"

I thanked him. That sure cleared it up.

Jacked Up

Super Bowl XIV in Pasadena, Rams vs. Steelers — for some strange reason my favorite Super Bowl of them all. Maybe it was because I had been tracking the Steelers all week, and they seemed worn out, tired, depressed, not in a good mood. Jack Lambert eventually emerged as one of the heroes of the game, intercepting a Rams pass deep in Steelers territory just when it seemed that L.A. would go ahead in the fourth quarter, but during the week he was feeling very low and ugly.

We're sitting in the bar of the team hotel. A couple of teeny boppers are making the rounds, and they let out a squeal as they spy him. "Jack Lambert! It's Jack Lambert!" They yelled. I'm thinking, *oh, brother*.

"My horoscope said I'm gonna run into somebody famous," one of them said. "Do you believe in horoscopes, Jack?"

"No," he said, staring into his beer.

"Do you know your astrological sign?"

"Yes," he said.

"What is it?"

"Feces," he said.

News from the Tent

One of the best teams for quotes was the Raiders. I remember making the rounds of the tent that served as their midweek interview area before they played the Redskins in Super Bowl XVIII. As the crush of reporters closed in on him, Howie Long closed his eyes, tilted his head back and uttered a stream of consciousness I've always remembered as a perfect Press Interview Day capsule.

"Give me a day to die ... are we in Kansas yet, Toto? ... I don't know where I am ... oh God, I'm in a tent ..."

And two tables away, Lester Hayes was leading the writers through this weird *Star Wars* angle: "I honestly can feel myself getting my power from the Force. When it is with me, I am able to play. I am very, very close to Obi-Wan Kenobi." And on and on in this vein, the writers dutifully writing down every word.

"How do you think up this stuff?" I asked him afterward.

"Aren't they amazing?" he said, wide eyed. "They wrote it all down. They were all serious. I could have told them anything. Wait till you hear what I have for them tomorrow."

Death in Detroit

Well, I've saved the best for last. People with long memories might recall that I became a cause celebre in Detroit before the '82 Super Bowl. On Tuesday we went to the Silverdome on a freezing cold day for Picture and Press Day. Except that they didn't let us in when they were supposed to. The cops kept us outside a fence, freezing. I gripped the fence and asked, "What's the deal?" "How'd you like this stick across those fingers?" was the answer. I guess Detroit cops don't like writers any more than anyone else does.

It was a nasty, mean place to have a Super Bowl, and next day I was one of the guests on *Good Morning America*, along with *The Detroit News* sports editor, Joe Falls, and when Charlie Gibson asked us how we liked it there, I let loose with both barrels. I mean heavy, heavy stuff.

I knew something was up when one of the technicians wanted to fight me after the show. "I'll bet you're one of those punks from New York," he said. "Nah, I'm from Hamtramck, (Mich.)" I told him.

"Like hell you are."

"Like hell I'm not."

And then they pulled us apart. In the car going back to the hotel, I said to Joe, "I think I might have said something I shouldn't have."

"I think you might have," he said.

Well, the city came down on my head, kaboom! I received two death threats. I didn't take them too seriously, my theory being that if someone wanted to kill me, he wouldn't tell me about it first. But my mother took it big. She'd read about it in the paper, and I guess she figured that the next picture of me would be with a tag on the toe.

"Maybe you ought to hire a bodyguard," she told me over the phone.

"Gosh, Mom," I said, "I looked in the yellow pages under B and I couldn't find any."

"Very funny, very funny," she said.

One columnist wrote, "I'm sure Mr. Zimmerman would like to hear from you, so here's the hotel he's staying at and his room number." Which, of course, produced round-the-clock crank calls. And you don't want to shut your phone down, not when there are two young kids back home.

But I learned a very interesting thing, the difference between male and female crank callers. Your typical male crank caller: "Is Mr. Zimmerman there?" "This is Mr. Zimmerman." "Oh yeah? Well, then, why don't you ..." And the parade of obscenities, followed by the phone being slammed down.

Typical female crank caller: "Is Mr. Zimmerman there?" And then the same routine, the same obscenities, but wait ... no hang up. Natural feminine curiosity kept them on the line, and, to quote an old Edward R. Murrow radio bit, "The Jungle Answered Back," I'd let forth with my own volley ... "Why don't you get ahold of your husband and ..." A much more satisfying exchange indeed, especially when I'd hear that intake of breath denoting the surprise at hearing a writer using that kind of language.

Next March the league meetings are in Phoenix. Curt Sylvester of the *Detroit Free Press* asked me for a quote, any quote at all from Phoenix. He said my name was still being mentioned in Detroit.

"Too hot," I said. "Wish I was back in Detroit."

And of course the letters followed. "You ass, when you were here you said ... and now you're saying ...", etc. Lots of happy Super Bowl memories, folks.

Chapter 6

Diary of a Madman

This column appeared on SI.com *on Aug. 16, 2001.*

Just came back from two weeks of nonstop AFC East training camp visits and, boy, am I tired. The teacher has given us the topic What We Did This Summer, which was always my favorite topic in composition class. Well, I talked to a guy who played against Bronko Nagurski. And ate in some swell restaurants. And clocked a national anthem in 1:56.87. And counted 1,032 steps from the entrance to Gate 91 in Newark Airport. And got into this big fight with The Flaming Redhead at the same venue because we always get into fights as air travel approaches since we hate airlines so much and are always in an ugly mood.

Saturday, July 29: We drive, hooray, to Bryant College in Smithfield, R.I., for the Patriots. Good mood all around because no air travel is involved. Set a record for different states' license plates recorded on the trip, 31, plus three Canadian provinces. We head immediately for nearby Providence and Al Forno restaurant, which is a hot spot now because the chef has been on Martha Stewart's show twice, and we arrive at 4:30 p.m., an odd time for dinner, granted, but a necessity, since the place accepts no reservations and it's filled up by 5:30. The outdoor garden dining is filled even earlier, and one of the extremely odd rules of this place is that they only serve their drink specials in the outdoor venue.

Why this strange rule? Who knows? They're a little strange in New England anyway. And what's so special about the drink specials? The mint julep. Never in my 103 years on this planet have I had one to match it. Frosty metal glass. Mint has been boiled in the correct way and it lines the bottom, blended with boiled sugar. Then a layer of crushed ice, then the bourbon near the top. You use a short straw and by moving it up and down you can experience all varieties of taste sensation with the julep. Oh, man. We have one, then bing-bang, another one, and by now the Redhead is starting to wave at the people at the other tables, so it's time to order food. Won't bore you with all the details, but the produce is local and fresh, which is they real key, I believe, and everything is delicious. Nice call, Martha.

Patriots' practice is a strange amalgam of wide receivers imported from all parts of the globe, plus glaring weaknesses in the offensive and defensive lines. The new wideouts, which I read will lift the passing game to undreamed of heights, are basically people from other teams that felt they needed to upgrade their wideout situations. Best looking one is ex-Brown David Patten, but that's nothing new because he always looks good in camp.

Later I ask Bill Belichick why the big rush for wideouts when he has Terry Glenn and the vastly underrated Troy Brown, who are certainly serviceable enough. Belichick thinks for a moment before deciding how to phrase his reply.

"I'm not counting on Glenn," he says. Well, the guy is currently out with a sore knee, but that's no big deal, is it?

"I'm just not counting on him," he says. "If he lines up for us, it'll be a bonus." This is strange news indeed.

"Is he gonna go in the tank? Is he gonna quit?" I ask.

"He's just a different person," the coach says. What he's trying to tell me, in code of course, and what I'm too dense to pick up, is something that surfaces a few days later, the four-game suspension, followed by Glenn's no-show, followed by his banishment.

I walk back from practice with Belichick on a shaded pathway, used by coaches, players and team personnel, but not open to writers, and which saves you roughly a quarter of a mile of the 1,310 steps between the office building and the press area at practice. When I arrive at the parking lot where the two routes join, I am on the privileged side of the chain and therefore warmly greeted by the security people who would normally tell me to take a hike. I am ushered through, and a young fan immediately asks me for my autograph.

"You don't want mine, I'm nobody," I tell him.

"Well, you were on the other side of the chain," he says.

"Anybody can get there if you pay them," I say.

"Daaaad! Is that true?"

"Don't listen to that guy," says the tough-looking daddy. "He's a moron."

Highlight of the trip is a conversation with Francis "Bucko" Kilroy, the Patriots' 82-year-old consultant, one of the founders of the art of personnel scouting and codifying. A gentle fellow, given to reflection and reminiscence, and how many people remember that at one time he was one of the filthiest and most feared linemen in the game?

"He committed the worst foul I've ever seen on a football field," Herb Hannah, the father of Patriots guard John Hannah, once told me. Herb was a starting tackle for the Giants in 1951. "We were playing the Eagles and after one play, when we were walking back to the huddle, Bucko came up behind our end, Bob McChesney, and smashed him in the back of the head with a forearm and laid him out."

So now we're sitting under the warm Rhode Island sunshine, watching practice, and Bucko is telling me about his rookie year, 1943, when the great Bronko Nagurski made a wartime comeback after a five-year layoff and he's lining up for the Bears as a tackle — against Bucko.

"A great holder," Bucko says. "So I punched him. He goes back to the huddle and asks someone, 'Who the hell is that guy?'"

"Oh, he's that wild-assed rookie. Stay away from him. He's crazy."

The drive back is more pleasant because we avoid the ugly Connecticut Thruway and take the older but slower Merritt Parkway.

"This is beautiful," the Redhead says. "Why didn't we come up this way?"

"Because we wanted to get to Al Forno before five," I tell her. Oh yes, we also ate at Hemenway's and Legal Sea Foods to complete the trifecta and thus ended our experience in fine dining on the AFC East circuit.

Wednesday, Aug. 1 (not to mention another visit on Aug. 8): New York Jets at Hofstra University, Hempstead, L.I. This is an awful 75-mile drive from my home in New Jersey, but I know it well because I used to make it every day during the decade or so that I was a Jets beat writer. Bad things always happen, traffic tie-ups, freakies. Once I nearly lost my life on the Cross Bronx Expressway, skidding wildly on squashed potatoes after a truck had dumped its load. You ever drive over squashed potatoes? Bet you haven't.

You have to stay alert for tie-ups as you're driving to Hempstead. You have to hunt for back roads. You arrive exhausted.

Things brightened up when I got to camp. It's always old-home week for me at Jets camp, always someone around that I knew from the old days. This time it was Wesley Walker, the former wideout, and Connie Nicholas, daughter of the Jets' former team dentist, niece of their famous orthopedist, Jim Nicholas. I knew her as a frisky little kid, frolicking among her heroes. Now she talks about her grown children. Or did she say *grandchildren*? I can't even visualize something like that. I'd missed, by a day, pass-rushing phenom Mark Gastineau, newly released from prison. He's back in custody now, but when he showed up at Hofstra he mentioned his religious conversion. "These days I'm sacking Satan" was his quote in the papers. I called the Elias Sports Bureau to find out if he'd get credit for that one on the record, but no, they wouldn't count the sack since it was shared by about 72 million others.

An open, friendly place, unlike the *Stalag 17* operation Bill Parcells ran. What a pleasure to actually be able to talk to assistant coaches. "If they hadn't let me talk to the writers when I was an assistant with the Bucs," Herman Edwards said, "I probably wouldn't be a head coach now."

Right away you get good feelings about this man. A players' coach, well-liked by everyone, but so was Pete Carroll, and the Jets laid down on him. Could this happen again?

"The veterans won't let it happen," Vinny Testaverde said, exactly the same quote I got from numerous veterans when Carroll first took over. The place bubbles with enthusiasm, but nose tackle Jason Ferguson is out for two months, and so is the No. 1 pick, Santana Moss. Well, Jim Haslett and the Saints shrugged off early injuries in camp last year and did just fine. Maybe history can repeat.

Thursday, Aug. 2: Now it's time to fly to Fort Lauderdale for the Dolphins. Here's a helpful word of advice: If you're booking a reservation, ask what the aircraft is, and if they say the code is 73-S, which stands for a Boeing 737-200, thank the person very kindly and book something else. Delta provided us with one of these horror machines. Doug Flutie couldn't fit into one of the seats. You have just about enough room to read a small paperback. A newspaper is a challenge. The seat in front of you presses firmly against your knees. If the passenger chooses to recline it, the pain will be exquisite. Howling, by the way, is not permitted on Delta. Or any other airline.

A brief interlude. You will forgive me, please, if my comments about the airlines and air personnel and air travel border on the irrational. I hate them, you see. Not a mild dislike, but an active, blazing hatred. If any other business operated like this business does, it would be out of business. Torture, relentless humiliation, lies, hypocrisy, deception — they've got it all. The topper, of course, is when you've just completed some miserable, full-aircraft, mooing cattle drive, and you're rushing to exit the plane like some trapped coal miner and you hear, "This is your captain. We hope you've enjoyed the flight," etc. I can't continue. I will point out little grace notes as they occur. One warning: If anyone mailbagging in a query chooses to take me to task for these sentiments — in other words, allies himself or herself with the airlines against your faithful narrator — I will take down your name and get even, somehow, somewhere. I'm not kidding.

Linda, bring me a glass of water, please.

Delta night flight from Newark to Fort Lauderdale. I don't count the steps anymore, from entry to gate, in Newark terminals A and B (Delta terminal) because they're all about the same, roughly 450-500 paces. Full flight. Lady in front of me tries to recline her seat. I'm holding it firmly in place. Sorry, no torture today, lady. She tries and tries, twisting in her seat to get a look at what the obstruction is. My eyes are on a far wall, my face a blank. I've gone through this drill before. A pro against an amateur. She gives up.

Finally we spill out into the muggy Fort Lauderdale air in various stages of stagger. We drive our rental car to our usual habitat, the Airport Hilton, only to find that in the space of a year something terrible has happened to this place. Filthy room, patches of stuff all over, gooey, grungy imprints of previous food, and hey, there's not even any toilet paper in the bathroom. We can stand everything except the latter.

Have you about had it with all this whining? OK, I'll hold off for awhile, repeat, for awhile. This is, after all, a football column.

Two figures dominate the Dolphins' practice, the defensive tackles, Daryl Gardener and Tim Bowens, each a No. 1 draft choice in the mid-1990s. For years people wondered when they were going to bust loose, and now it looks like they've finally arrived. Gardener had some magnificent games on my charts last year. If he hadn't gone down with a herniated disc in his back and missed six outings, he would have challenged Warren Sapp for the second spot on my All-Pro team. (The Saints' La'Roi Glover was No. 1.) Bowens has established himself as one of the league's sturdy two-gappers, a perfect counterpart to Gardener, who is probably the most remarkably built really big man I've ever seen. He looks like a gymnast, blown up to 6-foot-6, 310, with chiseled, rippling muscles and 8 percent body fat, a category that always has made me nervous, with the lurking fear that someday I'll have to hold still for a measurement of that dreaded statistic. ("Seventy percent body fat? How could you let yourself get that way?" etc.)

In the locker room, we get into a spirited debate about the best tackle tandems in the league. I throw out the names of Glover and Hand in New Orleans.

"Hand was a great pickup for them," Gardener says. "Glover works very hard, but he's undersized. Sometimes the double-team will blow him off the line."

I mention Sapp and McFarland on the Bucs.

"What helps them is that the defense is so exotic," Gardener says, "and there's so much slanting. Plus the linebackers are exceptional. I've seen that scheme just take out our offense and dissect us."

How about Darrell Russell and, uh, Grady Jackson on the Raiders?

"I like Russell's power and speed. To me he's the total package — when he wants to be, and that's the key to it."

I'm running out of tandems. Siragusa and Adams on the Ravens? Defensive line coach Clarence Brooks happens to overhear.

"Fate put 'em in the right place at the right time," he says.

To a man, the locker room choice is Bowens and Gardener, and this twosome just might be the best after all. It'll certainly bear watching.

In practice that day I see a sad sight. Jamie Nails, a starter for the Bills at right guard last year and an early cut this offseason, is standing on the sideline waiting for practice to end so he can try out. In almost five months, no one has picked him up. He looks like a guy who has crash-dieted and lost a lot of weight too quickly, with unusual hills and declivities on his body. He is unrecognized. No one talks to him as he silently watches practice.

I'd never met Jamie Nails, but I was filled with this feeling of sadness as I reflected on the jarring world of pro football and its sudden crash landings. One day, top of the world, chartered planes, locker room attendants to handle your gear, kids fighting for your autograph, and then in a heartbeat it's over, and you're just another guy wondering if you'll ever make a living at it again; you're out on your own. If I were a beat man covering the Dolphins, I might have done some kind of sidebar feature on this phenomenon. Instead, I went over to Nails and introduced myself and did a quickie interview and took some notes, just to let him know that at least one guy knew who he was.

Our Delta night flight back home was delayed an hour. "Weather in Newark," we were told, which could mean anything. Five raindrops, backed-up traffic, equipment failure, you name it. Then we got in the plane and sat at the gate for another two hours. Seems that a small aircraft had made an emergency landing and spilled some fuel on the runway. Those little blower things over the seats were barely functioning. The heat became crushingly oppressive. No drinks were provided. Why not, I asked the male flight attendant.

"We only have enough for our in-flight service," he said.

"Why don't you bring some more on board?" I asked.

"If you want to write a letter, you can," said this guy, whose name, I found out, was Ed.

"He's goading you," The Flaming Redhead said. "He's trying to get you to blow up and lose it. Stay calm."

Ed was way ahead of us. He took my name. He asked me if I was sitting in the seat I'd originally been assigned. How well I knew this drill. A race to see who could get off the first letter. *I noticed that the passenger in 19D was loud and offensive and disturbing the other passengers, etc.*

God help you if you get mad and raise your voice. Then that becomes the only issue. *Unruly, antagonistic, a danger to himself and others. We strongly recommend, your honor, that the individual be immediately committed.* Oh, I've been through that one about a million times. And they wonder why we hate them so much.

Wednesday, Aug. 8: A night flight to Rochester aboard a tiny US Airways prop plane. Destination: Bills camp at St. John Fisher College in Pittsford, N.Y. I like these little prop jobs. They seem like a throwback to a less complicated, happier era. I like Rochester, too, with its old-world elegance and the Eastman Kodak Museum, which Linda and I toured with great enjoyment last year. I like the little craft shop she found this time, Craft Company No. 6, which had a wonderful collection of signature kaleidoscopes, which are among the 800 or so things I collect (and yes, I did pick up a few exotic numbers).

I spent a shockingly long period of time with the new coach, Gregg Williams, a lover of football history, particularly on the defensive side of the ball, his specialty. We swapped Buddy Ryan stories — he'd studied under Buddy — and he laid out the complete plan for the Bills' new 4-3 defense, which involved more of a gap-penetrating style than the old 3-4, two-gap, and yes, new schemes are great — if you have good players.

Later I talked to one of my favorites, left defensive end Phil Hansen, a sturdy 11-year veteran who's seen more styles than Schiaparelli.

"Well, they still have me sinking down to a tackle on the nickel defense," he said, "at 262 pounds."

"What do you say to that?" I asked him.

"I say, 'Bring it on!' Oh, brother."

Yep, new style, and that'll solve everything. On offense it's once again the "New West Coast Offense" that everyone seems to be turning to — or away from. Except that their QB, Rob Johnson, at 6-4 and a skinny 212, seems like anything but a quick-read, quick-drop guy. But he says he's perfectly suited to it — hell, he'd tell me that if they put him in at blocking back — so who am I to argue?

I enjoyed watching tiny defensive line coach John Levra getting madder and madder as he put his guys through a three-man read and recognition drill conducted at a slower-than-desired pace under the sultry heat.

"See that?" Levra screamed at a rookie who took the wrong lane and got caught inside. "Do that and you'll get caved in and walled up and you'll foul up everybody." After practice I told Levra that that was exactly the story of my life. He gave me a "Who the hell are you?" look.

A snappy 232 steps from entrance to gate in the Rochester Airport. Fort Lauderdale had been only a few paces longer. Thank heavens for small airports.

Thursday, Aug. 9: That was not the case, unfortunately, at Newark for our 6:50 a.m. flight to Indianapolis and Colts camp at Terre Haute, Ind. This time it was Continental, which meant Terminal C and the dreaded Gate 91, a grueling 1,032 steps. Newark gates in the '90s are particularly dangerous for overweight air travelers shlepping two carry-on bags, and the prospect of it put both Linda and myself into a nasty mood. The trouble began in the always-under-construction parking area when a female security officer tried to get me to back up into a spot that had just opened up.

Cars shot by, my back-up was a zigzag. "Just back up like she's telling you!" the Redhead yelled at me.

"The rear view mirror's fogged up," I said.

"*You're* fogged up," she said.

Things got worse on the plane. "Our flight time in the air will be one hour and 32 minutes," the captain cheerfully announced, which is a deliberately misleading statistic because you spend half an hour on the ground, so the total time is really the scheduled two hours or so, all of which I made known, in grumpy 6:50 a.m. fashion, to the stewardess.

"What are you bothering her for?" the Redhead said.

"Because I want honesty," I said, "and she's part of the scam." And so for the next half hour, it was the cold, mad face, stare-straight-ahead routine for us, and when breakfast came around, I made my stand by declining the single muffin, minus butter. Later, of course, I grabbed two of them when the hunger became insurmountable, which caused peals of laughter from the Flamer and ended the war. A short, 289-step walk in the Indy terminal helped to restore me to my usual jolly self.

The Colts practice at Rose-Hulman Institute, which marked the third school that nobody ever heard of that we visited. It is held in a weird climate inversion kind of bowl that keeps the humidity way up there, so you are drenched in sweat even when the temperature is fairly reasonable. During my interviews I had to keep the notebook well away from my head because when I forgot the sweat dripped onto the pages, blurring the writing. The night practice was better, in a way, but marked by other hazards, namely mosquitoes. Last year I saw two of them drag a ballboy off the field, and one of them said to the other, "We'd better hide him before the big ones get here."

This time I was well-prepared, having liberally dosed myself with a can of bug spray, making a nice slippery time of it. The odor still clings to my notebook.

Easy angle on this team. Great offense, suspect defense, how's it going to change? Talked to every defensive player I could lay my hands on after first touching base with Peyton Manning, of course. A fine chap who will discourse meaningfully on any topic, with, thankfully, a lack of the usual cliches. I go back quite a ways with Peyton, back to the days when he was a small child listening to an interview I was doing for a piece on his father, Archie, in New Orleans.

"Who's your favorite player?" I asked him.

"Freddie Solomon," he said. "But my father is my favorite Saint."

The comments from the defenders I talked to pretty much revolved around the fine collection of athletes the club had put together. The most sensible came from Jeff Burris, the left cornerback ("Until you can control a game, you can't make a name for yourself, and so far the only names on this club are on offense") and Chad Bratzke, the right end ("Well, we have the athletes, but this is a hard game, a fast-paced game. It's a fight the whole way. We'll find out what kind of fighters we have.")

Terre Haute? Well, you won't find fine dining there. In the two blocks on either side of the Holiday Inn where we stayed, we counted 21 chains. Arby's, Hardee's, Long John Silver's, Taco Bell, Burger King and McDonald's, of course, Rally's, Denny's, the list is endless. Two China Buffets, Applebee's, Pizza Hut, Dunkin' Donuts, why go on? We ate at the hotel, at the Outback Steakhouse. I grabbed a bunch of the delicious, homemade cherry bars at the training camp. We got by. What the hell, I'm too fat anyway.

I don't want to label Terre Haute as a depressed area, not on two quick visits, but the real estate ads were stunners. "Beautiful large white Victorian, three stories," I read. I asked the Redhead to guess how much. "One hundred and seventy five," she said. "Sixty-two, five," I told her.

"Here's one," I said. "Two bedroom home with three-year-old furnace and 24 x 24 detached garage."

"Thirty thousand," she said, hitting what she thought was rock bottom.

I dropped the bomb. "Nine thousand, nine hundred."

There was a picture of a beautiful brick Presbyterian church, 9,800 square feet, priced at $149,900. Were they actually selling a church? This we had to see. So we drove over to look at it. A magnificent structure it was, occupying almost an entire block, complete with stained-glass windows and a huge pipe organ. Why were they selling it? Departed congregation? Moving to new location? What? I called the real estate company and talked to someone who told me, "They're just selling it, that's all. Of course, you'd have to do something about the two people who're living there. Kick 'em out, let 'em stay, whatever you want."

How about that beautiful big organ?

"I guess you could use it for parties if you wanted to." It was all so depressing.

Well, there were good things in Terre Haute. We found a country antiques place, and Linda bought three big cowbells. Why cowbells? "I've always wanted them," she said. "I love the sound they make."

For the second straight year, we bought a load of secondhand books at a fine store called Wabash Books. We visited the museum that once was the home of one of my heroes, the old labor leader, Eugene V. Debs. A wonderful place, uncluttered by those insulting Do Not Touch signs. They simply presented the objects and relied on your good judgment to leave the stuff alone.

On Saturday night I caught the Seahawks-Colts exhibition game. I sat in the scouts section, my favorite area in the press box. Next to me was a young Packers scout who'd had a brief career as an NFL linebacker. How did we differ? During the national anthem his right hand was on his heart, mine was on my stopwatch. I caught Colts cheerleader Sarah Steele in a depressingly long 1:56.87. "That might be the longest I'll clock all year," I told the scout.

It was Mark Rypien's night. Listed No. 3 on the Colts' depth chart, the 38-year-old former Super Bowl MVP, who'd been out of football for three years, saw more action than he or anyone else expected because the No. 2 guy, Billy Joe Hobert, went down with a concussion. Rypien responded with a masterful two-TD night, and boy, was it fun watching an old pro like that teach the youngsters all the tricks, picking the defense apart with short, quick stuff over the middle. Pick, pick, pick, surely the defenders would catch on and make him go outside, but they never did, and in the locker room afterward, he laughed like a kid as he showed me a weirdly swollen elbow.

"I'm getting hit again," he said. "Isn't it great?"

Yep, there are great things, for sure, on the camp circuit. If only you could avoid those damn airlines.

* * *

THE LONG AND WINDING ROAD
This column appeared on SI.com *on Feb. 6, 2007.*

My serious playoff action on the road began with a lonely trip to Indianapolis and ended in the rain in Miami. Why was the Indy trip lonely? Because usually The Flaming Redhead makes these journeys with me, at least to the championship round, but there were one-thousand-one-hundred-and-forty-eight reasons why she didn't make this one. That's right, $1,148 was what Continental Airlines wanted, round trip from Newark, when you don't book at least a week in advance.

"But how was I supposed to know ahead of time New England would knock off San Diego and the AFC championship would be in Indianapolis?" I asked the Continental ticket agent. "You're the expert ... you're supposed to know stuff like that," she said. Yeah, I guess so.

(Just kidding ... no one really said that ... c'mon ... I told you I was just kidding.)

So since I'll be going on a six-month sabbatical (from the magazine, not the web site), at half pay, we can't afford to start throwing around four-figure tariffs for 80-minute plane rides, and the Redhead stayed home.

What she missed was a trip out there on a plane filled with teeny bopper cheerleaders, heading to Indy for the Jamfest Cheerleaders Super Nationals, with 8,000 strong. It was like being on a plane filled with demented mice. Same thing on the plane ride home. Same thing in the hotel, the lobby, hiding behind potted palms, everywhere.

"Where's the newsstand?" I asked the desk clerk at the Hyatt, which was the press hotel.

"Through the lobby," he said, "if you can get through the cheerleaders."

On the second floor, they had what they euphemistically called a Press Lounge. A sofa and a few chairs and a table, supposedly with sodas and stuff. It looked like the kind of press lounge they might set up in Bulgaria. I stuck my nose in just once. Three guys in what looked like workingman's garb were bitching about the lack of bottled water, and a Hyatt lady was telling them, "We'll bring more." Adios Press Lounge.

Yeah, it was lonely. Had a meal at the Hyatt's rooftop restaurant, going round and round. Paid 14 bucks to watch Forest Whitaker chew up the scenery in *The Last King of Scotland* on the hotel's pay TV movie set-up. Well, it beat all those puff pieces and softball interviews on the NFL Network. Front page of *The Indianapolis Star* carried a story about the ketchup war between Heinz and Red Gold for the use of the term Red Zone. Wish Linda would have been there to read it. Flaming Redhead Zone?

Sometimes the sports section has stories and items that put you to the test, trying to figure out whether they're serious or not. The Outside View column in *The Star*, for instance, talked about "a series of simulations I've run this past weekend, with the Colts beating the Patriots five out of 10." Am I too dense to grasp this?

- My first two meals in Miami were at Joe's Stone Crab and the Porcao Churrascaria. I felt like I was tapped for the entire Super Bowl week. I'd been going to Joe's for about 40 years now, and it hadn't really changed, except that it was bigger. You didn't have to wait as long, sometimes not at all. Still the same sensational hash brown potatoes and creamed spinach. The stone crabs? Yeah, they're good, but I've never been a serious devotee. I just don't understand the magic of them.

  But somebody does because an order of the jumbo sized costs $72 on one of the more wide-ranging menus. Half a broiled chicken, for instance, still costs $5.95. "In 50 years, I think they've raised the price by about 35 cents," a waiter told me. Anyway, the Redhead had a Ginger Salmon for $19.95 that she said was wonderful.

  Porcao is one of those Brazilian Churrascarias where they come around every 30 seconds or so with different cuts of broiled meats, which you load up on until you pass out. Paramedic units are on duty. Outside the place, a group of cardiologists was getting ready to storm the doors. All I kept thinking, as I shamelessly indulged, was how evil I was, how I would pay for all of this, if not in this world, then in the next one.

  We were food-exhausted after only two days, but we still managed to put in an appearance at P.F. Chang's China Bistro, which always has been one of our favorites and, again, did not let us down, plus Versailles, which, unfortunately, has fallen on bad times. Not financially, judging by the huge mob that was there for this typically festive Cubano Sunday lunch. No, this still remains the focal point of Little Havana and environs. But the quality, which once was good, is now terrible. Everything tasted as if it had been sitting around for half a day and then warmed up. Something unfortunate has happened to this place, an owner dying or retiring, takeover by a son-in-law, something like that? Sad.

- I was waiting during Tuesday's Press and Picture Day for someone to ask the dreaded question, the one that always makes me shake my head and begin coughing: "What's the dumbest (or the weirdest, or strangest) question you've been asked?" Ted Hendricks gave it the definitive answer about a million Super Bowls ago: "That one right there," but it always returns, usually posed by some halfwit who thinks he or she is being so clever and original.

   The perpetrator surprised me this time. ESPN's Mark Malone, a former Steelers QB no less. "What's the strangest question you've been asked?" He asked the Bears' Olin Kreutz. The answer was drowned out by the sound of my groaning.

- Ran into an old friend with the Colts, Howard Mudd, who's been an NFL offensive line coach for 32 straight years.

   "I've got you graded in more than 20 games when you were playing for the 49ers," I told him.

   "Oh yeah? How'd I do?" he said.

   "Very well," I told him. He took the news calmly.

- At the Wednesday interview sessions at the team hotels, I caught up with Chicago defensive coordinator Ron Rivera ... this was a day before all the stuff was written about him possibly going to Dallas as head coach. A good guy. Former reserve linebacker on the Buddy Ryan championship defense. I asked him if, when he became a head coach, he'd allow the press to talk to his assistants, or if he were of the Belichick One-Voice school of thought?

   "I would owe it to them to let them get as much publicity as they could," he said, "to let the writers know all about them."

   Yaaay! C'mon Dallas. You're not gonna find a better head coach than him.

- Sitting on the dais and addressing the room at large, Brian Urlacher was asked how he felt about being the "face of the Chicago

Bears." "If I didn't have to talk to the media, I'd be real good with it," he said. I got up and left.

"You jumped the gun, as usual," Don Pierson of the *Chicago Tribune* told me later. "He was just kidding." Oh, comma, I see.

- Someone at one of the players' tables was reading the story about Andy Reid's son Britt getting busted for waving a weapon around. A veteran writer turned to me and asked, "Trivia question. Who was Britt Reid?" An easy one. The Green Hornet, on the old radio drama. "Kato, warm up the Black Beauty." "All right, Mister Reid."

- Mexican radio and Mexican TV was everywhere. "Do you know Spanish?" TV Azteca asked Colts' linebacker Rob Morris. "Only the bad words," he said.

- Wednesday afternoon I did my last *She Says, Z Says* video with Brooklyn Decker, the swimsuit model. Our first one outdoors. By the swimming pool. I push her in at the end. Tee hee. On Friday, as a favor to *Sports Illustrated*'s publicity director, I made the rounds with her at an area that I sincerely loathe, Radio Row in the Press Center. Hee Haw Central, Yahoo Valley.

"Well, Zim, it should be a great game Sunday ..."

"Either that or it won't." Blank stare. Interview is winding down before it's started. Get this stiff outta here!

So on Friday, Brookie and I toured the place. Let me tell you something about Brooklyn Decker. Last year, when she was in the swimsuit issue, she was 18. She had recently turned 19 when we started doing the video in October. I kid you not, when I was 19, I was an unruly thug with an IQ about 40 points lower than Brooklyn's. She is one sharp cookie. Funny, too. A lot of fun to work with, to bounce lines off of, and vice-versa, much of it unrehearsed.

She handled herself well during the radio stuff. I was, as usual, an obnoxoid. The best interviews were by three women from something (didn't catch the first word) Chix. They focused on Brooklyn's career, a refreshing change from all the football stuff. I got a couple of easy questions and then was given a felt tip and asked to sign some stuffed animal thing, as all their guests were. Sure, why not, but why get out of character and be a nice guy?

I inscribed it, "Keep punching ... your pal, Franz Kafka ..."

One idiot in a pseudo football jersey asked me if I "tried to get it going" with Brooklyn. I told him it would be like trying to "get it going" with my granddaughter. Interview over. See ya around.

- Blood was flowing at the Hall of Fame enshrinement meeting Saturday morning. I don't want to go too deeply into this thing because there were heavy repercussions. The Paul Tagliabue discussion set a record of 58 minutes. Two speakers began matters by endorsing him. I was the first of the anti voices. One of my points was that under his stewardship, and without his intervention, the rights of the press were eroded almost beyond recognition. Later I was told that I was a bit over the top. Maybe so. He didn't, as you know, reach level two, composed of 11 candidates.

- It always amazes me that when I come back from a Super Bowl, people always want to ask me about the halftime show, sometimes even the national anthem. OK, Billy Joel's rendition of the anthem was not the worst one I ever heard. But it was among the worst five. The halftime show? How's that again? Is that what you asked? Once again, please?

   I think my hearing is coming back, slowly, but I'm not quite sure. Just to be safe, I'm learning sign language. Halftime with Prince was LOUD! Never heard anything that loud. And that's all I can tell you about it.

- After the locker room stuff was over, I was walking back to the press bus, in the rain, and a security guy from the host committee offered to walk me over to the bus, under his umbrella, so I wouldn't get wet. People who have been whipped and kicked by authority figures all their lives are not used to this form of kindness. I was stunned. I politely declined, since the rain actually was refreshing after the locker room sweatshop, but this gesture will not be forgotten.

- On the plane home, Linda told me of an unusual thing. Seems that there's this company that had been granted the rights to manufacture a couple of hundred winning team hats and T-shirts, you know, things that said, "World Champion Colts," etc. These were handed out, in the postgame locker room to all people connected to the team, which meant that an equal number had to be made up in advance for the other team as well. So what happens to all those World Champion Bears items?

"Donated to charity," The Flaming Redhead told me, "but usually sent to some far off place. The article I read said that they'd turn up in places such as Romania and the African countries." Wow! What a great collection to have. Super Bowl I, World Champion Chiefs. Or maybe World Champion Falcons in Super Bowl XXXIII.

Maybe some day they'll appear on eBay. And I'll place the first bid.

Chapter 7

All-Time Teams

Editor's note: This all-time team was selected in 2007.

This is ground I've plowed many times. But I'm always finding something new. First, bear with me for a moment while I tell you why I don't like All-Star teams, Pro Bowl teams, Coach of the Year awards, Super Bowl MVP trophies. Because they're just promotions, NFL gimmicks to sell more T-shirts.

Pro Bowl voting is a popularity contest. I have seen high vote getters who spent two-thirds of the seasons on injured reserve. Players don't take the voting seriously, coaches are always busy with something else and fans pack the ballots. Very seldom is the Coach of the Year the Super Bowl winner because the balloting takes place at all levels, just about when the playoffs are starting. So it's always the guy who, amazingly, takes his team from 4-12 to the playoffs and many times not much further. Super Bowl MVP ballots are collected before the final whistle.

And as for All-Star teams by such organizations as the AP or the Pro Football Writers, well, these are better than most, but there's still the subliminal pull of the superstar, the comfort in the known entity. And that's why, and this will sound like the utmost in arrogance, I have faith in my own All-Pro team every year, compiled by so much tape breakdown that you would start laughing if I laid it all out for you ... my own team and very few others.

But unfortunately I must admit to the demon prejudice, that most personal of all human failings. I'm more careful about this than I used to be and I try to isolate it and eradicate it before it becomes an embarrassment, but let's face it. If you become passionate about something, sooner or later you're going to play favorites. The heroic run, the spectacular defensive play, especially on behalf of the team you happen to be rooting for, will take on a disproportionate significance. An example:

In 1985 I had picked Cincinnati, an eventual 7-9 team, to upset Dallas, which eventually won its division championship, in a late-season game. The affair wasn't close, 50-24, Cincy, and the Bengals ran for a million yards and especially notable was the job Cincy's 23-year-old, 300-pound left guard, Brian Blados, did on Hall of Famer Randy White. I didn't much like the Cowboys anyway ... America's Team and so forth ... and to see them beaten like that, and to watch the way the fat kid took on White, the most feared interior lineman in the game, just flipped me.

So I picked Blados on my *Sports Illustrated* All-Pro team, the only All-Star honor of any kind he ever achieved. And I left off John Hannah, one of the greatest offensive linemen in history, but a player, who after 13 seasons, had reached the end of the trail. And Hannah, with whom I had been fairly friendly, stopped talking to me.

"I mean Blados?" he said in our last conversation. "Are you kidding? Brian Blados?"

But picking an all-time All-Pro team is different. It's etched in marble. It's for the ages. It's something in which I've had a lot of practice because I've been doing it for, oh, about 63 years, ever since I got my first taste of the game in the World War II-era-Giants vs. the wartime combination of the Steelers and Eagles, nicknamed the Steagles, on Oct. 24, 1943, the day after my 11th birthday. The tickets were my father's birthday present to me.

Next year we went to the Polo Grounds on Oct. 22, the day before my birthday. Giants vs. the Cards-Pitts combination, referred to as the Carpets — they don't name 'em like that anymore. I started jotting down names of my favorite players, beginning with Al Blozis of course. The 6-6 tackle was the personal favorite of all New York kids who liked football. He'd been drafted into the army in December of '43, but he played three games in '44 while on furlough. I remember the deafening roar of the Polo Grounds fans when his name was announced. I remember reading about how he broke the army record for the hand grenade throw when he heaved one almost 100 yards at Fort Benning, Ga. I cut out the article and kept it.

And then in January, 1945, Lieutenant Blozis was killed in the Vosges Mountains in Alsace, venturing out, alone, to find a sergeant and private in his command who had gone out on patrol and failed to return. He immediately joined my all-time All-Pro squad, alongside Giant stars such as Mel Hein, the center-linebacker, and known entities such as Don Hutson and Sammy Baugh and remained on what became an ongoing list of All-Stars for a few years. It was only when the cold analysis of the dispassionate chartist, aged 17 or 18 or so, roughly elbowed sentiment aside, that Big Al became a former all-time All-Pro.

Actually I started charting games in 1947, and although players such as Blozis and Hein were at the time untouchable on the all-time list, the charts helped me pick my yearly All-Pro teams. For me they were significant because I was combining the NFL with the AAFC (All-American Football Conference). The bulk of the positions, at least on my club, were filled by AAFC players, which might have been a little unfair because those were the guys I was always watching in the flesh. In my neighborhood, at least, we dug the AFC and our Yankees, with the great triple threat, single wing tailback, Spec Sanders, and tiny Buddy Young, who would bring you out of your seat every time he touched the ball, and tough as nails Bruiser Kinard — now THAT's the kind of nickname a lineman should have — and in the last year of the league's existence, a tough, rawboned cornerback, defensive halfback is what they called them in those days, whose strangling style of pass coverage made him an immediate favorite of any New Yorker who loved football, and that was Tom Landry.

So those were the people who populated my All-Pro team, keyed, of course, to the magnificent Cleveland Browns, whom, in our hearts we just knew were better than anything the NFL had to offer. But I wasn't a fanatic on the subject. I understood, of course, the majesty of such people as Slingin' Sammy and Sid Luckman and Steve Van Buren, whom we would occasionally catch via one of the very early TVs, but it really couldn't compare to going out to Yankee Stadium and watching the Browns work behind Otto Graham and Marion Motley, who remained for many years the greatest player I'd ever seen, and Bill Willis, whose lightning moves brought a whole dimension to defensive line play.

When the leagues merged, it seemed as if the old boys club of the NFL deliberately tried to destroy the heritage of the AAFC. For many years statistics from that league were ignored on individual players' career totals, and it was only years later, when the AFL joined the NFL, bringing their statistics with them, that the AAFC numbers were allowed in by the back door. Thus many interesting statistics already had been mothballed. In 1947, for instance, Van Buren set the all-time single season rushing record of 1,008 yards. Sanders, though, topped it by 400, finishing with 1,432, a number that stood up for 11 years, except that it remained an asterisk number.

Do you know who the all-time leading punter is in pro football history, based on highest average? Well, if you said Baugh, because of all those quick kicks, you were right until 2003, when Shane Lechler forged ahead and eventually lifted Sammy's record a full yard, up to a gaudy 46. But you still haven't answered the question, and I doubt if you will because the answer is Glenn Dobbs, Brooklyn Dodgers and then L.A. Dons, in the old AAFC. His average for four years in that league stands at 46.4. A fluke, you say? An aberration? Oh no, a magnificent, 6-4, 215-pound, run, pass and punt tailback who worked out of a formation especially designed for him, an early version of the shotgun. He's not in the books because his 231 career punts fell 19 short of the minimum the NFL requires. And after his league merged, he played four years in Canada. But he missed some AAFC playing time because of injury one year, and just say he hadn't been hurt and would have gotten those 19 extra boots. What would the NFL records people have done? Probably increased the minimum requirement.

Way afield, I'm going way afield here, which is what happens once your hair has turned the color of the snows. My all time All-Pro team. Yes, it's here, the whole thing, based on more or less 64 years of pro football watching. At *Sports Illustrated* I have been asked for my all-time team at least half a dozen times, usually in connection with some spread they were planning or some promotion, and each occasion produced a spirited argument. "Eleven offensive players, please, 11 on defense, plus a streamlined special teams contingent, got that? Eleven, plus eleven, plus whatever."

No, certainly not. There are nuances at each position, power tackle and speed tackle, rush linebacker and strongside LB and coverage LB, and ... "Oh God, there he goes again."

"Look ... for the last time. It's for the layout. To fill a certain space, OK? Write the nuances in your memoirs someday."

Which is what I'm doing now. And why I have destroyed those meaningless 11 and 11s. OK, not destroyed ... I don't destroy anything ... but shoved deeply into a drawer. And without further preamble, here, then, is my all-time All-Pro, nuanced team. One note — I have seen every player on this list in the flesh except for Hutson, I think. My father swears that we saw him play in the Polo Grounds. If so, I don't remember it. What I DO remember, though, is the two solid days I spent in the Packers' film room looking at Hutson footage.

OFFENSE

WR — DEEP: Lance Alworth, Chargers, Cowboys, 1962-72
    Don Hutson, Packers, 1935-45
POSSESSION: Raymond Berry, Colts, 1955-67
COMBINATION: Jerry Rice, 49ers, Raiders, Seahawks, 1985-2004
TE — Dave Casper, Raiders, Oilers, Vikings, 1974-84
T — POWER: Art Shell, Raiders, 1968-82
SPEED: Forrest Gregg, Packers, 1956-71
    Ron Mix, Chargers, Raiders, 1960-71
G — John Hannah, Patriots, 1973-85
    Jim Parker, Colts, 1956-67
C — Dwight Stephenson, Dolphins, 1980-87
QB — OLD RULES: John Unitas, Colts, Chargers, 1956-73
NEW RULES: Joe Montana, 49ers, Chiefs, 1979-94
RB — Jim Brown, Browns, 1957-65
THIRD DOWN: Hugh McElhenny, 49ers, Vikings, Giants, Lions, 1952-64
FB — Marion Motley, Browns, Steelers, 1946-55
SHORT YARDAGE: Earl Campbell, Oilers, Saints, 1978-85

DEFENSE

E — POWER: Reggie White, Eagles, Packers, 1985-98
RUSH: Deacon Jones, Rams, Chargers, Redskins, 1961-74
    Rich Jackson, Raiders, Broncos, Browns, 1966-72
T — POWER: Merlin Olsen, Rams, 1962-76
SPEED: Joe Greene, Steelers, 1969-81
COMBINATION: Bob Lilly, Cowboys, 1961-74
OLB — STRONGSIDE: Dave Wilcox, 49ers, 1964-74
COVERAGE: Jack Ham, Steelers, 1971-82
RUSH: Lawrence Taylor, Giants, 1981-91
COMBINATION: Ted Hendricks, Colts, Packers, Raiders, 1969-83

MLB — Dick Butkus, Bears, 1965-73
CB — Jimmy Johnson, 49ers, 1961-76
    Deion Sanders, Falcons, 49ers, Cowboys, Redskins,
    Ravens, 1989-2000, 2004-5
SS — Ken Houston, Oilers, Redskins, 1967-80
FS — KILLER STYLE: Cliff Harris, Cowboys, 1970-79
RANGE STYLE: Willie Wood, Packers, 1960-71
COMBINATION: Larry Wilson, Cardinals, 1960-72
    Brian Dawkins, Eagles, 1996-2006

SPECIALISTS

K — Adam Vinatieri, Patriots, Colts, 1996-2006
P — Tommy Davis, 49ers, 1959-69
KR — Gale Sayers, Bears, 1965-67
PR — Deion Sanders
WEDGE BUSTER — Henry Schmidt, 49ers, Chargers, Bills,
    Jets, 1959-66

* * *

If this were England, Al Treml would have been knighted. I had been searching for Hutson footage for weeks, but all I'd come up with were highlight reels. Highlight films are OK for casual entertainment, but not for anything serious. What I wanted was raw game footage, every play, every move. This was for an *SI* piece I eventually did on the search for Hutson and Bronko Nagurski … what were they really like? I found my Nagurski footage at the Hall of Fame's film library. Two games, complete, and I was lucky to see them because, as far as I know, that's the only stuff on Nagurski that exists. Treml, the Packers' film director, was the keeper of the Hutson archive, though, and he said, "Come on out here. You can watch all the Hutson footage you want." God bless him. I spent two full days studying film, not exactly knowing what I would find. Hutson was a freak, with numbers like Babe Ruth's home-run totals that destroyed everything that existed until then.

I saw Hutson in his early years, the 1930s, when he played left end on defense and would occasionally have to rush the passer. What kind of a rush did he put on? Nothing that would terrify anybody. On sweeps and traps, he gave ground and did what he had to do without trying to unzip anybody. Later in his career, they moved him to defensive right halfback.

His helmet rode high on his head and he seemed a little awkward at times, an Ichabod Crane, until he was in full flight. Then he was a gazelle. He usually played the short side in the single wing and, when he lined up tight, he was a pass blocker, often having to face up to a defensive tackle, or an end, if he was coming.

"OK, T.O., on this play you've got to square up against Julius Peppers. Think you can handle it?"

I watched Hutson take down one of those big guys with the strangest looking block I'd ever seen. He threw a head fake, turned his back, flipped one leg in the air and made contact with his butt and back, a sort of reverse, reverse-body block. My God, I thought. What playbook did that come from? But his guy dropped. I saw him go back into coverage and break up a pass and I saw him intercept one, and then on the sixth play of the first reel that I watched, there it was. The play that was worth the trip.

The Packers were playing the Giants. Clarke Hinkle, scrambling, threw an option pass, sidearm, with two defenders in his face. Hutson was running a down and in. The ball was wide of the mark and high. He went up, the Giants' Tuffy Leemans went up with him. Hutson did a scissors kick in the air and kept going up … up … and stayed up, like Michael Jordan. He reached and, with his body fully extended, he snatched the ball away from Leemans, came down running and glided in for the score, a 62-yard touchdown. It was over in an instant, smooth, quick, decisive. Eleven years of that. Ninety-nine touchdowns.

Two plays later Hutson ran a deep sideline route. Tailback Cecil Isbell's pass was behind him. The defensive back was screening him off. With his momentum carrying him the other way, Hutson reached back, reached, reached — his arms seemed five feet long — reached past the defender, made his catch, kept his balance and scored. I ran the play back, frame by frame. It was an impossible catch. I'd only seen one other like it, Lynn Swann's against the Cowboys in the '76 Super Bowl, when his momentum was taking him out of bounds, and he corkscrewed his body and reached back to grab the ball inbounds.

I watched Hutson outjump two or three defenders, Randy Moss-style, on goal line fade patterns, I saw him catch deep passes so smoothly you couldn't believed it had happened. I watched him toward the end of his career when they ganged him with two or three defenders and played aggressively and sometimes chopped him down at the line. And still he led the league every year.

How did he rate, all time? Well, I watched that footage in the summer of 1989. Jerry Rice had been in the league for four years, and you knew he was great and would get greater, but no one could predict that he'd wipe everything off the books. Hutson wasn't a technician like Raymond Berry, the finest possession receiver I ever saw. He was more like Lance Alworth, the same explosive speed, the same hunger for the ball downfield, a monster at the point of the catch. And then the smooth glide as he raced for the end zone. I didn't have the heart to rate him above Alworth. As a young writer covering the AFL and rooting hard for its teams, I had seen Bambi simply tear up that league. No, in 1989 my two greatest receivers — Berry and Alworth — became three. Four now, of course, with Rice filling out the set.

Berry had done it for me with one play in the days when he and John Unitas were hot in the late 1950s. Of course, we always read about his meticulous attention to detail and how he would walk the field before the games and note every irregularity and the many hours he and Johnny U worked together. But one play put a picture in my mind that I never forgot.

It was in 1959, the year of my first newspaper job, on *The Sacramento Bee*. We used to go up to San Francisco on Sunday and sit in the end zone and take our shirts off and drink beer and yell our heads off for the Niners. Right under where I was sitting, the Colts had a second and goal on the 49ers' seven-yard line, and some sort of instinct told me to hold my binoculars steady on Berry and not to look at anything else on the field. In the next 2.5 seconds or so, I saw a tableau that still is so vivid in my memory … the perfect coordination of passer and receiver.

Berry ran straight at Abe Woodson, the right corner, and launched himself at Abe's knees in a head and shoulder block. Abe, figuring some sweep was on the way … there must have been some play-action simulating a sweep … fought to get Berry off him. Then, in an instant, Berry turned and hooked to the inside, and Unitas' ball was right there as he hooked. Touchdown. Six points. And the 49er fans gave poor Abe a tremendous booing. What the hell was he doing, a yard off Berry anyway? Perfection. Couldn't do it any better. He and Johnny U put together 13 years of that.

One story about Berry I have to tell. I've always loved it as kind of a capsule of how football people see the world, except that I never could find a place where it fit. When he was coaching the Patriots in the 1980s, some friends treated him to tickets to a Boston Pops concert to celebrate the team's Super Bowl season. Afterward they asked him how he'd liked it.

"You know the greatest thing about it?" he said. "All those musicians playing their instruments, and everyone just leaves them alone. There's no one coming along whacking them in the head, trying to mess them up, trying to mess up their timing."

Two of the prettiest sights in the game were Alworth running the deep post, and Rice winning the shallow cross, splitting the field like someone cutting a piece of pie, turning a five-yarder into plus-50. Bill Walsh called it "athletic arrogance." Rice called it confidence in a quarterback who would always put the ball exactly where it had to be, in front of him.

"I was blessed by having two Hall of Famers, Joe Montana and Steve Young, throwing me the ball," he said. "The whole idea when you're running any route but, especially the short crossing pattern, is to know that you're not going to have to break stride or reach behind you for the ball. If I'm watching a game and I see something like that, I have to turn away. You see a guy hitching up or turning back for the ball and you know something terrible's going to happen with those DBs cruising back there like sharks. I was lucky. Joe was a quarterback who'd never hang you out to dry, maybe the best who ever lived, leading you on the short cross. Steve came pretty close to that level."

It's too bad, at least for football voyeurs such as myself, that Rice chose to drag his career out forever because there are young fans who will always remember him as he was toward the end, who never will have seen him in his prime. But what the heck, he certainly earned the right to play it any way he wanted to. Especially after such a rough beginning. Coming out of college, his speed was suspect. The scouts clocked him in the 4.6 range, and even in 1985 that was a little slow for a potential first-round choice.

"The trouble with scouts," Bill Walsh said, "is that they don't time people in game situations."

And then, in his first year with the 49ers, he started dropping the ball. Now people really got worried. So did Rice. And then, in the space of a year, he just cured it. Worked through it. The thing I'll always remember about him is the smoothness with which he did things, the incredible ease. Year after year.

And the thing I'll always remember about Alworth was my feeling that somehow a child had become trapped inside him. I remember telling him something that Jets receiver George Sauer once told me after I'd seen him catch five square outs on a single drive and I asked him what was to keep him from catching 20 of those six and seven-yard outs, as long as the cornerback was playing off him.

"You couldn't take it physically," he said. "Your ribs wouldn't hold up."

"Oh man," Alworth said when I told him what Sauer had said. "I wish they'd throw *me* 20 passes a game."

"He always wanted the ball," his coach, Sid Gillman, said. "He never got it enough."

"He first showed up in our office in June, looking for an apartment," said Al LoCasale, who worked in the Chargers front office in the early 1960s. "He had a skinhead haircut. He looked 15 years old. I heard my secretary, Barbara, tell him from the next room, 'We're not giving you the money because we're not getting the paper.' She thought he was the newspaper boy."

I have learned one thing in my two decades as a Hall of Fame selector. Don't talk too much, otherwise what you say becomes meaningless, just more waves washing on the beach. That's especially true when you're isolating someone, for emphasis reasons, as the "best I've ever seen at the position." You can use that one, maybe once a year, for one player. Any more than that and you become a parody of yourself. So who have been my "best I've ever seen" guys at the Selection Committee meetings? J.J. Johnson, the cornerback; Dwight Stephenson, the center; John Hannah, the guard; were a few who made it. Cliff Harris, the safetyman; Tommy Davis, the punter; Richie "Tombstone" Jackson, the defensive end, were some who didn't, and I've just about given up on the last two. In 2002 my "best I've ever seen" was Dave Casper, the tight end.

Yes, indeed, John Mackey had been terrific, dynamic, an explosive force, but he had already been enshrined. I didn't have to worry about him. In making my argument for Casper, I mentioned that he never dropped the ball. Mackey had had occasional bobbles. Casper had been a tackle at Notre Dame. You think those guys know how to block? No tight end ever had those credentials as a blocker. And Casper came up in the era of the down-the-field chuck before the rules were loosened to protect the receivers. How many times had I seen him absolutely mugged on his patterns? And to combat the argument that he wasn't really that much of a downfield threat, I pointed to his 13.8 yards-per-catch average, better than the keynote tight ends of '02, Tony Gonzalez and Shannon Sharpe, better than that of Kellen Winslow, who'd been recognized as a serious figure running the deep seam routes, and to jump eras, better than Antonio Gates, the current king of the TEs. Well, Casper made it, I'm happy to report. Wish I were so lucky with some of my other guys.

He was an unusual person, given to outlandish statements, usually delivered with an, "I'm only telling you what everybody already knows," kind of indifference. I was talking to him in the locker room once, shortly after he had gone from the Raiders to the Oilers. This was after an exhibition game against the Jets. He was tying his tie and was about to leave, when a kid from the student paper at Hofstra University, where the Jets had their camp, asked him, "What do you think of Ken Stabler?" who'd been his QB on both clubs.

"The Snake?" he said, putting a final knot on his tie. "I don't think he's ever studied a gameplan in his life. He probably just throws it away as soon as he gets it. I'm not even sure that winning or losing means much to him; he's more interested in the game he can play against the defense, how badly he can sting 'em."

The kid was writing all this down like mad, and all of a sudden it dawned on me, "Holy hell? I've never heard this kind of stuff from a Raider or former Raider in my life." And I whipped out my notebook and began scribbling away. Innocent question from a young reporter, dynamic answer. That was Casper.

They have compartmentalized the offensive tackle position. Form two lines, please. Toe dancers on the left side, hogs on the right. Trying to get a left tackle to get down and do some serious drive blocking … why, that's like trying to hitch a racehorse to a plow. Quick feet are what's needed, quick feet … God, I'm tired of hearing that phrase. It's like they're describing kickers, or Thai boxers. So you will see high on the first round of the draft, dance masters, such as the Jets' D'Brickashaw Ferguson, whose flying feet will keep him in step with the right side speed rushers, many of whom are really linebackers with a hand on the ground but on running plays might wind up being driven four yards into his own backfield. Oh sure, there are exceptions, such as Baltimore's gigantic LT, Jonathan Ogden, whose drive blocking is better than his pass protection, but they are exceptions.

And on the right side, well, you'll find players with more girth, except in the wallet department because bangers don't get paid as well as dancers do. You'll find sturdy people, but they'll be lower draft choices, or perhaps failed left tackles or guards that just morphed over from their regular spot. Honest citizens who can block for the run but might need a bit of help if they're lined up against speed rushers.

Thus, one of the toughest positions for me to fill on my annual All-Pro roster is offensive tackle. Usually, I wind up with the players with the fewest negative grades, not the real studs. But I'm tilted the wrong way, I've been told by scouts, because I'm instinctively drawn to people who can knock an opponent off the line, whereas it isn't really the checkmate that's desired in this ultimate NFL chess match. It's a whole series of drawn games, ties, pass rushers who are nullified.

So my eyes wander nostalgically toward the past, where my No. 1 tackle is Art Shell, the Raiders' Big Brahma, oversized at 300 pounds in an era of 260-pound linemen, dynamic coming off the line, impregnable as a pass blocker.

"Came at me like a freight train first time I faced him in practice," Howie Long said. "Busted my cheek open, gave me a scar I still have."

And here's the odd thing: Shell played the left side. OK, you could say that he blocked for a left hander, Kenny Stabler, for most of his career, but he was the LT before Stabler was around. He's my power tackle. And the two speed tackles on my all-time team ... and believe me, I tried to break the tie and I couldn't ... both played the right side, Ron Mix and Forrest Gregg. But that's the way it was in those days. The best tackle played the right side because the best defensive end was lined up left — Gino Marchetti, Willie Davis, Deacon Jones, Tombstone Jackson, etc. Best against the run, best against the pass ... they had no designated weakside rushers in those days. So why was Shell on the left side? Because the Raiders always were a left-handed running team. It was part of Al Davis' philosophy.

Mix and Gregg were lean 250-pounders, skilled, smooth, a pleasure to look at for an afternoon. Watching them was like a clinic. They could pull out, if they had to, execute any one of the intricate set of drive blocks they had in that era, lock onto the speediest rusher. "The most perfect football player I ever coached," Vince Lombardi said about Gregg. Mix's coach, Sid Gillman, toned it down a bit, merely saying that Mix was the finest offensive lineman he'd ever seen. Do I just sound old, reminiscing about these greyhound tackles while having to watch, every Sunday, 330-pound jumbos with 50 pounds hanging over their belts? Just one more story.

The Jets' defensive left end, Gerry Philbin, was a mean, hard-bitten, undersized competitor who did it on desire and a persistent hatred of his opponent. He made it a point of honor never to talk to opposing players.

"Come on, Gerry," I said to him one day. "There must have been one time when you said something out there, I just know it."

"OK, there was, but it was the only time," he said. "We were playing the Chargers the year after we won the Super Bowl. I was putting on a rush, and Mix caught me just right and knocked me on my ass. As I was getting up, he said, 'Hey, great Super Bowl, Gerry.' I said, 'Thanks.' That was the only time I ever said anything. But you'll notice that Mix did his job first before he said anything to me."

Guard was the easiest position on the board for me, except for running back, where Jim Brown is unchallenged. Once I wrote a piece for *SI* in which I called Hannah the finest offensive lineman who ever lived. It was a very hard choice that I had to make between Hannah and Jim Parker and, I think if I had it to do over now, I'd choose Parker. It stirred up some controversy, which made my editors happy. A decent contingent of players who had had to line up against Hannah backed me up. The most sensible objections I heard also came from football people, some of whom said that you have to choose a tackle for that kind of designation because the pass blocking duties were much tougher. I remember Mike Brown, the Bengals' GM, held that view, as he lobbied for Cleveland's great tackle, Mike McCormack, as the all-time No. 1.

But maybe I'm just too seduced by the running game, by a lineman's ability to dig down and get under his man and drive him off the TV screen over and over again, and that's what I saw Hannah do … better than anyone I'd ever seen. And when you talk about pass blocking, in which Hannah certainly got stellar grades, who are the great pass blocking guards in history? Name them, please. A guard pass blocks in a phone booth, or at least in a fairly congested area. Now if someone were to ask me the same question I just posed, I'd hold up one finger. Jim Parker. Greatest pass blocking guard who ever lived, and to strengthen the claim, just look at what he did when he moved one position to the left and lined up at tackle. The same thing, All-Pro as a guard, All-Pro as a tackle. Forced even the guys behind the TV cameras to isolate on him, in the '59 NFL Championship

Game, when he gave an unforgettable performance against the Giants' Hall of Famer Andy Robustelli. After a while it became an item of fascination for the network, the lesson in how a tackle controlled a rusher, hailed as the first time TV isolated on this match-up, complete with replays.

Yeah, maybe Parker was the best lineman ever. At any rate he and Hannah made my guard choices a slam dunk, which is always joyful duty for a selector. I visited Parker in Baltimore a few years before his death in 2005. He wasn't well, and I'm afraid my questions didn't make him feel any better. I asked him what he thought of the current standard of line play in the NFL.

"Ooooh," he said, grabbing his stomach. "Every time l think of that, I get this pain right here. I look at those techniques and what do I see? I see no technique. I see big fat slobs just playing slob football, pushing, grabbing, and then my stomach starts hurting again. Oooh, why'd you have to ask that?"

Hall of Fame project number ... what ... for yours truly? Two, three, five? Dwight Stephenson, center, Miami Dolphins. Freddy Smerlas, the Bills' nose tackle, was one of those guys of the opinion that no human being with a heartbeat could ever block him. Except for one.

"Dwight Stephenson was like no other center who ever played the game," Freddy said. "You play against him, and it's like you're hit by a bolt of electricity. It's like something just flashes through you. You never know where he'll be coming from."

That was exhibit one in my argument for Stephenson at the Selection Committee meeting. Argument No. 2 was something Howie Long had told me. He said that when they faced him, the Raiders' gameplan was for him to come down hard from his defensive end spot and crash Stephenson, to foul up his blocking angles and keep him from getting to the next level and nullifying a linebacker. It was like a wham block by a motion tight end, in reverse.

"First time I've ever been involved with a gameplan aimed at the opposing center," he said.

Argument No. 3 was, well, the old standby, "Greatest I've ever seen at the position," which I hoped wasn't wearing a bit thin, but what the hell, it was true. Stephenson made it down to the final six, when only a yea or nay vote was necessary, and he didn't make it. I found out when I was driving back to my hotel and, when the news came over the radio, I got dizzy, literally, and had to pull the car over and stop. I mean, who the hell had been the assassins who had dinged him at the very end?

"They're like murderers in a dark room, hiding behind a door with guns in their hands," I wrote, which is the kind of analogy you draw when you're close to a mental breakdown.

Next year I asked for a show of assassins. Who are you? One fellow actually came forward and said, "The test of a lineman is longevity," he said, "and Stephenson's career only lasted eight seasons."

"Jesus Christ," I said, "can he help it if Marty Lyons came up behind him and took him out at the ankle and ended his career?"

Well, something must have kicked in because that next year he made it. Thank God.

Some people have trouble choosing the greatest quarterback of all time. I don't. As long as you understand that all time means split time. Old rules and new rules. Old rules meant a basic lack of rules when it came to protecting the passing game, which the NFL's Competition Committee regarded as their Holy Grail after defenses such as the Steel Curtain Steelers threatened to turn it into a mere memory.

Defensive linemen could head slap their way into the backfield and take down a quarterback any way they could, as long as they did it in fairly reasonable proximity to when he delivered the ball. Pass defenders could mug the receivers all the way down the field. Bump and run cornerbacks made the bump a real serious thing, not just a funny name. The Rams had a system called the Axe Technique, which meant chopping receivers down at the line and then chopping them again when they got up. The Chiefs had a corner named Freddy "The Hammer" Williamson whose modus operandi was a karate chop designed to stun his opponent.

And in this world, which now appears primitive but seemed perfectly natural at the time, John Unitas was king. There had been many great passers in the league: Sid Luckman, Otto Graham, Sammy Baugh, Norm Van Brocklin and some QBs who showed inspirational courage. Unitas was a combination of both. Then there were the supreme intellectuals of the game, the great play callers, exercising a skill that is now lost when everything is called from the sideline or the press box. Only a handful of quarterbacks call their own game now ... make that only one that I know of, Peyton Manning, and he is tightly wired to his offensive coach, Tom Moore. But in those days we talked of the great "Field Generals." What would they be now? Field Lieutenants? Captains maybe? Dutiful followers of the chain of command.

Writers mentioned Johnny U's genius on the field, the way he could bring his team back time and again. Teammates and opponents alike talked about his toughness, his ability to function at the highest level under the most severe punishment. The stories have become legendary. The old Colts talk about the time Doug Atkins bloodied John's nose, and Alex Sandusky, the guard, scooped up some mud and stuffed it up his nose to stop the bleeding, and the ref stuck his head in the huddle and said, "Take all the time you need, Unitas," and Johnny U told him, "Get the hell out of here so I can call the play." The Rams' Merlin Olsen said, "I don't know if I could do it, stand there week after week and say, 'Here I am, take your best shot.'"

But that was then, and this is now, and any defensive lineman so bold as to come near a quarterback's head would first get a flag and then, probably, a hook and would watch the rest of the contest on the TV in the clubhouse. Quarterbacks are protected. So are receivers. And O-linemen. No more head slaps, no more mugging down the field, not too many bloodied quarterbacks, although it can happen in what are termed accidents.

Joe Montana arrived at the dawn of the new era and played his career as the rules evolved into what they are now. He had the ability to bring teams back, as Unitas did. He never had to call his own game, certainly not with Bill Walsh running the show, and he never really had to absorb the punishment Unitas did. He was a better athlete. I mean, Unitas never high jumped 6-9. Many of his most famous plays came at the tail end of some daring escape, most notably the touchdown pass to Dwight Clark that beat Dallas and got the 49ers into their first Super Bowl. Unitas' precision passes to Ray Berry were a thing of beauty, and he had great touch and accuracy on his long throws; Montana might be the most accurate short passer who ever lived, especially throwing the slant or the shallow cross.

I have been asked to select one of them as the greatest ever and I can't do it. Could Montana have played in an era in which toughness was at such a premium, such as the Unitas era? Probably. Could Unitas function in today's game, in which everything came in from the sidelines? No. He would have been a coach's nightmare, growling and cursing and changing up all the bench calls until the team either changed its methods to accommodate him or shipped him off to a rare bird such as Tom Moore, who would have geared the system to Johnny U's rare ability to see things during the course of battle that the coaches missed.

"They've taken the game away from the quarterback," is something he told me many times. "The quarterback just stands there waiting for something to come in from the bench, and the team stands around, and ah hell, I just couldn't have put up with that." He spoke with passion and anger and in that regard he was almost directly opposite to Montana, who always seemed to have an air of wonderment about him. So what's the big deal, anyway?

The one thing they had in common, though, was the ability to raise their game to the highest level when the stakes were highest. When I asked Unitas about it, he'd just about reconstruct the situation play by play, such as the winning drive in overtime against the Giants. There was even a certain anger in that: "Oh hell, anyone could see ..." etc.

Montana never seemed to know quite how he accomplished what he accomplished. Once, when I was doing a two-part series on him for the magazine and I had what I knew would be my longest one-on-one shot with him, I worked myself into a near-frenzy trying to unlock the door. *(Editor's note: This feature appears in Chapter 10.)* But how does it happen? How do you manage to lift your game, and then lift it again if you have to, until you're right at the top when you're under the most pressure?

He shrugged, smiled. I mean, it really was a game, after all. They do say "play" football.

"I don't know ... better concentration, maybe," he said. I felt like Macomber, the coward, in Hemingway's story, "The Short, Happy Life of Francis Macomber," when Wilson tells him, "Doesn't do to talk too much about all this. Talk the whole thing away."

"He never told you, did he?" said Matt Millen, who was Montana's teammate toward the end of his career. I said no. "He doesn't know," Millen said. "He just goes out there, plays, completes passes, wins. It's just so natural to him."

Unfortunately, I never saw Jim Brown play in college. I was in the army, stationed in Germany, during his senior year at Syracuse. Which didn't mean that I never saw him as an athlete. In Brown's sophomore year, I saw Syracuse play basketball in the Garden, and early in the game, the first sub who came in for the Orange was a 6-2 guard with muscles in his arms like melons. Hmmm, now that's an unusual looking basketball player. I saw him take a charge, and the guy who tried to run him over bounced once and wound up on his backside. This was who? Oh yes, Jim Brown. Then it clicked. I said to my buddy, "Isn't that the guy from the Manhasset on the Island, the one they said was the greatest high school lacrosse player in history?"

"Yep, that's him," he said.

Brown was a 220-pound, bruising fullback in college. At least that was his reputation. In the NFL he was a whole lot more, of course. He weighed 228 and ran with the grace of a jungle cat ... until he smelled his prey, then he would strike quickly with explosive force. He never missed a game. He retired at 29. His running skills have been documented so many times in so many ways that there is very little to add. I covered him only once in a locker room, in 1963, when I was writing an opposing team sidebar on a Giants-Browns game in Yankee Stadium.

He was standing on a bench, talking to a small semi-circle of writers. He had run for 123 yards and two touchdowns in a place where, traditionally, he had had problems. He had his head tilted back as he answered their questions, coldly, arrogantly. He was literally looking down his nose at them. He had just come out of the shower, and water was dripping on their notes. I didn't like the looks of this scene, so I decided to talk to the offensive linemen, Schafrath, Wooten, Hickerson. No one else came over. They were glib, funny, friendly, a pleasure to deal with. Folks, I think I've hit on something here.

I still remember the headline the *New York World-Telegram & Sun* put on my piece: "Don't Forget Those Toughies Who Clear the Way for Jimmy." This is really apropos of nothing, except that it set me up for covering big games for the rest of my career. You don't need to talk to the superstars to find out what happened. Well, Brown is my walkaway choice for greatest runner ever. Any arguments?

One addendum: Give me a play to run on third and 10, and I'll go with the throwback screen to Hugh McElhenny. The King. A crazy legs, the Barry Sanders of his day. The play would give you minus two or plus 40, but guaranteed, no one would forget it.

I've told the following story so many times. It became a chapter in my book, *The Thinking Man's Guide to Pro Football*, and the chapter was labeled "Strictly Personal: The Greatest Player." The player was Marion Motley, fullback for the Browns for four AAFC years and four full seasons in the NFL. I originally wrote it in 1968, kept the honor going when I did the revised *Thinking Man's Guide* 15 years later. Now, in my old age, I've learned to shy away from flat-out pronouncements such as that one ... I mean, can I say that he was better than Jerry Rice or Reggie White or Lawrence Taylor or Jim Brown or Joe Montana or John Unitas? Well, I don't think so. Maybe I've undergone a deconditioning process by reading so many lists by so many people who never saw even a handful of the players they're trying to line up and rate, one through 10, or 25 or 100 or however many their editors tell them to rate. Nah, keep me out of that race and let me just say that Motley is my all-time No. 1 fullback and a terrific competitor. But the story of my attempt to track him down for my greatest player chapter bears repeating.

Motley first had been seen through the eyes of a 14-year-old, eyes that grew wider with each viewing. That was the Motley of the All-America Football Conference, a player not many NFL followers saw because when the Cleveland Browns were merged into the NFL Motley was 30 years old with two bad knees. He was a shadow of the old Motley, but he still was good enough to earn All-Pro honors, which might be an indication of what he had been in his old AAFC days. I've deliberately tried to keep from cluttering up this section with statistics, but I'll make an exception for Motley and give you just a taste of what his rushing stats looked like in his four years in the AAFC, not receiving, although he was effective enough on the screen and swing passes to average 14.3 yards per catch from 1946-49. To put this in perspective, Gale Sayers averaged 11.7 for his career, O.J. Simpson 10.6, Jim Brown 9.5, Payton 9.2, Barry Sanders 8.2. Only three pure runners among the mob of backs in the Hall of Fame ever topped Motley's average, and the leading pass catching backs of the current era, Marshall Faulk and LaDainian Tomlinson, average 9.0 and 7.3, respectively.

Now take a look at Motley's eye-popping rushing figures:

Regular Season/Championship Games

Year	Carries	Yards	Average	Carries	Yards	Average
1946	73	601	8.2	13	98	7.5
1947	146	889	6.1	13	109	8.4
1948	157	964	6.1	14	133	9.5
1949	113	570	5.0	8	75	9.4
TOTAL	489	3,024	6.2	48	415	8.6

An 8.6 playoff average, 6.2 for the regular season? These are statistics for a will 'o the wisp 185-pounder. But Motley weighed between 232 and 238 in this period, plus he played situation linebacker on defense and blocked for Otto Graham in pass protection. That's the way they did it in those days, fullbacks took on the blitzers, and when they reached Motley, set four-square and big as a lineman, that was the end of the rush. Or as Weeb Ewbank, who was an assistant on the Browns in those days, put it, "Motley takes the romance out of the blitz."

If you want to say, well, OK, that was against inferior competition, think again. The AAFC was every bit as good as the NFL. Everyone knows what happened when the champion Browns met the champion Eagles in the 1950 opener, one of the most meaningful games in league history. Browns 35, Eagles 10.

Well, I saw Motley in his AAFC glory days and sadly watched him as his skills gradually declined in the NFL and by 1968 I had him squarely in my gunsights for the greatest player chapter. The problem was getting him to sit down for an interview. He had been burned by Paul Brown, who had promised him a job on his staff and then stiffed him, burned by people outside the football community. He was gun-shy.

I finally tracked him down in Miami during the week of the Jets-Colts Super Bowl. He was down there to help with a fund-raising campaign for the NFL Alumni Committee, to try to get a pension installed for former players who were broke and needed help — the same battle as now, almost 40 years later. I made an appointment to meet him in his hotel. He was gone when I arrived. I re-scheduled it for the next day. Again, gone. I was getting desperate. We were onto Saturday, with the game the next day. I made an appointment to meet him at 8 a.m. I showed up at 6:30. When I came to his room, he was putting on a green sweater, getting ready to take off for a golf tournament. I told him who I was and why I was there.

"I've talked to a lot of guys who said they were going to do stories on me," he said, "but somehow I never get to see those stories. They say they'll send them, but they never do."

I didn't know what to do. If I missed him that day, well, gameday was out, then everybody scattered, and the chapter would be due. He was almost out the door. The only thing I could think of was to sound off in a pure stream of consciousness.

I told him I was in Kezar the day Norm Standlee tackled him near the 49er bench and he crawled all the way across the field and out of bounds to save a timeout.

"Pulled a muscle in my leg on that play," Motley muttered.

I told him I was sitting in the end zone for the '47 championship game against the Yankees, when he ran 51 yards for a TD, right at me, with Harmon Rowe riding his back for the last 10 and punching him in the face. I told him I was in Yankee Stadium the day he knocked Tom Casey out of football. Casey had been a 175-pound defensive back for the Yankees, the only man I ever saw stop Motley, head on, when he had a full head of steam. He woke up in Bronx Veterans Hospital. He never played any more football.

Motley smiled. "I see him every now and then," he said. "He's Dr. Thomas Casey now and he lives in Shaker Heights, right outside of Cleveland. We kid each other about that play. He'll say, 'You S.O.B., you ended my career.' And I'll tell him, 'I couldn't help it if you got in front of me.'"

He looked at me hard. "Young man," he said, "you've got quite a memory." And then, and the memory stays very fresh in my mind, he slowly peeled off that green sweater and lit a cigarette.

"Now what is it that you want to know?"

The interview went well, and I got what I needed. I sent him an inscribed copy of the book, but, unfortunately, there's only so much you can tell somebody, and how could I tell him that he was an early idol of mine, shortly after the death of Al Blozis, the record grenade thrower, that I had seen that incredibly tough looking picture of him in *Pro Football Illustrated* 1947 edition, with his lower lip sucked in and what looked like a scar running down one side of his face and I had saved it for more than 20 years? The advent of the face mask created one interesting phenomena in football. It changed the aspect of players' faces. It took away the real tough guy look of the early stars. I mean, do you ever see anybody nowadays with a face like Bronko Nagurski's? What you see is a collection of baby-faced, weight lifting 300-pounders. Could I tell Motley that what I saw of him on the field was even tougher than that picture of him? Nah, not done, not cool. Better move along.

One of the saddest things you can say about a player, something that combines admiration with melancholy, is that he "plays too tough for his body." Usually the statement defines a runner, and it is marked by fearsome collisions. Larry Brown, the old Redskins' runner, was a perfect example of the species. So was Paul Hofer ... anyone remember him? An early Bill Walsh tailback on the 49ers, real kamikaze runner. Neither of them made it past 29. But Earl Campbell did. He lasted all the way to his 30th birthday and he was as ferocious as any of them — and bigger. He punished tacklers; they punished him. Today he can barely walk. But man, when he smacked in there with that amazing takeoff speed of his and his 240 pounds, bodies flew.

One of his most famous plays came against the Raiders, when Jack Tatum was the most feared hitter in football. It was a goal line play, Campbell exploded into the line, Tatum took a run at him and met him full force, Campbell stiffened, made it into the end zone, held onto the ball and collapsed. Six points.

"Toughest play I've ever seen by a back," the Raiders' strong safety, George Atkinson, said. "Man scored a touchdown when he was unconscious."

We have flipped over to the defensive side of the ball and we're entering the world of specialization. This is what drove the editors crazy, my battery of designated skills. I wish to apologize, for those and for the various ties I've awarded, but there really are different positions within one label.

Reggie White moved around all over the line during his career, but he always came home to the power side, left defensive end, because he could play the run, could stand up to a tight end with double-team intentions, could penetrate and throw a large shadow over the quarterback's primary field of vision, the "front side," it's called.

Once I watched Eagles game film with him in his home in the Philadelphia suburbs and he pointed out the minefield he had to dance through on practically every play. It was like watching a matador trying to take on three or four bulls. They set him up, turned him, dove at his knees, hung out and waited for blindside hits, and I realized that this wasn't just a big guy getting by with a variety of moves, speed rush, bull rush, his patented "hump move," etc. It was a case of agility translating into survival. One particularly vicious-looking play against the Giants, when his back was half turned and one of the tackles drew a bead on the back of his knee and White just turned his body at the last minute to avoid the death blow, got me to instinctively cry out, "Watch out!" He got a laugh out of that.

"Is this normal?" I asked him.

"Not against every team," he said. "With some others, though … every game, every play."

The argument against Deacon Jones and Richie Jackson is that they had the head slap to help them on their way to the quarterback. My argument is that even without that move they would have found a way to get in because they were such great competitors, such great athletic specimens. Neither argument is right or wrong; it's just the admiration I share about the days when I was watching these two great players.

I think Deacon made more crawling sacks than any player who ever lived. When he was knocked off his feet, the argument was just starting.

"The main thing is to keep going," he said. "If I get blocked, I'll claw my way in, even if I have to crawl."

He was a run player, too, of course … they all were in those days when the ground attack was big, not just a change of pace. Not many disputed the claim that he was the greatest defensive end of his era.

But Jackson occupies a special place in my memory because 1) no one ever heard of him, since he was an outlander from one of the AFL's backwater franchises, and 2) he has never reached any serious level of Hall of Fame consideration, despite my lobbying for him every year in the preliminary balloting, mainly because knee injuries took the heart out of what could have been a glorious career. Two stories stay with me. The first one was told to me by Stan Jones, who was the Broncos' defensive line coach in 1967. The team had gotten Jackson, a nondescript linebacker and tight end for the Raiders, in a five-player trade.

"I was sitting on the porch of our dorm after dinner," Jones said. "He pulled up in this old jalopy he'd driven nonstop from Oakland, 24 hours over the mountains. I looked at him and told him, 'You seem a little big for a linebacker. I think we'll try you at defensive end.'

"He was 26 years old. He'd been in the minor leagues for a while. He just stared at me and said, 'Mister, I'm gonna play somewhere. I've driven as far as I'm gonna drive. Here's where I make my stand.'"

And he did. He became Tombstone, one of the most respected DEs in the game.

"He was our enforcer," said Lyle Alzado, who'd been on the same defensive line. "If a guy was Hollywooding you, you know, trying to show you up, they'd move Richie over to him, and he'd straighten the guy out. The Packers had this 6-8 tackle, Bill Hayhoe. I faced him when I was a rookie, and he was grabbing me, jerking me around, making fun of me. I was having a terrible time. Richie said, 'Lyle, is he Hollywooding you?' and I said yeah.

"He moved over for one play. That's all it took. He knocked him to his knees and split his helmet wide open. Remember that famous picture of Y.A. Tittle on his knees, with blood dripping down his nose. That was Hayhoe. They had to help him off the field."

Howie Long will not get many votes for the all-time team because it's generally picked by sack totals, and his were not impressive. Oh, he'd line up on the power side and jam up the run and then move inside and face the meat grinder when he was called upon. He'd do all the nasty things, and if they awarded sack statistics in a fair manner, by sacks caused, not inherited, his totals would be out of sight because he flushed a million quarterbacks into other peoples' arms. He just never was a great tackler himself. He used to register a certain amount of bitterness when he'd read about some defensive end who was being plugged in as a wide or open side pass rusher.

"Just once in my life I'd like to see what that's like, spending a whole season rushing from the open side," he said. "What's the record for sacks in a season?"

One more DE and then I'll let it go. This concerns a freak player who could rush the passer and do very little else that endeared him to his teammates. Mark Gastineau of the Jets, hated by his fellow linemen because he would not run his inside stunts, taking it inside where the big boys lived. "I'm doing my thing," he'd tell them. But man, what a pass rusher.

First of all, he had speed in the 4.5s to go with his weight, which was in the 290s. I've watched him in practice during half-line drills put on a relaxed kind of rush, with a dreamy look on his face, and come in untouched. I mean clean. Over and over again, and I'll swear that it looked as if he were just walking fast. The problem was that offensive linemen simply could not judge his speed or his change of pace. A freak.

Defensive tackle is a confusing position these days. You've got nose men playing a zero-technique, two-gap defense, and three-technique tackles, playing a one-gap, plus all manner of varieties. You've got base players such as Atlanta's 350-pound Grady Jackson who might be on the field for only the first play of a series, and "reduced ends," such as the Steelers' Aaron Smith, who would line up as a tackle, on the last one. It makes it confusing when you're trying to pick an All-Pro team because first you have to locate your guy on the field, after you've made sure he was there in the first place.

If you want, you could get real technical and pick a battery of players, one for each technique, or you could get lucky when someone makes it easy for you by excelling in all of them.

Such a player was Pat Williams, who started his NFL life as a sleek, mobile, 270-pound Buffalo Bill and gradually grew to a sturdy Minnesota Viking in the 320-330-pound range. In 2005 he had one of the greatest seasons I've ever seen a DT have. He could play the nose, and I saw him leave a trail of destroyed centers around the league, including Chicago's All-Pro Olin Kreutz. He could move outside the guard in the three-technique and penetrate quicker than he could be blocked. He wasn't like one of those typical, situation fat guys who gets yanked after his base, first or second-down play, and spends the fourth quarter on the bench, sucking oxygen. He turned it on for all four periods.

I named him my Defensive Player of the Year. I thought he was the most impressive power tackle I'd seen since the heyday of Merlin Olsen, and do you want to know what kind of postseason awards he reaped? None. Sackers get the glory. He had one. Of course, after he had established his credentials he got a steady diet of double-teams, but that was OK. He still collapsed the pocket and forced the QB onto other peoples' sack statistics.

I've picked sacking tackles on my All-Pro team, but only if their run grades measured up. That's why I never was as high as other people were on Alan Page, who has more sacks than any tackle in history. Against the run he was a liability. Pure rushers who, like ex-Viking John Randle, said they'd "pick up the run on the go," were persona non grata. He never made the *Sports Illustrated* All-Pro list.

"All you're doing," said Mike Giddings, a high-powered personnel consultant for 13 NFL teams, "is neglecting the most dominant interior rusher in the game. And that's what the game is, whether you like it or not: pass rush and pass protection."

My reasoning, which I tried to explain to him, was the following, and I had seen this so many times: First play the enemy runs is a trap at Randle. He's so far out of position he takes himself and the guy next to him out of the play. Plus eight for the opponent. Second play is a draw aimed at you know who. He's upfield and moving fast, when the back goes by without stopping to wave. Plus five. Third play is a pass, and Randle, showing a remarkable spin and burst move, sacks the QB for a six-yard loss and pounds his chest to deafening roars (if it's a home game). He has his sack and he can retire for the afternoon, and a season of those kind of games would give him 16 sacks, a huge number for a DT. All-Pro, of course, but to me he is seven yards in the hole ... 13 allowed, six accounted for.

Now look at my trio, please — Olsen, Lilly and Greene. No excess weight hanging over the belt, skilled in all phases of the game, never off the field. Am I being simplistic? A lost soul crying for a less technical age? I don't care. These are my guys. Lilly's game represented near-perfect technique. A grabber and thrower. "Hands that were so quick that you just couldn't beat him to the punch," Dolphins guard Bob Kuechenberg said. A roughneck only when aroused or held to the point of madness. Tom Landry used to send weekly game films to the league office with special notations marked, "Holding fouls against Bob Lilly."

Greene's style was at variance with his name, Mean Joe. He could get nasty out there, but his game was based on quickness. So fast off the ball was Greene, so quick to penetrate, that the Steelers created a new alignment in his honor, "the cocked nose tackle" set up, in which Greene attacked the center-guard gap from an angle, or a tilted position. The bully boy on that defensive line, in fact the most feared player on the whole Steel Curtain Defense, was No. 63, Fats Holmes, the only player on that unit, oddly enough, who was never chosen for a Pro Bowl.

"After the game, just look at the condition of the guy who had to play against Fats," Chuck Noll said. "That'll tell you what kind of a player he was."

Playing against Greene, the major fear was embarrassment, the whiff, the total miss, which happened more often than offensive linemen would like to recall.

Olsen was the quintessential bull rush tackle. Oh, you've got bull rushers now, but he did it play after play without letup, collapsing the pocket, piling up the run, breaking down the inside of the line while his teammate, Deacon Jones, mopped up outside. He was also one of the cleanest defensive linemen in the game. He hated nonstop holders, and especially cheap shot artists. The name of Cardinals guard Conrad Dobler would get him furious, even by casual reference. Once I told him that my newspaper, the *New York Post*, was doing a Dobler feature. And Merlin, who played all those gentle giants on TV once his playing career was over, showed some real fury.

"If you're the one to write it," he growled, "I'll never speak to you again."

Another time he admitted that Dobler's filthy tactics had forced him to do the only thing he ever regretted in 15 years of football.

"I arranged it with Jack Youngblood, the end playing next to me," Olsen said, "that I'd set Dobler up and Jack would crash down from his blind side and cave in his ribs. Except that we weren't very good at it. Dobler smelled it coming. He sensed it and turned at the last minute, and Jack wound up hitting me, and Dobler just laughed at us."

"We should have practiced it a little more before we used it," Youngblood said.

The year was 1968. I had just covered the Penn State-Miami game in State College, and I was in the Nittany Lions' trainer's room talking to Mike Reid, the junior defensive tackle. Miami DE Ted Hendricks would win an award for top collegiate defensive lineman that year, next year would be Reid's turn, and we were discussing how a player as freaky looking as Hendricks could be so good. I mean, he was 6-7, 215, and his technique was to kind of lean over things and pluck ball carriers out of space with his inordinately long arms. Even his nickname was freaky, "The Mad Stork," not exactly designed to put fear into people, unless they were parents with too many kids, worried about more coming.

"He's, well, the kind of guy you wouldn't mind going down into the pit with," Reid said, "but I don't think you'd ever get a clean block on him either."

It proved to be a remarkably accurate forecast of what Hendricks' life as an NFL linebacker became. He didn't leave a trail of shattered bodies or a memory of ferocious hits, but he just played everything so well. He was seldom out of position, he could move backward and knock down passes with those long arms, or rush forward and smack them back at the quarterback. Everything was done from a plane of high intelligence ... he had been a Rhodes Scholar finalist in college.

My lasting memory? Somebody, sorry but I can't remember who, ran a reverse at him. Now this just wasn't done, but it was tried, and Hendricks sniffed it out immediately, and when the ball carrier had finished moving parallel to the line of scrimmage and was ready to turn upfield, there was Hendricks, just standing there. All momentum had been lost. They faced each other. Hendricks shrugged and held out his hands, palms up, like, "OK, now what happens?" A huge roar went up from the Raider crowd, which always cherished such moments. The runner dropped to a knee. Second and 16.

For a guy who played such a correct, technically sound game on the field, he was pretty wacky off it. I found out when I spent a hilarious week on Oahu's North Shore one off-season, trying to do a piece on Hendricks, who was an instructor at John Wilbur's football camp. It's hard to remember everything that happened or to read the notes I somehow managed to take. l seem to remember a place called Juju's and something about fright masks and an amateur hour type of evening … not sure I was involved in it or not. I do remember asking him about his place of birth, Guatemala City, where his father had been stationed.

"You've never seen flowers like that in your life," he said and then proceeded to name the species of Hawaiian flora in our area. Then he got this faraway look.

"You know something," he said. "I really should have been a florist."

OK, Hendricks, nicknamed "Kick 'em" by his Raider teammates for one lamentable lapse of judgment, is my all-purpose outside linebacker. And now we move to the field of specialization. Jack Ham was the best pure coverage linebacker, with second place going to … oh, I guess I'd have to say Chuck Howley of the Cowboys' Doomsday Defense. Ham lined up on the left side of the Steelers' defense, which was kind of unusual because usually that was reserved for the strongside LBs skilled at playing the tight end.

Maybe it was Ham's instinctive ability to cut through traffic and stack up the power sweeps to the right, a big part of NFL offenses in those days, that kept him there. Maybe it was because Andy Russell, the RLB, was also an open side kind of player, but it worked out just fine. Ham was such a force in coverage, and against the wide plays, that even the All-Pro and Pro Bowl pickers, who usually grade linebackers on sack totals, could spot his greatness. He blitzed very seldom.

Coverage was so instinctive to him that it never seemed like much of a big deal.

"Jack and I were sitting next to each other on the bench," Russell said, "and we were talking about the market, and he was telling me about some stock he really liked. Then we had to go out on defense. First play they ran, read the pass and dropped into his zone, deflected the ball with one hand, caught it with the other as he stepped out of bounds, flipped it to the ref and overtook me on our way off the field.

"'Like I was telling you,' he said, as if nothing at all had happened, 'you ought to look into that stock; it's really a good deal.'"

Ham and I were once talking about Lawrence Taylor. "Sometimes," Ham said, "I think his playbook was written on a match cover." In other words, LT's coverage responsibility, so important in Ham's scheme of things, was almost zero. His career interception total was nine. Ham's was 32. Taylor, basically a defensive end in college, wasn't really a linebacker at all, although he is generally acclaimed to be the best ever. He was an outside rusher who would occasionally line up in a stand up position, the finest in history at this special role created by Bill Parcells and Bill Belichick on the Giants.

Later in their careers both coaches searched for other players to fill this role, which turned a 3-4 defense into a 4-3 and back again. Parcells tried it with Greg Ellis on the Cowboys; with Belichick's Patriots it was Willie McGinest and then Rosevelt Colvin, basically down linemen who would stand up at times but really were pass rushers at heart. Taylor, of course, was the greatest.

I've already written how LT, toward the close of his career, became introspective, even philosophical about the game. A couple of years from the end of his career, we got into a talk about how a player knows when the end is coming.

"I'll tell you how I know it," he said. "The power rush starts going. That's the thing that people never realized. I'd get sacks in lots different ways, but the best came from straight power, driving right into a guy and lifting him because he didn't expect it from someone who weighs 245. It's the starting point for everything, the base of operations. But when you feel that going, and right now I do, then you can tell things are coming to an end."

I lobbied hard for Dave Wilcox at the Hall of Fame Seniors Committee meeting. His was an almost unnoticed skill as the eras changed, playing the tight end, actually nullifying him, avoiding getting hooked on running plays, the typical modus operandi of the classic strongside linebacker. I think the quote that swung it for him was one from Mike Ditka.

"Wilcox was the reason I quit when I did."

I had ammo from Mike Giddings, the super personnel guy, who'd been Wilcox's linebacker coach on the 49ers.

"Strongside linebackers get hooked to the inside now on running plays, and it just doesn't seem to matter," he said. "How many times do you think Wilkie got hooked? Never. It was a point of honor with him."

That was part of it, of course, but trying to get him the nomination as the senior candidate and then getting through the major enshrinement voting based on a platform of not getting hooked, well, I think half of them would have looked at me as if I were telling them that he stayed away from the ladies on Bourbon Street.

No, I think the strongest thing that emerged, in addition to the Ditka quote, was a battery of testimony that Giddings provided, statements from just about every Niner who ever lined up behind Wilcox about how much he had done for their careers. Plus, of course, many quotes from opponents who respected the world of old fashioned values that he represented. And to the credit of the selectors and the Seniors Committee members, there was just something about Wilcox and the humility he showed in doing a specialized skill better than anyone else ever had.

Oh, he could rush the passer if he had to. Giddings mentioned the game in which they decided to turn him loose on the quarterback, and he had three sacks and two forced fumbles. It was just that he was too valuable in his regular job.

At one time middle linebacker was such a glamour position that All-Pro teams would have two, sometimes even three MLBs on them. The TV special, *The Violent World of Sam Huff*, brought the position into focus but what a cast of characters. How about if I give you 10 names, each of whom was called by some publication or rating service, the best ever at one time. Dick Butkus, Joe Schmidt, Ray Nitschke, Willie Lanier, Mike Singletary, Lee Roy Jordan, Tommy Nobis, Chuck Bednarik, and most recently, Ray Lewis and Brian Urlacher.

Believe me, each one had his supports, and I can even throw in a couple more and make a case for them — Jack Lambert, the first MLB with really deep, downfield range, and Sam Mills, a personal favorite for his absolute genius on the field and ability to lift the performances of everyone around him.

OK, Butkus is my No. 1, and I've spent many wee hours in press rooms and bar rooms waging the same battle over and over again. About 15 years ago, when run-stuffing middle backers started getting the hook on what were considered passing downs, I heard Butkus described as a player who would be on the field in base downs but not when it was time to throw the ball. That one has picked up momentum, and my only answer is to look at the people who are advancing it.

Butkus came up in 1965. That's 42 years ago, as of this writing. In 1970 he suffered a serious knee injury that never was properly treated by the Bears and resulted in a six-figure settlement when Butkus sued them. He never was the same player after that, although, out of habit, they still put him on the All-Pro teams for two more seasons. So let's say that his last good season was 1970, before he got hurt, which was 37 years ago. I look at some of the people who are issuing these pronouncements on what downs he would or would not play, and they weren't born while he was in his prime. Or maybe some of them were in grade school, or teenagers. See what I'm getting at? They just don't know nuttin' about nuttin.'

Butkus had a reputation as some sort of Cro-Magnon who beat offensive linemen senseless and then did the same to ball carriers.

"Not true," said the Packers' Jerry Kramer when I talked to him about Butkus. "The last thing he wanted to do was take you on. He tried to get rid of you as quickly as possible, so he could be in the best position to make the tackle. And when he was, yeah, the runners suffered."

Sure, everyone knows he was hell on wheels against the run, but pass defense seems to be the point of contention. He didn't have the range downfield of Lambert or Singletary. He wasn't required to because the Bears wouldn't put him in zone coverage that would send him deep. He couldn't close on a shallow receiver as Lewis could in his prime; Ray was the best I've ever seen at that, but he didn't get tied up in traffic, either, as Lewis occasionally would. He destroyed traffic, anything that would slow him down on his way to a tackle would infuriate him. The MLB's usual coverage responsibility in those days was second man out of the backfield, and speed usually wasn't that big a factor because the assignment didn't usually have him turning and running downfield with the back. By the time the second man out would turn upfield, the rush would have arrived.

Butkus covered the swing and flare routes, short stuff over the middle, and he knew angles and how to get through traffic, and his coverage left nothing to be desired, even when he had to hustle downfield. He was fast enough. He had what Vince Lombardi called "competitive speed," plus great instincts. But if I had to say what he did best, it was operate without a decent pair of tackles in front of him.

Lewis had a pair of 350-pound monsters, Tony Siragusa and Sam Adams, to keep the blockers off him in the '01 Super Bowl. Urlacher played behind Tank Johnson and a very solid two-gapper, Ian Scott, and, for most of the season, Pro Bowler Tommie Harris in 2006 and, a few years before that, Pro Bowler Ted Washington. Butkus' tackles were nondescript guys such as Dick Evey and John Johnson and Willie Holman and Frank Cornish. He never played behind a Pro Bowl tackle in his entire career. And yet he could cut through whatever line scheme they had going against him in a flash and get rid of the blockers and gather himself for the thundering hit. Yeah, I'll stick with him.

They are legislating the cornerback position out of football. Interference rules get tighter every year, a push to produce more passing and scoring and offense that Tex Schramm and the Competition Committee started many years ago. The worst thing is that there's no consistency to the calls. Basic things that coaches teach get flagged by one officiating crew, allowed by another. Players such as Champ Bailey, labeled a "shutdown corner," still get beaten deep on occasion, when the Broncos are actually manning it up and not hiding in a Cover-2, everyone's blue plate special these days. No, cornerbacks might have good streaks, or even a good run for a full season, but the following year they could come back and go into shock.

Here we go again ... all together now ... "It's not the way it used to be!" OK, since my team dwells, depressingly, in the past perfect tense, let's bring it as up to date much as I can. Deion Sanders. Timed in the high 4.2s. Greatest closing speed of anyone, ever.

In 1994, when Sanders was 27 and presumably at the peak of his game, he had one season with the 49ers. I asked Merton Hanks, the free safety and a fellow with whom I was fond of discussing football and personnel and one thing and another, what he would write if he were doing a scouting report on his famous teammate.

"Don't let him bait you into throwing the quick out against him. He'll let two or three go and then take the next one back for six. It's a cat and mouse game with him, and you're not going to win. Don't throw the deep sideline route on him. With the sideline for protection, he'll either smother it or pick it off. You could try a deep post, just to keep him alert, but that's risky, too, because it'll look like a completion, and then he'll close fast enough to get the pick.

"So what does that leave? You could try to run a pick play on him, but he'll yell so loud that the officials will watch for it from then on and you won't get it again. You could drag him across the middle on a shallow cross. He doesn't like it inside much, but you'd better make sure your quarterback leads the guy just right because if it's a little bit off, a little bit behind him, Deion's gonna grab it. If you complete a couple of those, you might force them to protect him in a zone, but anyone who coaches him has to know that's the stupidest thing to do with him because he gets bored in zone coverage and loses a little concentration. But ... if somehow you can manage to get them in some kind of a zone ... well, it's a big if. That's how you get ready for Deion, the 'if' approach. Hasn't worked too well so far, has it?"

Here is the problem with Jimmy Johnson, whom I will say without reservation is the greatest defensive back who ever lived: For the first eight years of his career, no one knew who he was. The 49ers weren't in the postseason, they weren't on national TV, he didn't have big interception numbers (the only ones that define a cornerback) because everyone was afraid to throw at him. I was working in New York, as beat man covering the Jets for the *Post*, and the AFL didn't face the NFL in the regular season in those days. I did have a friend, though, named Mike Hudson who'd been my classmate at Stanford and worked for the UPI in San Francisco during this period, a Niner fan, like me, and I'd get periodic letters from him saying, "You've got to see this cornerback we've got, J.J. Johnson. I've never seen anything like him."

I remember seeing him once or twice during that period of 1961-68, his first eight years in the league, and I couldn't record much of anything because he didn't make any plays, and the reason for that was that no passes were thrown in his direction, or if there were, they amounted to maybe a couple of quick outs or something like that. That should have been the tipoff right there, but where's the sign that says a former lineman had to be a keen evaluator of pass defenders?

Then the Niners got good with three straight playoff seasons, 1970-72. And a year or so before that, someone must have grabbed their PR director, George McFadden, by the throat and told him, "You've got to do something for J.J. He's 31 years old, and no one's ever heard of him." So in 1969, when Johnson already had passed his 31st birthday and had completed eight years in the league, the Niners press book listed an unusual statistic for him — passes thrown into his coverage, passes completed, yards gained. The numbers were 25 of 74 for 250. Broken down for his 13 games (he missed one), the average was 5.7 passes (and there was no way of telling whether this was in man or zone coverage), 1.9 completions for 19.2 yards per contest.

Next year the press book did the same thing, and the two-year stats came out to a per-game average of 5.9 passes, 2.1 completions, 23.1 yards. I phoned my buddy, Mike.

"Did he give up any TDs?" I asked him.

"I never saw him give one up."

Well, something must have kicked in because he made All-Pro for four straight years, starting in '69, and led the defense on three straight division championship teams. By now I was watching him every chance I got and I'd never seen anyone as smooth and graceful in his pass coverage. The Niners PR staff stopped listing those good stats after two years, but I saw games in which the opponent only threw at him two or three times. In '71 he broke his wrist in the ninth contest and played the rest of the season with a cast on, and they still were afraid to test him, and when they did, he'd knock the ball down with his cast.

The fade started coming in '73 when he banged up his knee and, for that season and the following three, he slowly declined. But come on now ... those were his 13th through 16th years in the league, at age 35 through 38. I would talk to him by phone from time to time. A proud, dignified, humble person, a little sad, maybe, but able to hide his bitterness at being overlooked during the prime years of his career.

Then I became a Hall of Fame selector. Johnson's name would surface briefly and then sink. I couldn't understand it, but a decade and a half after his career ended, he was still hardly known. I became strident, shrill, "You've got to understand that this guy..." etc. Wrong approach. After getting stiffed a few times, J.J. issued a statement that he would appreciate it if his name no longer would be proposed for enshrinement, just as Harry Carson did recently. Oh, my God. Something had to be done.

In 1994 my pitch was that this was J.J.'s last year as a "modern" candidate. After that he would go into a dismal swamp called the Seniors Pool, in which many were swallowed but few emerged. One per season, out of all the great, unrecognized names of history, would be pulled out of that groaning mass, that Dante's vision of hell, and presented for possible enshrinement. And that was the fate that would befall the greatest cornerback in history unless you, the selectors, acted and acted now.

Well, he made it. I saw him at the Pro Bowl in Hawaii. There was no more talk about how his name shouldn't have been proposed, etc. He was in tears. I was in tears. End of story.

Dr. Z was born in Philadelphia but grew up in New York City.
(Charles Zimmerman)

Paul was always motivated by food.
(Charles Zimmerman)

Zimmerman practices during his days playing football at Stanford. He later transferred to Columbia.
(Linda Bailey Zimmerman)

Paul continued playing rugby into his late 30s. (Linda Bailey Zimmerman)

Paul is in his mid-40s, before he began writing for Sports Illustrated.
(Linda Bailey Zimmerman)

With his ever-present cigar, Paul visits one of his favorite destinations, Navarro Beach in Mendocino, Calif. (Linda Bailey Zimmerman)

Paul is never afraid to embrace his eccentricities. (Linda Bailey Zimmerman)

The hats may change, but the cigar remains a fixture. (Linda Bailey Zimmerman)

The Flaming Redhead gets a kick out of this picture. She likes to call it his "crazed" look.

(Linda Bailey Zimmerman)

For a Sports Illustrated *photo spread, good friends, Paul Zimmerman and Peter King, pretend to squabble.* (Heinz Kluetmeier/*Sports Illustrated*)

Thankfully, Paul Zimmerman and Peter King resolved their fabricated disagreement. (Heinz Kluetmeier/*Sports Illustrated*)

At age 72, Paul was still working for Sports Illustrated.
(Linda Bailey Zimmerman)

Dr. Z's football office features a treasure trove of information and collectibles.
(Heinz Kluetmeier/*Sports Illustrated*)

One month after his initial stroke, Paul is with Linda Bailey Zimmerman at Kessler Institute for Rehabilitation. (Linda Bailey Zimmerman)

Six months after his stroke, Paul attends a fund-raiser. (Linda Bailey Zimmerman)

Paul and Linda Bailey Zimmerman are surrounded by good friends, Matt Millen (far left) and Peter King (far right). (Arthur Frank)

A gathering of confidants includes from top left to right: Barbara Neibart, Joel Bussert, Ann King, Peter King and bottom left to right: Arthur Frank, Paul and Linda. (Karen Robbins)

Paul holds the 2014 Emmy he won for NFL Films Presents: Yours Truly, Dr. Z. (Linda Bailey Zimmerman)

In the old days, the strong safeties were sturdy fellows who were expected to lock onto tight ends but still had to be gifted in zone coverage downfield. Free safeties were wispy guys with tremendous range. Then the monster safeties arrived, 220 to 230 pounds, strong or free, it didn't matter. The big free safeties followed in the wake of the early "killer" types, Jack Tatum, Cliff Harris, the Chicago pair of Gary Fencik and Doug Plank. They were what Al Davis used to call, "obstructionists," a euphemism for roughnecks. The big strong safeties could either play "in the box," as fourth linebackers in the base defense, or they could man the actual LB spot in nickel defenses.

At 6-3, 198, Ken Houston was a big strong safety in his era. You didn't find many of them over 200 pounds. Even the Raiders' intimidating pair of Tatum and SS George Atkinson weighed in at 200 and 180, respectively. The AFL knew all about him because he was the finest SS the league had ever produced, not just a big sticker, as most of them were, but a gifted cover man, too. But so what? AFL? AFC? It was all bush league to pro football's Old Boys Club. Even when Houston set a record for career interception TDs, which was broken by Rod Woodson 30 years later, nobody got very excited.

Then he was traded to the George Allen Redskins. At 28 he wasn't exactly a member of Allen's Over the Hill Gang, but he finally got the exposure he needed to stake a reputation as the best ever at a position that still is not fully understood. I mean the 2006 AP All-Pro team didn't even have a strong safety on it, preferring to go with two frees. Strong, free, what the hell's the difference? Well, there is to me.

I'm still waiting for someone to come along and stake a claim at the position. Troy Polamalu looks promising, but he hadn't done it long enough. Ed Reed has switched from strong to free. Roy Williams is a big sticker, thus a popular Pro Bowl vote getter among the players, but he's not a cover guy. Nope, Ken Houston it is, until someone comes along to challenge him.

When I first started covering football free safeties were what I call "range" types, players who patrolled vast patches of territory, basically small, wiry guys with tremendous ball instincts — Jimmy Patton, Yale Lary, One-Eyed Bobby Onion, Willie Wood. Paul Krause, bigger and a bit slower, was the demon interceptor, but he wasn't the tackler these other people were. It was hard to evaluate these players, at least it was for me, because we never knew what their responsibilities were on any play. So you let the interceptions do the work for you, if you were lazy, or you stacked up a whole pile of quotes, if you wanted to make it a popularity contest.

I lean toward Wood as my range type because I just saw him as a more dynamic athlete, with an eye-catching burst to the ball and a good measure of toughness. Emotionally, though, I'm drawn to Larry Wilson, who first popularized the safety blitz, a technique deemed insane at the time. So I've given him a designation termed, "combination," since he was a terrific player in space, a fearless hitter and a safety whose techniques were near perfect.

But I can't just neglect the dominant safetyman of our era, the Eagles' Brian Dawkins, who does everything: blitzes, hits with real force, locks onto tight coverage downfield and, here's the thing that swings the election for him, seems to have an electric effect on everybody around him.

That brings us almost home in this complicated category, but now it's time to talk about hitters because the free safety position appears in many guises, and it would be unfair to neglect the killer-type free safeties because they can influence things in dramatic ways. Who was the greatest hitter who ever played — at any position? I've been asked that question on a million mailbag columns for the *Sports Illustrated* website. In my *Thinking Man's Guide*, it was an easy one to answer because all I had to do was shut my eyes, and I'd see Hardy Brown, an undersized, mean-spirited linebacker sending someone to dreamland.

They said he did it with a shoulder he could pop like a coiled spring. Some of the blows I saw him deliver looked more like forearm pops. The blow I remember best came when Brown's 49ers played the Rams in Kezar, and little Glenn Davis, Army's famous Mr. Outside, caught a swing pass, and Brown popped him with the shoulder and he went down and stayed there. They took him out on a stretcher, and I had my binoculars on him and I can still see that deathly white face with the eyes closed. I thought he might be dead.

"Hardy Brown," Y.A. Tittle once said, "had a shoulder that could numb a gorilla."

I don't know whether or not he could exist today. Technically a shoulder or forearm shot is not illegal, but too many of them aimed at the head would, I'm sure, generate some kind of legislation, "conduct unbecoming," or "conduct becoming hazardous," or something like that.

The Colts' middle linebacker, Mike Curtis, was nicknamed "The Animal" for obvious reasons, but I'd have to put him behind Brown in the mayhem sweepstakes ... except for one memorable shot I saw him deliver. In a 1971 playoff game against the Dolphins, a fan came out onto the Baltimore Memorial Stadium just as Miami was about to run a play, grabbed the ball and started prancing around. Curtis' blow, forearm to chest, sent him flying a good five yards. I interviewed him in a police holding area after the game.

He was still a bit drunk ... he'd taken a bus down from Rochester and had been drinking the whole way. He showed me his jacket. "Unzipped it, top to bottom," he said. He seemed proud of it. Two weeks later he filed a lawsuit.

"Read and react. Everyone else just stood around, Curtis sprung like a panther," Colts center Bill Curry said. "I felt like telling that fan, 'That's what I have to face in practice every day.'"

I don't think the big guys generate enough speed to be considered the game's most devastating hitters ... OK, maybe the Broncos' left defensive end "Tombstone" Jackson, who could split helmets with his head slap, might figure in there somewhere, but I think that free safety has to rate as the player generating the biggest hits, replacing linebackers.

Nowadays I'd give the nod to the Redskins' free safety Sean Taylor, taking over from the Cowboys' Roy Williams. But the all time No. 1, and I hate to go this route because I'm only reinforcing a negative, is Jack Tatum. The shot he delivered to Patriot wideout Darryl Stingley that paralyzed him was not, I believe, a clean blow, and I've argued this a million times. The pass was off target, Stingley was on his way to the ground when Tatum drilled him. He didn't have to do it, but when someone has been trained in the guard dog mentality his whole career, don't be surprised if he bites.

The first time I saw Tatum in the flesh was in the 1971 Rose Bowl, Stanford against Ohio State. The L.A. papers had been going with a pregame angle I thought was kind of silly: "Will Stanford dare to throw into Tatum's territory?" I mean, you don't just give up on an area of the field. Tatum played the open, or wide side cornerback in Woody Hayes' defense. Right, and someone is just going to avoid it. Silly Southern California angle.

Stanford had a bunch of clever, pass catching backs, and on the game's second series, Jim Plunkett threw a five-yard swing pass to one of them, Jackie Brown, to the wide side. Oh oh. Tatum came up to meet him. It took 10 minutes to run the next play because an ambulance came out on the field to collect Jackie Brown and take him away. Right out there, red light flashing, while the Stanford guys stood around and watched. There were no more short passes into Tatum's territory.

A footnote: I just looked at my play-by-play chart to make sure. Brown actually came back into the game and scored two touchdowns. But by running, not pass catching.

Were NFL players actually afraid of Tatum? Yes. Here's a letter I received recently from his teammate, Todd Christensen, the All-Pro tight end:

"When I first came to the Raiders, I was a scrub, and as you well know, these are the guys who play offense for the defense, and vice-versa, on alternating days. So it was defensive day, and I was lined up in the slot to catch a slant. Plunkett timed it right, but so did Tatum, who had clearly lined me. He came in a blaze of color so fast that I actually shrieked a little 'aaahhhh' and then at the last second he veered off.

"He came over to me and said, 'Don't worry, young buck, I was just getting my timing down.' I am not ashamed to tell you that fear made its way into my constitution."

Tatum is not my all timer. Cliff Harris is. His hitting was not quite on par with Tatum's ... no one's was ... but Harris was a well respected intimidator. Plus a fine cover guy. He started his NFL life as a cornerback. And I don't think any player ever studied the science of hitting as he did.

The first time I ever got to know him, we had dinner at his restaurant in Arlington, Texas. We finally closed it at 2 a.m., and most of the time we had talked about an elaborate diagram he had drawn up, which I labeled, "Cliff Harris and the Science of Hitting." He had been an engineering major in college, and his chart was filled with notations such as "point of maximum impact." It's been a while, but one thing I remember is his note on the swing pass, that the maximum impact does not come when the catch is first made. The idea is to wait until the back turns and starts upfield, then deliver your blow.

He used to hate the grades the coaches assigned. All it did, he said, was to induce a play-it-safe mentality. Don't take chances, don't screw up your grade.

"I see a teammate in trouble and I gamble," he said. "I leave my assignment and cover for him and I've guessed right and I knock the ball down. I grade a zero on the play. Same thing with a receiver coming across on a shallow route. I let him catch the ball and then I knock him out. Again, a zero on the play for allowing the completion. But the guy is out of the game."

Harris has been up for the Hall of Fame a number of times. I've spoken on his behalf each time, but I've failed. He is now in the Senior Pool. Pray for him.

The last time I made up this list, Morten Andersen was my kicker, based on all-time numbers and percentage and whatever. But I've simplified it and zeroed in on one category. Clutch kicking. The greatest clutch kick I've ever seen was Adam Vinatieri's 45-yarder in the howling snowstorm against Oakland that got the Patriots into overtime and subsequently into the Super Bowl, where his 48-yarder at the final whistle beat the Rams. Two years later his 41-yarder with four seconds left beat Carolina in the Super Bowl.

Thus he was 3-for-3 on the three most important kicks in the team's history. A miss on any one of them could have affected the lives of many people. I don't want to bog this down with a parade of numbers during Vinatieri's whole career, but they are of Hall of Fame quality. Pressure kicking is the story. Just ask Mike Vanderjagt, who has the best lifetime percentage in history. When faced with the biggest pressure kick of his life, though, a 46-yarder that could have put the Colts into the AFC championship, the result was a badly skunked low line drive, way wide right. The Colts got rid of him after the season.

Have you ever heard fans consistently cheer a punter and never boo him? Yes, if you've watched the Giants' Jeff Feagles knock them out inside the five-yard line. Yes, if you were a 49ers fan in the late 1950s and 1960s when Tommy Davis was punting. Yes, emphatically yes, if you were sitting anywhere near me in the Kezar Stadium end zone, with the wind blowing in your face, watching Davis trying to get the Niners out of a hole … "Come on, Tommy! Please, God, let him get one off"… and hearing that sweet KABOOM! as he rockets another one into the gusts in the windiest stadium in the league. A high hanger into the wind, 48 yards from scrimmage, 4.8 on the stopwatch. Week after week of that, game after game.

Punting out of the end zone, into the wind, what's the hang time? That's one of many ways I judge punters, probably my favorite way. Davis was the best and he's my man. For years Sammy Baugh, with his phony gross average built on quick kicks, the old bounce and roll play, was the all-time career record holder. Davis was second in gross yardage, punting in the worst conditions in football. Then Shane Lechler came along and forged to the lead with his 46.1 average. Nope, Shane doesn't do it for me. A middle of the end zone punter. Before they started calculating net yardage, it was a hidden statistic. Then finally bowing to the insistence of ex-Giant and Jet punter Dave Jennings … I mean he had been begging for it for only 10 years or so, but the Elias Statistics Bureau, in its infinite wisdom, moves at the pace of a 10K run at Fat Farm, USA … they started counting net, and the guys who couldn't place the ball were exposed.

Lechler led the NFL by three yards on gross average in 2006, but he was 12th in net, which means that either 1) he couldn't keep the ball out of the end zone, which was true (19 touchbacks, high in the league and nearly double those of his nearest pursuer) or 2) the punt coverage team was crummy (true again … the Raiders' 12.9 yards allowed per punt return was third worst in football). But he'll probably make the Hall of Fame some day if he keeps his gross up there. Ray Guy, a middle of the end zone punter with a lofty hang time, keeps coming up at the enshrinement meetings. Why I don't know. His career gross average is lower than that of anyone in the game today. They didn't keep net in his day, but Peter King, a fellow selector, figured it out once, using old play-by-play sheets, and it was very anemic, something like the low 32s.

Glenn Dobbs of the old AAFC, with the top gross average ever, would be an exotic choice, but he really didn't do it long enough, and I didn't get to see him punt more than a couple of times in his career. Nope, it would take someone with an absolute thunderfoot to dislodge an emotional favorite such as Davis.

I'll be really brief with the return men since the numbers speak such a loud message. Right now Chicago's Devin Hester is a one-year wonder. A few more seasons like his rookie year of 2006 and we'd have to take him seriously. Gale Sayers has the best career kick return average in history. But it was a short career. Dante Hall has run a lot more kicks back, but they've got the same number of TDs, and Sayers' average is more than six yards higher. Sayers is my man.

Jack Christiansen, who doubled as the strong safety on the great Lions' secondary nicknamed Chris' Crew, burst onto the scene with rookie and second-year seasons the likes of which never have been duplicated — punt return averages of 19.1 and 21.5 yards with six touchdowns. He coasted in on those figures to give him the second best career average in history. Well, I guess he's my pick, even though Chicago's great scatback, George McAfee, was three-hundredth of a yard higher. In the modern era ... Hall was impressive for a while, but I've always liked him better returning kickoffs. So I guess that's it, except for one man.

If I were down to my last punt return of the game and I needed a single effort to get me back in position to win it ... that was it, one last shot ... who would choose to be back there waiting for that kick? I can think of only one name, Deion Sanders. He might retreat and lose yards, and I'm sure that's what brought his average down during his career. But that scene has been repeated just so many times, Sanders back there, kind of waving his hand from side to side, maybe clowning a bit, the crowd tense, expectant, the punt team nervous, and then, oh my God, he just might ... wait a minute, they've got him pinned. But those instincts of his, the excitement he generated.

His return average couldn't match Christiansen's. Career TDs were the same, six. But I just can't get that picture out of my mind. I'm switching votes. Is it too late? Sanders is my all-time NFL punt returner.

If you wanted to break down the members of the special teams suicide squads into specific areas of expertise, as Buffalo coach Bobby April does, I'm sure you could give me a pretty efficient set of operatives, all going at a fully proficient level, pick one. But there's a certain romance attached to this position, so for old times' sake, I'll go with Henry Schmidt, one of the cast of unforgettable characters who decorated my *Thinking Man's Guide*. I draw from it now.

I began covering the Jets full time in 1966. Schmidt was a reserve tackle. He was in his fourth pro camp and by the time he hit New York he was just about playing out the string. His salary was $15,000. His face was craggy and lined, and it was painful to watch him getting out of the team bus after a 15-minute airport trip. His battered knees cramped and aching, he would hobble like a 60-year-old man.

When the Jets finally cut him, I was surprised to see that he was only 29. He looked like 40. And then I remembered who Henry Schmidt was. He was the greatest hot man, or wedge buster, that I'd ever seen. I had watched him in his rookie year with the 49ers in 1959. He was inordinately fast coming down the field for a guy 6-4, 254 pounds. The Niners fans loved him, but when he'd hit the wedge and splinter it like kindling, it would draw a gasp, rather than a cheer, from the crowd. Usually the ball carrier would be part of the mob that Henry took down on his wild attacks. When people saw that he was actually able to get up and walk off the field, that's when the cheers would come.

Seven years later I saw what all that wedge busting had done to Schmidt. The only miracle was how he had managed to survive as long as he did.

"The problem," Jets linebacker Larry Grantham explained to me one day, "was that Henry was terribly nearsighted. He'd just aim at the biggest cluster he could find. Then someone fitted him with contact lenses. When he actually could see what was coming at him, well, that was it for Henry as a wedge buster."

This ends the sad story of Henry Schmidt. And thus ends the roster of my all-time team.

* * *

BEST DEFENSES OF ALL TIME

Entitled "Curtain Falls on Ravens Defense," this column appeared on SI.com *on Feb. 8, 2001.*

Post-Super Bowl, I did a one-pager for the magazine in which I tried to put the Ravens' defense in some kind of perspective and compare it to some of the great units of the past. Since I didn't want to rent a U-Haul to bring my library down to Tampa, I had to do it on general impressions. Now, more than a week later, armed with my full battalion of charts and reference books, I've tried to come up with a more thorough breakdown.

It can be frustrating work, especially when you're dealing with statistics. The encyclopedias and yearbooks are inconsistent. So are the press books. So, basically, I tried to avoid a heavy reliance on numbers and concentrate more on the individuals, as I remember them.

I chose eight great defensive units of the past for my breakdown and comparison — Detroit's in the 1950s, when the Lions won three NFL titles, stretching into the early '60s; the Lombardi Packers of '60 through '67, when Green Bay won five championships, including two Super Bowl victories; George Allen's L.A. Rams' Fearsome Foursome units of the '60s; Buffalo, the dominant defensive team of the early AFL; Minnesota's Purple People Eaters of the late '60s and '70s; the Cowboys' Doomsday Defense of the '60s and '70s; Pittsburgh's four-time Super Bowl champion Steel Curtain of '72 through '79; and the Chicago squad of the mid-'80s.

I know I'm neglecting many fine defenses — the Giants of different eras, the champion Colts, the early Paul Brown teams in Cleveland, Denver's Orange Crush — but I have to draw the line somewhere. The teams I chose basically had continuity and the ability to put their stamp on the game for a number of years.

Detroit Lions

Defensive Hall of Famers: **four**. S Jack Christiansen, MLB Joe Schmidt, CB Dick "Night Train" Lane, S Yale Lary, with a fifth, CB Lem Barney, appearing in 1967 as the run of great defenses was on the decline and a sixth, T Alex Karras, an occasional finalist in the balloting.

Defensive Pro Bowlers: **13**, but I'm including a 16-year period, 1952-1967, and it was easier to make the Pro Bowl in those days because there were fewer teams.

It's almost impossible to compare the Ravens with these units because the game was so different. The running attack dominated; the Lions didn't even fully go to a 4-3 until 1956, six years after the Giants introduced the alignment. Detroit preferred to stack its young middle backer, Schmidt, behind a massive 360-pound nose guard, Les Bingaman, who kept the blockers off him. Sound familiar? Schmidt adapted nicely to the 4-3, though, and put together seven more Pro Bowl seasons from '56-62.

Schmidt ranked with Sam Huff and Ray Nitschke as the first of the game's great middle linebackers, the defensive glamour position of the era, slightly predating Dick Butkus, Tommy Nobis and Willie Lanier. Schmidt wasn't a bruiser; he was a precision player, a sure tackler with great instincts for the ball. Very similar to Ray Lewis in those skills, but without Lewis' blinding speed.

The array of DBs that the Lions put on the field in those years, though, was truly astounding — Chris' Crew, featuring Hall of Famers Christiansen and Lary at the safeties and Pro Bowler Jim David at the left corner, then Lane, Dick LeBeau and Barney, all All-Pros. I saw the Lions through very young eyes, and my vision was slightly blurred because I always seemed to be rooting for the teams they were facing — the Browns in the title games of the '50s, the 49ers in the '57 playoff, etc., but I remember being very impressed by Detroit's front four, featuring Pro Bowlers Karras and Darris McCord and later Roger Brown, and especially one nasty customer who never was selected but should have been, Gil "Wild Horse" Mains. Also impressive was Detroit's Pro Bowl right linebacker Wayne Walker, another sure tackler who fit in well with the system.

On personnel, these teams could match up with anybody. You can't compare them with the Ravens, though, because of the difference in team speed and the types of offenses faced.

Green Bay Packers

Defensive Hall of Famers: **five**. E Willie Davis, T Henry Jordan, MLB Ray Nitschke, CB Herb Adderley, FS Willie Wood, with a sixth, OLB Dave Robinson, appearing on Seniors nominating ballots.

Defensive Pro Bowlers: **11**.

Nitschke, a raging terror at MLB who would race sideline to sideline with more speed than people gave him credit for (he was a fullback at Illinois), was the emotional leader. Wood, a far-ranging safetyman, and Adderley, one of the great pure man-to-man corners, have appeared on some all-time NFL teams. Robinson arrived on the later Lombardi units, and he was one of the first great size (6-foot-3, 245 pounds) and speed outside backers.

It was a great cast, built around a solid, ball-control offense (Lombardi's background was as an offensive coach), anchored by a fine line and another gifted cover corner, Pro Bowler Bobby Jeter.

I wouldn't even try man-to-man matchups with the Ravens, or even a unit-by-unit comparison, again because the eras were different, but I'll tell you one area in which the Packers have a great advantage: class. There was none of the swaggering, trash-talking crap that so demeaned this Baltimore team. The Packers played for a coach who expected them to conduct themselves as champions and they never failed to. It doesn't seem to be much of a priority with Brian Billick.

Los Angeles Rams

Defensive Hall of Famers: **two**. Merlin Olsen and Deacon Jones.

Defensive Pro Bowlers: **seven**, covering the '60s.

Everything was keyed to the great play of the front line, the Fearsome Foursome: from left to right, Jones, Olsen, John LoVetere — later replaced by Rosey Grier, later replaced by Pro Bowler Roger Brown and, finally, Lamar Lundy. It was a well-integrated power unit with two Hall of Famers playing side by side and destroying one side of the line, the right tackle playing the run and the 6-7 Lundy coming up with the frequent big play.

The outside backers, Maxie Baughan and Jack Pardee, were George Allen warhorses who put together a few Pro Bowl seasons between them. The middle backers, except for Les Richter in the early years, were basically journeymen, and there wasn't tremendous speed in the secondary.

But when the front four was on a roll, this could be a punishing defense, very hard on quarterbacks and runners. I include it because those are the moments I remember and because Olsen and Jones are on my all-time team. Some people feel that this outfit was overrated because it never won a title, never even played in a championship game. Maybe the critics are right. I don't care. It holds special memories for me. As a unit the Ravens were better, again because of the speed.

Buffalo Bills

Defensive Hall of Famers: **zero**, but DT Tom Sestak has been an occasional Seniors candidate.

Defensive AFL All-Stars: **10**, and I didn't include 1965 because the entire team was credited with All-Star status that year. How did this happen? Well, that year the championship Bills played the AFL All-Stars in a one-year format that was later dropped. The success of the effort depends on how serious the stars took the game. I don't know because I didn't see it, but the Bills led at the half, 13-6, before finally getting overrun by depth and stars such as Joe Namath and Lance Alworth 30-19.

In a league geared toward wide-open offenses and passing frenzies — a sales vehicle to compete with the buttoned-up NFL — defense wasn't at much of a premium in the attempt to sign the superstars. But the Bills built an impressive unit that got them into three championships (they won two) from 1960-66.

I covered the AFL in those days. The front four of Ron McDole, the vastly underrated Sestak, Jim Dunaway and Tippy Day could have competed with anybody. Butch Byrd was a terrific corner and George Saimes a gifted free safety. All three linebackers were AFL All-Stars at some point, including Mike Stratton, who made the thunderous hit on the Chargers' Keith Lincoln in the '64 title game. In two championships against Sid Gillman's explosive San Diego offense, the Bills held the Chargers to 135 and 119 yards passing and seven points total.

Compare them to the Ravens? I can't. I won't. You can't make me.

Dallas Cowboys

Defensive Hall of Famers: **three**. T Bob Lilly, FS-CB Mel Renfro and T Randy White, with MLB Lee Roy Jordan and FS Cliff Harris appearing on ballots.

Defensive Pro Bowlers: **11**, stretching over a very long period.

The true Doomsday Defense began in the mid-1960s, when the Cowboys appeared in their first of two straight NFL title losses to the Packers, and stretched through the early '70s, when Dallas won its first Super Bowl. When the Cowboys made everyone furious by labeling themselves America's Team, the Doomsday sobriquet was quietly dropped.

It's tough to isolate one period of the 13-year run (1966-78) in which the Cowboys made 12 postseason trips, appearing in five Super Bowls (winning two) and two early NFL title games. I think their greatest teams were in the early '70s, when the young stars of the '60s reached full maturity and Tom Landry, who ran both offensive and defensive gameplanning, put together a beautifully integrated, cohesive unit.

Superstars? Where to begin? Eight Cowboys put together five or more Pro Bowl appearances apiece. The immensely gifted Lilly and run-stopper Jethro Pugh led a line that later plugged in White and pass-rush specialist Harvey Martin. Jordan should be in the Hall of Fame. Few middle linebackers ever have been as sound against the run. Chuck Howley ranked with the Steelers' Jack Ham as one of the great outside backers in coverage. Renfro and Cornell Green were DBs with 15 Pro Bowls between them, and safeties Harris and Charlie Waters put together nine entries.

For five years, though, they were known as the team that couldn't win the big one. Then the Cowboys won it in '72. Then they won it again in '78. They didn't put up overwhelming numbers, but they were probably the smartest defense ever to take the field. They're still another team that I can't compare to the Ravens, but be patient, I'm getting there.

Minnesota Vikings

Defensive Hall of Famers: **two**. S Paul Krause, T Alan Page, with DE Carl Eller a frequent candidate.

Defensive Pro Bowlers: **nine**, during the period of 1969-76, in which they appeared in four Super Bowls.

When people mention the Purple People Eaters, they're talking about the line — from left to right, Eller, Gary Larsen (later Doug Sutherland), Page and Jim Marshall. The linebackers and DBs didn't eat anybody, they watched the front four do it. Three members of the foursome put on a tremendously intense pass rush, while Larsen or Sutherland stayed at home. It was criticized as unsound against the ground attack by some, but the Vikings' linemen were such good athletes that they could pick up the run on the go. Until the Super Bowl. That's where the formula broke down. In their four losses, first to the Chiefs, then to the Dolphins, Steelers and Raiders, Minnesota's defense gave up an average of 215.5 yards rushing. Uh oh.

The linebackers were sturdy workers through the years, the DBs basically undistinguished except for corner Bobby Bryant and Krause, the NFL's all-time leader in interceptions. But the longevity and durability of that line was truly amazing. During a six-year period from '68 through '73, the same foursome took the field without missing a game. Eller, Page and Marshall played for 11 years with only two missed starts (both by Eller).

Regular-season points were hard to come by against this unit. From '69 through '71, they gave up a record 133 points (for a 14-game season), then 143, then 139, and only 38 TDs in the three years, 10 by rushing. It's tough to figure why they always took the pipe in the Super Bowl, but there it was. I'd give the Ravens the edge because they elevated their game when the stakes were highest.

Pittsburgh Steelers

Defensive Hall of Famers: **four**. T Joe Greene, MLB Jack Lambert, OLB Jack Ham, CB Mel Blount, with E L.C. Greenwood and SS Donnie Shell getting occasional consideration.

Defensive Pro Bowlers: **12**, during their eight-year playoff/Super Bowl run of '72 through '78; **13** if you want to count LB Robin Cole, who started in '78 and made the Pro Bowl a few years later.

This ranks as the greatest defensive team I've ever seen, and the one little patch of territory that I've singled out is in 1976, when the Browns' Turkey Jones body-slammed Terry Bradshaw in game No. 5 and put him out of action until the next-to-last contest. The defense was called on to hold the fort while rookie Mike Kruczek ran the show for most of the way. What it did was to run up nine straight wins, including five shutouts, with the enemy scoring a total of 28 points (two TDs and five field goals ... for you mathematicians out there, subtract a point for a missed conversion and it'll come out). Nine quarterbacks were faced during that span — including six who made the Pro Bowl at some time during their career, two of them Hall of Famers — and not one of them completed 50 percent of his passes against that Steelers defense. This is my performance chart for that unlucky bunch of QBs:

23-6 vs Cincinnati: **Ken Anderson**, 13-for-31, 2 INTs, 129 yards.

27-0 at New York Giants: **Craig Morton**, 11-26-1, 97 yards.

23-0 vs San Diego: **Dan Fouts**, 10-28-1, 122 yards.

45-0 at Kansas City: **Mike Livingston**, 11-25-4, 198 yards.

14-3 vs Miami: **Bob Griese**, 9-21-0, 144 yards.

32-16 vs Houston: **John Hadl**, 9-20-2, 134 yards.

7-3 at Cincinnati: **Anderson**, 10-26-1, 145 yards.

42-0 vs Tampa Bay: **Steve Spurrier**, 4-10-1, 58 yards; **Terry Hanratty**, 1-4-1, minus one yard.

21-0 at Houston: **Dan Pastorini**, 13-29-1, 95 yards.

Eight defensive Steelers were chosen to the Pro Bowl that year, the same number as the year before. At one time Pittsburgh put a unit on the field, in which 10 of the 11 players had Pro Bowl credentials. The only one who never made it was RT Fats Holmes, and he was one of the most feared players in the league. The front four was magnificent; the LBs featured two Hall of Famers — the pair of Jacks, Lambert and Ham — and the right backer, Andy Russell, an All-Pro. The secondary hung in a double zone and met the receivers with murderous tackles, as Baltimore does to a certain extent.

I rate the 1974-76 Pittsburgh units as No. 1 of all time. Then there was a drop-off, although they still won two more Super Bowls. Defensive line compared to Baltimore's? Steelers are better. Ditto linebackers, although

Lambert probably wasn't as good as Lewis in pure lock-on coverage, whereas he was very effective in the zone downfield. DBs? Again Pittsburgh. Team speed and cohesiveness? Well, that's where Baltimore excels, but I'll stick with my All-Star cast, which was the fastest unit ever to play — up to that time.

Chicago Bears

Defensive Hall of Famers: **1**. MLB Mike Singletary, with DT Dan Hampton a near miss this year and FS Gary Fencik an occasional nominee.

Defensive Pro Bowlers: **10**, from '84-88, when the Bears appeared in the postseason five times, winning one Super Bowl. To clarify — I'm counting players who made it at some time in their career and who started on these teams, i.e. Fencik, who made it in '80 and '81 but was an integral part of the later clubs.

Buddy Ryan's 46 defense attacked and punished, with the idea of unhinging the quarterback through relentless blitzing, plus throwing up a blanket front to smother the run. In 1986 the Bears gave up 187 points, a record for a 16-game season until Baltimore broke it this year. It was a ferocious plan — "Neanderthal football," Bill Parcells called it — but it was unsound in spots, too. For instance, it put tremendous pressure on the cornerbacks, and the Bears' corners through this period were only average.

In 1984, the year they lost to the 49ers in the NFC championship, the Bears allowed 15.5 yards per completion, third highest in the league. In their Super Bowl season the number was down to 13.3 — better, but still ninth highest. But as the Ravens did this year, they reached an absolute frenzy in the postseason of '85, shutting out their first two opponents, the Giants and Rams, and crushing New England, 46-10, allowing an average of 111.3 yards per game for the trio.

Compare them to the Ravens? D-Linemen Hampton, Steve McMichael and pass-rush specialist Richard Dent, better than anything the Ravens have. RT William Perry, worse. Linebacking trio of Singletary and Pro Bowlers Otis Wilson and Wilber Marshall, better than the Ravens' trio, although again, Singletary couldn't cover man-to-man as Lewis could, although Singletary was a fierce blitzer and valuable in occasional zone-coverage downfield. Raven corners were better; Bears safeties — Fencik and Dave Duerson — were better but not as fast as Rod Woodson and Kim Herring. Ravens were better on overall depth and team speed. The verdict — a tie.

Baltimore Ravens

Well, their achievement this year has been well documented. A team that played inspired football, raising its performance right up till the end. Held the enemy to under 200 yards in three out of the four postseason contests, one touchdown and an average of 4.8 points, with one TD coming on a kick return. Much credit to the defensive coaches, Marvin Lewis for his scheme, DL coach Rex Ryan, Buddy's son, for getting career years out of tackles Tony Siragusa and Sam Adams, who hadn't been doing much for a while.

But so far it's a one-year thing, and who knows what free agency will do to this unit? The old timers kept it going for an era.

* * *

BEST QUARTERBACKS OF ALL TIME
Entitled "Fitting Favre into History," this mailbag column appeared on SI.com *on Sept. 28, 2007.*

With a landmark record about to fall this weekend, and I'm talking about Dan Marino's mark for career touchdown passes, we'll designate our leadoff hitter as **Steve of Germantown, Md.**, who says, "It seems an appropriate time to ask if you would rank Brett Favre among the 10 best quarterbacks of all time."

I want to be fair about this. I've been repeatedly accused of being anti-Favre and I think the reason for my grumpiness is the announcers and fans have fallen so much in love with him during his career that they've been blind to his failings, such as the careless interceptions. How many times have I heard, "Well, at least he's having fun out there," as the offense trudges off the field, following still another pick?

But placing him in the pantheon of the all timers, well, I'm going to have to think it through, and why not right now? To me, his most remarkable record is never having missed a contest since he became a starter in the fourth game of the 1992 season. That's 16 years worth! Strictly on a skill level, I can't think of any other Hall of Fame quarterback who had a stronger arm, with the possible exception of Terry Bradshaw, who was a national schoolboy record holder in the javelin. Emotionally, Favre is a wild stallion who, at best, in the Super Bowl seasons, inspired all those around him ... at worst, drove his coaches crazy.

He's the kind of player who needed a periodic restraining order ... hey, why am I past-tensing him? Who needs — present — a periodic restraining order, and let's face it, coaches have been afraid of him. Mike Holmgren wasn't. Maybe Mike McCarthy, the current edition, isn't, since I keep reading how he's telling him to choke it off and play it safe. Now, how does he compare with the all timers?

John Unitas and Joe Montana, my twin No. 1s? Both better than him. Otto Graham, my No. 3? Ditto. How about the moderns, Steve Young, John Elway, Troy Aikman, Marino? Hmmm, more careful from an interception standpoint, Aikman and Young, higher-percentage passers, all except Aikman higher in yards per completion — which is a very telling stat in my book. Victories? Super Bowls? Uh uh, I don't count those in. They're team stats, not QB stats.

How about the old timers, Luckman and Sammy Baugh, for instance? No, I can't do it ... Sid Luckman, who played a full game on defense vs. Brett Favre? No, forget it. I forgot Norm Van Brocklin and Bradshaw and Y.A. Tittle, and the ultra moderns, such as Peyton Manning and Tom Brady, and ... OK, I'm cutting it off right here. That record of 16 years without missing a game does it for me ... Favre goes into my top 10, all time, probably around eight or nine, when I get it all worked out. OK?

Progressing in regimental fashion, we'll stay with the quarterback questions for a while. **Rick of Boulder, Colo.**, thinks one of the most overrated statistics for QBs is fourth-quarter comebacks, a big hoo-ha out there in Elway country; but Rick feels that maybe it was some earlier screw-ups that can put a team in a comeback mode to begin with. Yep, I sure agree with that; in fact, I think trying to isolate any one stat (except Favre's durability) is a mistake. My least favorite stat is passer-rating points, a system keyed almost entirely to completion percentage. Step right up, dinkers, and collect your reward.

From **Brandon of Austin**: Rex Grossman gets benched. But no one ever calls for Drew Brees, with numbers that are almost as bad, to get the hook. How come? Three reasons — 1) Brees is better, 2) Brees has done it, and Grossman hasn't and 3) Exactly who would you go with if you benched Brees ... Jamie Martin with eight starts out of 13 years in the league? Free-agent rookie Tyler Palko?

Let's stay with the Saints. From **Myshall, Carlow, Ireland**, comes **Padriac**, a fan of the Saints, namely Paul, Peter, Vincent and Sebastian ... OK, ha ha, a fan of the New Orleans variety who wants to know what's wrong, actually? The secondary has been exposed. So has the offensive line. That's two big areas of need, and if they make the mistake of trying to fit Reggie Bush into Deuce McAllister's role of heavy-duty back, that'll be three areas. But I can't believe they'll do that, not with Aaron Stecker simply thirsting for action. Thanks for what you wrote about my work, mate.

And thanks to you, as well, **Dan of Sammamish, Wash.**, who likens Bush to Rocket Ismail, a fantastic college player who never did much in the NFL. Ismail remains a mystery to me. He was the greatest collegiate kick returner I ever saw. Led the AFC in his rookie year with the Raiders, then kind of flattened out. I remember thinking he shouldn't be messing around at wideout. Let him do what he does best. I liked Bush better as a receiver than as a runner last year. Now I don't know what he is.

Question No. 2. Is the Cowboys' Marion Barber another Robert Newhouse? No. Newhouse was a chunky-legged little banger. He was the featured runner only once in his 12 years with the club and in that he has something in common with Barber. Style-wise, Barber is different. He's a two-gap runner with great instincts and competitive fire, a powerhouse, going for the first down. Why he plays behind Julius Jones, a guy he's infinitely better than, I'll never know.

Let's whip overland to San Diego, whose Chargers provoked a question from my E-mailer of the Week, **Garth Stewart**, who comes from, well, from **Seattle**. A rather innocuous query, but it's clothed in ancient history, which I love, thus, on this self-serving basis, a cherished award is rather frivolously given. "I continue to ask this question as relentlessly as the elder Cato calling for the destruction of Carthage. Did San Diego fire the wrong man? The wheels are coming off the bus." If history truly repeats, Civis Stewart, then you shouldn't be too anxious to get rid of Norv Turner. Carthage was destroyed, as Cato urged, but three years after he died at age 85. Do you really want to wait that long? By the way, I don't fire coaches here on *SI.com*. Call it feather-footing, but it's one game I refuse to play.

Closer to the action, **Chris of La Mesa, Calif.**, wants my "overall opinion of Philip Rivers and the Chargers." What I wrote in my rankings column still holds. They seem like a one-man team, Antonio Gates, whose circus catches kept bailing out an erratic Rivers. The Packers crowded the box to stop LaDainian Tomlinson and collected Rivers in the same box. He could have won the Green Bay game with one play, late in the contest, when the Chargers were protecting a four-point lead with two-and-a-half minutes left. Third and three on his own 28. A first down gets the Pack out of timeouts, and one more play runs into the two-minute warning. Another play and the clock runs way down, and another first down and the game's over. What does Rivers do on third-and-three? Overthrows Vincent Jackson on a sideline pattern, and that's a big guy to overthrow, 6-foot-5, 241 pounds. On TV Phil Simms makes this goofy pronouncement: "He played it smart." Huh?

Punter Mike Scifres, and here's an area you won't see discussed that much … anyway, punter Mike Scifres, one of my favorites last season because he was usually good for a five-second, high hanger, in the clutch, let's go with a 3.69 weenie that nets 29 yards, and the Pack is set up. The great firm of Merriman and Phillips, which has been quiet all day, and their lassitude this season has been still another problem, remains dormant. Green Bay scores its TD, Rivers still has enough time, but he throws three straight misfires — the third one a pick that comes back to the San Diego two, and it's all over. The worst thing was that the great handicapper, Z, had San Diego as his lock of the week. You ask me about Philip Rivers? Phooey, I say!

On to less strenuous topics. **John of Atlanta** doesn't much care for the last minute timeout that nullified game-winning field goals two weeks in a row. He asks about a proposed rule that says that if there's a stoppage in play, then no timeout can be called after the play clock winds down to 10 seconds. Well, the league told me that timeouts were called well in advance, but the whistles weren't heard because of the noise, so the ball was snapped and the ball kicked anyway. I'm not so sure. Didn't look like that to me. Yeah, I'll go for that 10-second rule. That last-minute sneaky timeout, which the league claims doesn't really exist, frankly stinks.

My column, The Meaning of the Game, drew some positive responses and one negative. First eat your spinach, then you'll get dessert. Nostalgia is overrated says **Joe D. of Lynnfield, Mass.** Do I really want to go back to the good old days of racism, sexism and toryism (OK, the last one is mine)? "The world isn't better or worse, just different. Football today is not football of yesterday. So what? It is what it is."

What a tough person. Is there no romance in your soul, sir? No dreams of the snows of yesteryear? Do you really love the hype, the wrestle-o-rama that is today's presentation? You say you don't, but you accept it because it's here. So are certain political figures whom I can't accept. So is terrorism. Besides, when I wrote of the past I was careful to point out this was an old-man's vision, misty-eyed but not really clear. Do you wish to strip me of all my memories?

Well, **Bill from Clearwater**, where the water is truly clear, liked the piece. So did **Andy of Baltimore** and **Alan of Omaha** and **J. Tyler of Terre Haute**, and these are not chaps to mess with. Note to JT — my favorite thing in Terre Haute is the Eugene V. Debs museum, honoring one of my heroes. My least favorite is the motel where we stayed while covering the Colts' camp. Within a two-block span on either side, we counted 32 chain restaurants. We chose Outback. Next to the Hardee's and Arby's and McDonald's and Burger King, it seemed like the Four Seasons.

Andy of Baltimore asks if Brian Billick runs one of the most media-friendly operations. Yeah, he's pretty good about access, maybe because he once worked in the 49ers' PR office. Herman Edwards is very good in that department, too. Alan of Omaha feels that all the dirt-digging types, epitomized by YouTube style of journalism are a big reason why the game has turned nasty. I guess so. Maybe it's just the overall crush of journalistic bodies, mine included.

From **Alfred G. of Santa Monica** — Fox's No. 1 team of Joe Buck and Troy Aikman worked a game that neglected to include starting lineups. A mistake, or something deliberate?

I asked that same question — to someone on the production team of the show. His answer was that they had ditched them, but were "working on something new." Oh, I see. Why tell people who's on the field? WE ARE THE GAME holler the networks. How about showing the starting lineups, instead of all the Fox announcers in action that day? Freakin' arrogance, I calls it.

Tim of Arlington shoots me this teaser: You're a GM. Pick one but not both and tell me why. Terrell Owens. Randy Moss. My answer is that I'd pick the one least likely to go into the tank, if the team loses a few. Owens. The other guy might just spend half the game at the concession stand if the team were going badly. Thanks for your kind words and your concern about the book, and your pledge to buy two.

Nice of you to want my book,
Publishers feel that I'm a shnook;
Fantasy football, "now that's got class,"
So I say, stick it up your ...

Michael of Salt Lake City feels that a great team in a division elevates the whole level of that division because the other clubs are so intent at trying to beat it, hence the quality of the AFC South. Why wouldn't they want to be better, just to be better and go as far as they can? But I'm not discounting your theory entirely. I think teams' drafts are based on the toughest people they have to play twice. If you're in the same division as Indy, you'd better have some serious cornerbacks. When he was with the Giants, Bill Parcells used to load up on guards. Why? Because all the other teams in the NFC East played a 4-3 and had at least one fine tackle — Eric Swann in Phoenix, Randy White in Dallas, Dave Butz in Washington, Jerome Brown in Philly.

From **Guillaume, le grand auteur de Los Angeles**: Arizona switches from a lefty QB to a righty, back and forth they go, so how does this affect the traditional LT-RT designation, with one, supposedly the tap-dancing pass blocker, protecting the back side and the other one the pounder on the front side? They just make the best of it, besides the differences aren't as great as you'd think. It would be too upsetting to disturb these guys' comfort zones by having them switch during a game after working all week on one side. And *merci pour votre sentiments.*

Ditto to **Joel of Longmont, Colo.** He wants to know what happens when a first-round draft choice just departs the board, as will take place if New England has to give up theirs. Well, if I worked for the Players Association, I'd say, hey, you can't just remove a man from the work force, but I'm sure that management has made certain there's a provision in the contract for it. As far as the effect on salaries, well, an agent would ask for first-round money if his guy is the 32nd pick, or the first one in the second round; the team negotiator would say, sorry, pal, but he was still taken in round No. 2. And back and forth they'd go, a little give on each side, a little take, and how we do worry about the comings and goings of the millionaires, don't we?

Chapter 8

Urgent Dispatch from Comrade Kalugin

A fairly comfortable time after Mikhail Gorbachev's Perestroika had changed almost all the rules of the Cold War and turned many of the KGB's most fearsome operatives into willing comrades of the West, at least in theory, *The New York Times* ran a lengthy sketch of Oleg Kalugin, who had been the agency's youngest major general in its history. The story began on the front page and continued with a jump inside, occupying a massive wall of print.

Normally one of these gigantic *Times* monoliths has a numbing affect, but I read every word avidly for two reasons. No. 1, it was written by no less a master of spywriting than John Le Carré, whose thrillers I've loved for many years, and No. 2, I had known Oleg when he was 24 years old. He had been my classmate.

Oleg's career had been a contrast of light and dark. The dark side involved many KGB operations that would have drawn shudders, even gasps from our easygoing Class of 1959, Columbia University Graduate School of Journalism, if we could have seen what our handsome, smiling confrere would be up to some day. One particular nasty one that I remembered at the time — because it had been so bizarre — involved the dissident Bulgarian journalist, Georgi Markov. He had been eliminated by the Bulgarian secret service, which had loaded an umbrella with poison pellets and then had an operative shoot Markov with them, as he brushed into him.

I was a bit stunned to learn that Major General Kalugin had been in charge of the operation, although years later in an interview he was quoted as saying that he didn't actually implement it himself ... the Bulgarians did that … he just supervised it. This was during Oleg's "Hallelujah, I've Been Saved" period after he had become a Soviet dissenter and enemy of the KGB and a valuable friend of the United States. His contrasting emergence into the light.

Le Carré, a.k.a David Cornwell, is, of course, an old pro and a former intelligence operative himself and, while acknowledging Kalugin's many contributions to the West, he gave the impression that he wasn't entirely buying the act. Perhaps it was Oleg's insistence on how his deals had been betrayed by the slothfulness of the KGB, thereby driving him to our shores, that bothered the writer. I know it bothered me. But I sensed the picture of a guy saving his own behind, getting out while the time was right, and I guess Le Carré did, too.

So I decided to write to him, care of *The Times*, if that was indeed the way you reached someone of his stature, and give him the benefit of my memories of Oleg and the Class of '59, high above the banks of the Hudson, just in case it might be of any use to him in future writing on the subject. This was not exactly dry material. It had its share of snappers, as you will see.

Now I've always considered myself a team ballplayer, and my first loyalty went to my team, Time, Inc., the parent company of *Sports Illustrated*, which paid, and still pays, my salary. So as Oleg's name began to take on significance, I tried to pitch my little narrative to the powers that ruled the Time empire. I received one callback, expressing annoyance that a Cro-Magnon from the world of sport, pro football no less, actually had the audacity to, etc. etc. I remember how, in desperation, I actually invaded the office. Their editor, who later quit the magazine, citing inability to accurately express himself under its system, told me he'd let me know if anyone were interested. I counted four times that he looked at his watch, a typical managerial tactic to let you know you're wasting his time.

Finally I wrote a note to the assistant managing editor at *SI*. "Doesn't anyone even want to hear the stories about this guy?" I had mentioned a line in *The Times* that described Oleg as attending Columbia, "masquerading as a student," while actually practicing his spy trade. "Hell, we were ALL masquerading as students," I said. Later the editor told me he'd gotten a chuckle out of that line but hadn't felt the need of passing along my note.

So off to the master of Smiley, and Leamas *Who Came In from the Cold*, went my Oleg stories, and quicker than I would have suspected came John Le Carré's reply. "What fun about Oleg," he wrote, followed by a thank you for permission to use of the material, if ever needed, but "you must write it all some day." And then, he gave me a sense of what I had guessed about his feeling for General Kalugin:

"You know," he wrote, "I had the impression that sometimes, listening and watching, that he really wasn't real to himself."

* * *

September, 1958: We had heard rumors that Columbia was about to host the first Fullbright Exchange Scholar from Russia, but we weren't really sure. We found out on opening day when the foreign students introduced themselves to the class and gave a little talk about "Journalism in My Country." I can't remember them all; there were maybe a dozen or so. A few South Americans; the usual Gupta from India; one guy from Canada who'd show up every now and then to play for our intramural basketball team; lovely little Guiti Nashat from Iran (or was it Persia then?), who captured the heart of Mike Claffey, a tough Irishman from Queens with whom I'd been a copy boy on the *Journal-American*; poor Silvia Pakains, originally from Latvia, later a victim of an unsolved murder by, we suspected, a very weird countryman of hers. And Oleg.

Compactly built, handsome in a sandy-haired, Slavic kind of way ... he looked like future Olympic sprint champ Valeriy Borzov. Friendly. Smiled a lot.

The speeches that day were mostly haphazard things, with English not always perfectly handled ... "Waal, in our country we try to, ah, write sometimes better style ..." Oleg blew them all away. His English was perfect. In precise, outline form, he described a journalistic system of integrity, logic, freely expressed ideas and clarity of purpose. Beautifully done. Total bullshit, of course, but we saluted the effort. Don't forget, this was not too long after the Soviet tanks were in the streets of Budapest.

When class broke up, we hustled Oleg down to the West End Bar & Grill on 113th and Broadway. "I want to see what a few Rheingolds do to him," said 6-5 Charley Wilson, who jumped center for our hoopsters. They didn't do anything to Oleg except make him a little happier, but they put

Charley and a few others down. I'm sure Oleg was thinking, "Beer? Child's play."

He fit in well. He was socially adept, never coming on too strong, never really holding back. I'm ashamed to say that we never tried to see how he would handle himself in a far reaching political debate ... it might have been interesting ... but there was a certain amount of shyness that kept things away from political heaviness. We'd talk about beer or the weather or school or women. I'd guess you'd have to describe his demeanor as smooth, kind of the way you'd imagine people at an embassy would handle themselves. I never saw him lose his temper, or even show serious annoyance. When we had some really interesting interview candidates to practice on ... Harry Truman, for instance, gave us a lesson in how to become browbeaten, whipped dogs, in the face of a really tough subject ... Oleg never, to my recollection, asked a significant question. He was friendly to the female members of our class, even cordial, letting his well-developed charm carry him along without ever making an obvious play that I noticed.

He never let on that he was married.

Basically, he represented a huge puzzle to us. Was he just a friendly, charming guy who happened to be a Russian, or was there something perhaps a bit more sinister involved? When he wasn't around, we'd concoct elaborate stories about him. What if he were a spy? Could they really have sent a young spy over to join our class and spy on America? Or on us? The idea was flattering.

But what could he be spying on us about? Hell, Oleg, just tell us. We'll play a cat and mouse game, report to control, leave messages in a tree or behind a loose brick.

"Urgent dispatch ... stop ... from Comrade Kalugin ... stop," Mike Claffey used to intone in a beery attempt at a Russian accent. "Can report with certainty ... stop ... that the meatballs at the West End are 40 percent filler ... stop."

And then I had read, 40 years later, that he'd been recruited by the KGB six years before he came to Columbia. So what exactly would he tell them about us, or New York? Columbia J-School students are sloppy drunks? Cheating was rampant during the midterm exam on laws of libel?

Actually, what he was doing, or so he said, was not spying but "reconnaissance." I read this in a January, 1998 interview from CNN Interactive's Cold War production team.

"It was a reconnaissance trip," he told them. "I was supposed to make as many friends as possible, to prepare fertile grounds for my future work, to familiarize myself with the United States and its way of life."

Oh, he familiarized himself, all right. Too familiar. Especially with the all night movies on 42nd St. He fell in love with them, which was no great surprise to me, because, growing up in New York, I had fallen in love with them a long time ago. One night a bunch of us crammed in the subway and headed down to 42nd St. to show Oleg what the real New York was like. By 1958-59 it was no longer the real 42nd St. that once had captured my childhood, the 14, 15, 16 movie theaters ... who could even count them all? ... that occupied one long block between 7th and 8th Aves., the Lyric, the Gotham, the Apollo, Republic, New Amsterdam ... how about one with that neon light circling around like he old camera? ... and of course the Laffmovie with the hysterical laughter of the fat woman and the funny distorting mirrors in front. Oh my God, was it wonderful ... Vincent's, with its 10 cent malteds, Hubert's Museum and Flea Circus, where my father once had taken me to see the legendary Jack Johnson. If there was real sleeze going on, prostitution and drugs and the like, it was pretty well under cover, even when we took Oleg there. All that came later.

So we took Oleg to Hubert's, and that didn't impress him much. They had those kinds of shows in Moscow, too. But then he got a look at that lineup of movie theaters and he flipped. A couple advertised triple features. There were old B films, and worse, from 20 years ago, a few current Westerns, plenty of low class horror films ... *Son of Kong* would be back there every month or so ... anything the theaters could latch onto cheaply. And some of the theaters were all nighters. People would sleep in them. I think that's what got him most of all.

Maybe we had underestimated Oleg, completely pegged him wrong. Maybe underneath it all he was a Steppenwolf, a night person, Poe's Man of the Crown. Sitting up there in the balcony that first night, listening to the snoring around him, hearing the occasional shout or growl from a demented 42nd St. regular, set off by the drone of the ice cream vendor working the aisle downstairs, well, maybe what just clicked with Oleg was something all his KGB training hadn't prepared him for, the real voice of the people, or one unique segment of it, socialism in the raw, New York style.

As an undergrad at Columbia, I had known 42nd St. addicts. The night before an exam, they'd be sitting in the balcony of the Gotham, watching

Claude Rains turn himself into the Invisible Man in 1933. Oleg had the look. I could tell. "Where you going tonight, Oleg?" "Oh, I think I'll drop down to 42nd St."

I just knew he was spending some nights there. His bright, boyish good looks were fading. He was becoming worn, turning into an old man before our eyes. Occasionally someone would drop a hint ... "Say, Oleg, about Jersey City," and he'd hold out a hand to stop the conversation. No kiss-and-tell guy was he.

Dean Barrett, the head of the J-School, was frankly worried. I mean, he couldn't flunk a Russian, the first exchange student ever. But there was this matter of class attendance. I liked Dean Barrett. A good natured chap, very frank. Once he told me how I became a member of the class of '59.

"One phone call from Lou Little," he said. "Just one."

Mr. Little was Columbia's legendary coach who had beaten Stanford in the '34 Rose Bowl, whose Columbia Lions had halted Army's long winning streak in '47. At Columbia he was God. He'd torture you on the field, but if you ever shed a drop of sweat for him, he'd help you any way he could, afterward.

"Mr. Little, I can't take that Zimmerman kid, not with those grades," Dean Barrett told me.

"Take him. He's a good kid." And the argument was over. That's how I got to J-School. And now, six months later, Dean Barrett was flashing me a worried faculty look and wondering how he was going to handle the Oleg situation.

The folks back home handled it. Word must have reached the Politburo that their fair-haired boy was hitting a few highway dividers on his way down the road. Who arrived one day but Mrs. Oleg? His wife, whom I later learned was the daughter of a famous Russian general, a hero. Seemed like a very nice person but spoke no English. We'd have one of our usual parties in someone's apartment, and Oleg would be there, of course ... he tried not to miss any, even in his ragged period ... and he'd be socializing all over the room, as usual, and there in a corner would be Mrs. Oleg, sitting there without benefit of conversation, arms crossed, her eyes staying on her husband. And his class attendance was just fine thereafter. And he graduated right along with the rest of us. The old cap and gown bit, hip hip hooray, and off to the KGB we go for some deep cover.

In reading about his career, his martyrdom at the hands of the Russian tyrants he fought against and then his valuable service to the USA, I've often been tempted to give him a call. There's a phone number listed for the agency he heads in Washington, the Centre for Counter Intelligence and Security Studies, known as the CI Centre. Actually, I tried it a couple of times, left a message, got no response. Which figures, of course. He probably wouldn't even remember me, and, even if he would, what would there be to talk about? Old times?

"Say, Oleg, Dean Barrett really was annoyed when he heard about that Bulgarian reporter and the umbrella bit. He said, 'We didn't teach him THAT at Columbia.'"

Nah, better leave it alone. But it is kind of an interesting story, is it not?

Chapter 9

Olympics

Editor's note: Paul Zimmerman covered five Olympic Games, starting in Tokyo in 1964. Three of them are included in this memoir.

Mexico City 1968

Mexico City in 1968 began with a massacre. There had been reports that some student activists had been shot in demonstrations 10 days before the Olympics began, but filtered through government agencies, the numbers, as usual, were seriously minimized. A few, a handful, no one knew for sure. When I got there, students I talked to told me as many as 300 had died and thousands were wounded. History has put an official number on it of 270 dead, 2,600 wounded, but we'll never really know for sure.

People have wondered how the 2008 Olympics could have been awarded to China, given its record of human rights violations. There has been a list of pseudo-demands that these matters be addressed or ... or what? The games would be withdrawn at the last moment? Nations would drop out? What a joke! The story of Olympic organizers and national directors turning a blind eye to political events, no matter how grisly, no matter how hideous, is an old one. The Games Must Go On. The slogan has been repeated proudly. It has been flown as a banner. It ignored Hitler's rise to power and glorified the rule of Nazi Germany in the Berlin Olympics of '36. It hardly blinked as the USSR crushed the Hungarian revolution when political divisions split China, Korea and Germany into hostile camps. It overlooked racism in South Africa, the growing poison of steroid and hormone abuse that, in its most repulsive phase, deliberately created a race of dwarfed female gymnasts; it overlooked murders outside the gates in Mexico City and inside the compound itself in Munich.

Amazingly, the impact of the killings in Mexico City never really was felt in the outside world. Even today, when reference is made to the '68 Games, the focus is the Tommie Smith-John Carlos black glove demonstration on the victory stand. But 270 people, students mostly, were murdered by government troops, shot down in a limited enclosure called the Plaza de las Tres Culturas basically because the games were to start in 10 days, and the president, Diaz Ordaz, didn't want unsightly things such as proposed student demonstrators presenting a bad image of the country to the rest of the world. So he had them killed.

I didn't realize the extent of what had happened when I arrived in Mexico City less than a week after the killings. No one did, or at least none of the sportswriters. Except for Chris Brasher. To this day he remains the finest journalist I've ever worked with. Bespectacled, studious looking, he'd hardly have been taken for the great athlete he once was — Olympic steeplechase champion, pace-setter for Dr. Roger Bannister in the greatest mile race ever run, when his Oxford teammate became the first man to break the four-minute barrier. He wrote a column for the *New York Observer* in those days. He was a digger, a fellow who couldn't be intimidated by the power elite, and he was at his best at the Olympics, as I found out when we became friends in Tokyo.

A few days before the Opening Ceremony I got a call from Chris Brasher. "I'm going down to the Plaza of the Three Cultures to look around. Do you want to come?" So we took a walk around the plaza. There were bullet holes everywhere. And policemen, who seemed uneasy about our taking notes. Somehow Chris had rounded up a couple of university students who said they had been there during the killings.

"Bloodstains," one of them said, pointing to a dark patch on the wall. "They couldn't clean them all up. This was where many were shot. Mixed in the crowd were government provocateurs. We had been warned about them. They were identifiable by a white glove on one hand. They'd raise the glove, then move away, and then shots would follow."

I tried calling a few members of the Mexico City Organizing Committee. Either unavailable, or they knew nothing about what I was referring to, or all of a sudden, my college Spanish was incomprehensible. I spoke to a few International Olympic Committee delegates. The basic sentiment was, "We're not here to talk about politics. At every Olympic meeting, you hear all sorts of stories." Foolishly, I tried to reach Avery Brundage, the IOC president. I had left a couple of messages. Older writers, especially nationally famous columnists, had quoted Brundage on occasion. They usually took care of him in print. The hardest adjective they used to describe him was "crusty," or occasionally they'd refer to him in a favorite descriptive of doddering journalists, as a "curmudgeon." Mention generally was made about his unyielding dedication to the spirit of amateurism.

It was Brundage, as head of the U.S. Olympic Committee, who had practically bludgeoned America into attending the 1936 Olympics in Berlin. There had been a protest movement growing about honoring a regime that was rumored to be waging wholesale persecution of Jews, including prospective members of its own Olympic team, but Brundage had gone to Germany on a two-week blitz tour to see for himself. "Are the Jews treated fairly?" He said when he returned. "Yes, they are." History has exposed this awful lie, but Brundage's influence and pervasive anti-Semitism even reached into the heart of the American team. Until the day he died, Marty Glickman, a Jewish sprinter from Syracuse, felt that Brundage had pressured the American track coach, Dean Cromwell, into scratching at the last minute Glickman and Sam Stoller, the only two Jewish athletes on the team, from the sprint relay, although they had qualified.

"It came from Brundage," Glickman said. "He didn't want to offend his German hosts."

I had done a research project on Brundage, a proud member of an ultra right-wing group called the America First Committee, whose primary objective was to keep America out of a European war. In 1940 student members of this committee had circulated a petition that said, "We demand that Congress refrain from war, even if England is on the verge of defeat." But even the America Firsters couldn't put up with Brundage after he addressed a German Day rally in Madison Square Garden three weeks after the Berlin Games and told 20,000 sieg-heiling bundists and sympathizers, dressed in their brown shirts and swastikas, "We can learn much from Nazi Germany." They severed relations with him.

"The Olympics must go on," became the mantra of this blind demigod. Those with short memories praised him for it. World War II signaled the postponement of the 1940 Olympics, despite Brundage's vehement protests. Japan had invaded Manchuria in 1937, the same year as the infamous "Rape of Nanking," when the butchery of the emperor's imperial troops resulted in the death of 100,000 to 200,000 civilians (estimate of Japanese researchers) or 150,000 to 300,000 (Chinese accounts). And where was the proposed site of this Olympiad that Brundage struggled so hard to maintain? Tokyo, of course.

I had written all this. I had written about his visit to the USSR when it was seeking re-admission to the games in 1952. It hadn't taken part since Czarist times, preferring to hold its own competitions, called Spartakiads, and there was some opposition to a state-run system of rewarding its athletes, especially when the Olympic committee paid so much lip service to the principles of strict amateurism. The format was the same, the blitz tour by Brundage, the carefully orchestrated visits to see only what his hosts wanted him to see, gifts ... this was a new thing ... icons, elaborate examples of traditional Russian art ... and how Brundage, an important collector of art objects, loved his trinkets.

When he returned he was glowing with praise. America certainly would do well to copy the enthusiasm and dedication of the Russian athletes. The state-run system? "That's their way of life," he said. Oh yes, politics and sport do not mix.

Would I get a response to the questions I wanted to put to Brundage, specifically about the massacre at the Plaza? Not likely. Which doesn't mean I didn't see the man himself. I saw him one day when I was driving on the Periferico, the highway ringing the city. I was in the right lane, minding my own business when all of a sudden there was a huge clamor of sirens and horns and flashing lights. Motorcycle cops came shooting by, cars with official Olympic markings, and in the middle of it all, a black limo with Brundage seated in the rear, back straight, eyes staring straight ahead, the perfect example of the Olympic ideal on its way to clear up some matter of utmost urgency. A few minutes later, I saw a similar entourage, this time in the lanes approaching. Same noise, lights, fanfare. Same limo containing Brundage, eyes still fixed on the near horizon, posture still erect. The motorcade had missed its exit, so now it was doubling back. I led my piece with the scene as a metaphor for the years of Olympic direction exerted by this man: Avery Brundage. Rushing to Nowhere.

I got that one transmitted, but when I tried to write about what I had seen and heard regarding the killings, there were problems. It was one of the early stories I filed from Mexico City. One or two previous ones had been sent. But all of a sudden, the transmission facilities were down when I tried to send this one. No one knew when they'd be restored. Again Chris Brasher came through for me.

"The government's tampering with the transmission," he said. And then he got me in touch with a Pan Am pilot he knew, who hand carried some of my pieces back to New York and turned them over to a messenger at the airport. And then the games began, and transmission was restored.

I had come from a 1964 Olympic world that had been daisyland, but now the real world was intruding. I was faced with the kind of dilemma every newspaper writer experiences, the matter of emphasis. To cover the world's greatest sporting event and gloss over its terrible preamble, as some other writers had infuriatingly done, would be unthinkable. And yet, how long does one keep flogging it when it was obvious that the government was pretending that it never happened, and none of the Olympic delegates I had mentioned it to were inclined to take any kind of stand or even afford it more than passing recognition, if that?

There comes a time when you can become a Johnny One Note to your readers. Yes, we agree with you. Yes, it's deplorable. But please, not day after day of this. Cover the Olympics for a change. I had worked for a couple of years on the *New York Post* with Leonard Shecter, who did a magnificent job of co-authoring Jim Bouton's hilarious baseball diary, *Ball Four*. But Shecter also wrote a lesser known work called *The Jocks*, the very title of which suggested his dislike of the sport itself. Almost every review I read of it used the buzzword "iconoclast" to describe Shecter, but I had a better descriptive for him. Bitter. Yes, he destroyed images, but he destroyed other things as well. Sports people didn't like him. He didn't like them. His life on the beat was not easy. *The Jocks* was his get-even work, and it made for uncomfortable reading. Yes, much of what he wrote was true, but it was so mean-spirited that the effect was like listening to a non-stop complainer. Is that what I wanted to be, a kind of spider, slinking around the periphery of the Olympics?

I had loved sports all my life. Sports got me to college, gave me an education, even an under-the-counter entry into journalism school, when Lou Little the football coach at Columbia, told Dean Barrett of the J-School, "I don't care about his grades ... take him; he's a good kid." But people such as Brundage were destroying sport at its highest level. Could I just suck it up and go back to the basketball arena and the track stadium? Well, yes. I was getting paid. And I loved the panorama of the sport itself. But what would happen as the games wound down would make the question academic and create one of the most memorable incidents in Olympic history and would turn the massacre into a footnote, in retrospect.

You remember brief snatches of exhilaration, brief bursts of emotion in the 1968 Olympics. I was sitting among the British track writers on the day that England's Dave Hemery won the 400-meter hurdles, and when he crossed the finish line in a world record time of 48.12, they let out a roar that shook their one little area. British reserve? Not that day. The explosion that came from that collection of properly dressed journalists in their 40s and 50s was something I wish someone would have captured on film. Sometimes, in the bustle of too many events going off at once, you lose track of something, a high jump attempt while a race is in progress, a qualifier in the discus. But some instinct made me lock into Bob Beamon every time he ran down the long jump runway, and I saw his 29-2 ½, which remained the world record for 23 years, and it was as close to athletic perfection in both grace and explosive power as I'd ever seen. Only Jim Brown, on some of his more spectacular runs, could match it in my eyes.

And then there was this one persistent reminder, this nagging substrate, that this wasn't the best of all worlds, that the ugly taint of nationalism involving a country that had committed a terrible crime would hang over the entire competition. You'd be in the boxing or basketball arena or at the swimming pool. And all of a sudden, someone, perhaps a fan, more like a government plant, would stand up and launch a cheer for the host nation, and others would join in. I'm not sure I have it exactly right; it would start off something like an old college football yell of the 1920s, "Alla-vee, alla-vay!" And it would end, "Mexico, Mexico, Yay! Yay! Yay!" Over and over again. I was frankly sick of it, sick of that pistol government and its phony nationalism and government thugs. And then came the incident with the black glove salute.

It had been building up for almost a year. In 1967, under the leadership of Harry Edwards, a sociology professor at San Jose State, a Black Athletes Boycott Committee, later changed to Olympic Project for Human Rights, was formed. The purpose was to organize a boycott of the '68 Olympics unless certain demands were met, including Brundage's resignation, the appointment of one black member to the American Olympic Committee, a restoration of Muhammad Ali's championship, etc. Proposed Olympic boycotts had enjoyed some recent success. In May of '67, Brundage had gotten the IOC to readmit South Africa, which had been expelled in '64 because of its apartheid policy. Thirty-two African nations threatened to boycott the games. The number eventually grew to 40, and the IOC backed down. Brundage was tougher against the Edwards group, though.

"If the American Negroes boycott the Olympics, they won't be missed," he said. The boycott died from lack of support by the athletes themselves, but something clearly was in the works. It broke, of course, when San Jose State teammates Tommie Smith and John Carlos won the gold and bronze medals, respectively, in the 200 meters and staged their symbolic demonstration on the victory stand. Eyes turned downward, one black gloved fist raised, the right for Smith, left for Carlos, shoeless but wearing long black socks, the Olympic Project for Human Rights medallion on their chests, they presented an imposing picture during the abbreviated version of the national anthem that's traditionally played at the games.

It has become an event frozen in time. People who weren't there have spoken about it intimately. Many others claimed to be present, as they had for other landmark events such as Dwight Clark's catch against the Cowboys in the NFC championship or the Lou Gehrig farewell in Yankee Stadium, or Bill Bradley's 42 against Michigan in the Holiday Festival Tournament in the Garden. I've read dozens of versions of how writers were personally affected by the brief Smith and Carlos tableau ... I guess "chilling" was the most common descriptive although you'd find a "disgraceful" here and there, not as often as Harry Edwards would have you believe, but it was an adjective leaned on by the right wingers among us. I also saw one or two "inspirings."

I am looking back through my set of clips on the incident. What did I call it? I didn't call it anything. I speculated that Smith's gloved right hand and Carlos' gloved left hand probably meant that they had only one pair of gloves between them. Was I chilled? Outraged? Honestly, no. I felt that I had seen a puzzle solved. I knew something would happen, I just didn't know where or when. Then it happened and it was up to me to cover it and try to present it as clearly as I could from as many angles as possible, and then, when some air had been put under it, I could sort it out and provide an overview.

I even found my old notebook. There was a smattering of boos as Smith and Carlos walked off the stand. They looked grim, but Australia's Peter

Norman, the silver medalist who had specifically requested — and worn — the Olympic Project button in support, looked pretty happy, probably remembering the way he got it.

"I asked for one," he said later. "Before we went to the stand, Smith asked someone he knew in the crowd for his button. The guy refused. Then Carlos took over. He said, 'Hand that thing over.' And that's how I got my button."

I filed three first-day pieces, at least that many follow-up stories, plus a column. I remember it was a nonstop hustle for quotes. I was covering the games by myself. You had to keep moving. I did a feature on Norman, a fascinating character who taught school in Melbourne during the week and worked for the Salvation Army on weekends and would even race, wearing a Salvation Army shirt. I covered the post-event press conferences. Carlos was rambunctious ... I had known him when he used to compete as a New York high schooler in the meets at the 168th St. Armory.

"Now you've done it," I said when I had a moment alone with him.

"Man, don't I know it?" he said. "But you know ... it feels good."

Smith was quiet and deliberate. "The totality of our effort was the regaining of black dignity," he said, slowly, so that the journalists, especially the foreign ones, would get it right. I talked to both their wives. "Does the American Negro ... ?" a European writer began, but they quickly corrected him. "Black! Black!" they said, one-two, quick-march. That was way before the term "African American" joined the vocabulary.

There was breaking news to report, a response from the American Olympic Committee to find out about, from the track team, the IOC ... but not Brundage. The black athletes had requested that he not be on hand to give them their medals, and he had retired from the fray. How about other demonstrations? A few runners, including 400-meter man Lee Evans, another San Jose Stater, had worn the long black socks, "pimp socks," they used to call them in some neighborhoods in New York. The black socks, unaccompanied by shoes, Smith had explained, represented the poverty of the black people. Would black socks worn by others be considered a protest? And if so, what was the official position? And how about the black berets? The 400-meter men were rumored to be considering wearing them on the stand during the playing of the anthem. Would this be bad enough to get them ... get them what? (Actually they did wear berets, but since it was raining at the time, it went down as a standoff.) I know it sounds silly, looking back at all this, but at the time it was rush, rush, get your stuff filed, think about it later.

I know I had to get into the Olympic Village as soon as possible. If there was to be any action, it would start there. I had a car. The village had two gates, each one manned by a couple of security guys. I had made a goofy pass, consisting of various TV logos pasted in a montage on a piece of 8 x 11 poster board. I would put it on the dashboard, with my press credential and driver's license attached to it, mumble "Televisa Europa," to the guards and keep moving. There was no up and down security arm. That was the key: to keep moving while they were scratching their heads. One time Brent Musburger, who now does the college football for ABC but was a Chicago newspaperman in those days, was in the car with me. He nearly blew it for me because he was laughing so hard. To this day, whenever he sees me, he'll greet me with, "Televisa Europa."

It was in the village that the word came down that Smith and Carlos had been banished from the team and the country and given 48 hours to clear out. I had gotten some early quotes from U.S. Olympic Committee president Doug Roby about how he had issued an apology to the Olympic organizers, and he hoped that would cover it. Or maybe he was expecting the demonstrators to issue some apology; it wasn't certain. But 12 hours later, Brundage or, it was rumored, an official from the State Department, had gotten to Roby and firmed him up at the punishment level. I had been there when Smith and Carlos first came back to their dorm. They passed two coaches along the way.

Hilmer Lodge, the Chairman of the Track and Field Committee ... good natured, fatherly, for many years a much beloved figure in West Coast circles ... went with his basic instinct.

"Hey, Tommie, great race," he said. Smith had suffered a groin strain in the semis and had gutted it out in the final, setting a world record.

Stanford coach Payton Jordan, the American Olympic head coach, turned his head away abruptly as they passed. A day later, as word leaked out that Smith and Carlos had been expelled, the village was opened to reporters, and the American compound came alive. Any black athlete was immediately surrounded, actually anyone wearing a U.S. sweat suit. On the steps of the American dorm sat a big, smiling kid waving a tiny American flag. George Foreman, 19, soon to be Olympic heavyweight boxing champion. Your opinion, please.

"Don't have one," he said. "I'm just having a good time here."

I have scattered notes on events that happened so fast that I didn't have time to date them ... Carlos heckles a Roby press conference from his eighth-floor dorm window ... hangs a sign, "Brundage Must Go"... two more signs from athletes' dorms, "Wallace for President" and "Win in Vietnam"... Carlos and wife exit the village ... Parisian newsman sticks his head in the window of his car. "We're weez you, Carlos," he says.

The overview piece I wrote when it was all wrapped up was that the USOC and whoever got to it could have handled it with intelligence instead of the heavy boot. A protest? Well, OK, isn't America supposed to be all about the spirit of protest? How about a nice dignified statement, "We certainly don't agree with what they did, but here in America we recognize a person's right to protest?" But this was Roby's official position, prompted by the mounting criticism of athletes and officials from more than 100 nations, and expressed in a single mimeographed page:

"We recognize that these incidents may be the result of granting athletes what might be considered excessive freedom in the cause of human rights, freedom granted by some of our coaches and managers during the four weeks in training before coming to Mexico."

Short and blocky, bull-necked with a head that looked like a concrete block and contained about as much brains, that was Roby. I wrote in my notebook at the time, "Where do they find these guys?"

I talked to Edwards about it some years later. He said he celebrated when he read Roby's statement. "It isn't often that your enemy presents himself so clearly," he said.

Press reaction to the incident never really has been accurately presented, I believe. The athletes themselves, even one as reflective as Smith, described how they had been vilified by the press. Not entirely true. Sure, the conservatives took them on and waved the flag, but overall, Roby and Brundage got just as much, if not more, heat by the way they had handled the whole thing. And European newsmen, especially the British, were almost overwhelmingly in Smith and Carlos' corner.

Somehow it rubbed me wrong, though, when a young British writer showed me a think piece he had written about America and its miserable black-white relations, going back to slave days, based on this incident. Of course it was and still is a legitimate concern, but it was also an easy angle at the time to neglect any progress that had been made and paint, with a very heavy British brush, the primitive state Americans found themselves in. And besides, wasn't England's whole history of involvement in the slave trade about as bleak as ours? As I said, it was just a personal thing, an annoyance. Maybe the piece deserved to be written, I felt, but not by you, Jack.

Edwards, who got his PhD and became Dr. Harry Edwards shortly thereafter and whom I've dealt with for many years since then (he became the 49ers' consultant and liaison man for black players), was a different story. When I read his quotes about the hostile press, I got on the phone immediately.

I reminded him about the story I had worked on with him about the boycott of the track meet sponsored by the restricted New York AC in the Garden earlier that year, 1968. I reminded him of all the sessions I had covered in Harlem, all the press conferences in storefront offices, H. Rap Brown, who was later convicted of shooting two police officers, standing up there telling us that he'd "blow up the Garden" if he had to. I reminded him of how the New York press covered all that, tongue in cheek about Brown's statement … I mean, he didn't get the name, Rap, for nothing … and how the treatment of the prospective boycott, which proved successful, was generally evenhanded and fair. Was this part of the press he had singled out as being ready to vilify Smith and Carlos?

I don't remember exactly what he said, but it couldn't have been too bad because we have remained cordial. Through the years it's just that I'm so tired of seeing the press demonized for propaganda purposes. But that's another story.

Munich 1972

Munich was about the murder of 11 athletes and coaches. Everything else was a subplot. But it was a subplot with substance, with bitterness and mind-numbing inefficiency and pettiness by an American team that became the world's laughingstock, a grotesque counterpoint to the tragedy of death. It was about indifference to human misery, from the athletes to the very top of Olympic officialdom, on a scale that I wouldn't have thought possible if I hadn't seen it for myself.

And that's what finally did it for me, what finally drove me out of this miserable arena three days before the competition officially ended. I'm sure you could find contributing factors — too many days of non-stop crises that broke some of the best and toughest reporters, too many nights of one and two hours sleep, taking a rifle butt to the head by a line of German security guards, watching a fellow reporter thrown down a flight of stairs when he tried to do his job, yes, by that same set of pseudo-policemen that botched the attempt to rescue the doomed athletes. I wasn't tough enough, you say? Maybe you're right, but you see it just came down to the fact that I didn't care anymore how high they jumped or how fast they ran. I wrote about the awfulness of human behavior that I watched, from a very close vantage point — too close, maybe — and then I came home.

The first crisis was taking place before I even got to Munich. The African nations and individual black athletes wanted Rhodesia kicked out for discriminatory policies. They were urging white American Olympians not to compete if Rhodesia was still in.

"Yeah, Lee Evans talked to me about it," said Milt Sonsky, an American javelin thrower who happened to be Jewish. "I told him, 'I can see it now. I can see myself trying to get you guys to boycott the Olympics because Russia doesn't let Jews leave the country.' You know what they'd tell me to do?"

Rhodesia was kicked out at the last moment over the strong objections of International Olympic Committee president Avery Brundage, who had yet to recognize that any kind of discrimination ever had existed in an athletic nation, be it Germany under Hitler or South Africa under apartheid. But Sonsky had touched on something deeper on the American team, torn into factions by its strange, moody coach, Bill Bowerman of the University of Oregon. He had organized a set of practice meets the week before the competition started, a procedure no one liked. He had conned Vince Matthews, a 400-meter man, into believing that if Evans beat him in one of those competitions he could take away his place on the team, even though Bowerman knew it was impossible. The entries already had been announced. The team was a seething mass of hatred and petty jealousies spurred on by the coach.

"The way it is here," Sonsky said, "the weight men stay with the weight men, the conservative guys with the conservatives, the blacks with the blacks. I've never even been introduced to Jim Ryun. I don't think he even knows who I am."

The Rhodesia situation was just calming down when crisis No. 2 broke. American sprinters Reynaud Robinson and Eddie Hart, each of whom had won his heat in the opening round of the 100 meters, missed the start of the second round five hours later. Blew it. Missed it cold. The word from the track and field staff was a noise like an oyster. Larry Merchant, our lead columnist on the *New York Post*, and I got our asses over to the American dorm in a hurry. The athletes we talked to were in a state of shock, as puzzled as we were.

"Could you see this happening on the Russian team?" said George Frenn, the weight thrower.

"They'd have somebody out back with a pistol to his head."

On a bulletin board downstairs, we got our answer. The schedule that was posted was a year and a half old, a preliminary listing at best. But it never had been updated. Exact times for the start of each event were vague. Some of them, including the heats of the 100, had been changed. Bowerman's staff hadn't even seen fit to get them corrected.

We were on the second floor when the police arrived. They wore the powder blue blazers, the color deliberately selected to denote friendliness and softness, the epitome of "The New Germany, heralding what will be known as The Carefree Games," the PR brochure had said. They were led by an American in a business suit, powder blue, of course, in keeping with the motif. I had seen this guy before. Fairly young, thin, soft-spoken in a kind of a sneaky, lisping way. I couldn't quite figure him out. An intelligence operative of some sort? Didn't really seem the type, but who knew? He did serve as a kind of half-assed commandant of the security group. All I knew was that he gave me the creeps.

"Out of here," he said. "Out."

"Look, we're trying to do our ..." Larry said, but he never got the "job" part out. One of the powder blue security guys had him by the armpits and in one yank heaved him down the flight of wooden stairs. Larry, who now announces the televised fights for HBO, stands about 5-6. He literally flew, bounced a couple of times, and came to rest at the bottom of the staircase. By this time I had my glasses and watch off, my fake front tooth, on what's called a "flipper," out and in my pocket.

"Get their press IDs," the CIA guy, or whatever the hell he was, said. Ohhhh no you don't! To part with that meant never ending hardship during the Olympic duration. Down the stairs I went. They didn't try to stop me. Larry was on his feet by now. They had his press pass. I got him out of the dorm, a bit shaky, but he was a tough little guy and he turned out to be OK.

Except that he didn't get his credential back for a couple of days, each one involving reporting to the security HQ until they figured that he'd learned his lesson.

"Heil Hitler, you bastards!" Frenn was yelling. "Zieg heil, you sons of bitches!" An athlete actually on our side? Wow!

By now the place was buzzing, writers, photographers, TV cameramen, all outside the American dorm, looking for answers, trying to pin this monumental foul-up on somebody, anybody. Stan Wright, the assistant track coach, took the fall. It was his job to get the sprinters to the stadium. Robinson and Hart caught their share of heat as well. Pampered athletes, who couldn't even find their way to the bathroom unless someone led them there, was the general tone. I laid it off mostly on Bowerman, plus the American Olympic brass that couldn't even assign someone to making sure they had correct schedules.

That night Wright faced the few writers who had been told about the informal press conference that had been arranged at an ABC-TV studio. That's the way they did things over there. Everything sotto voce. He took the blame. He mentioned that the schedule was mistaken. "My God," I said to somebody. "They still don't know the one they have is obsolete."

Hart was supposed to say his piece after Wright got through. It would be the only statement we'd get from one of the runners. It never happened. As soon as Wright finished, Ralph Boston, the former long jump champion who was working this Olympics as a "runner" for ABC, grabbed Hart, pulled him outside, and they took off, sprinting to a pre-arranged sub-studio where Howard Cosell was waiting for an exclusive interview. A beautiful double-cross.

I can feel it right now, standing outside, watching them disappearing, finally yelling like a disgruntled suitor heaving a shoe at the wedding procession, "I'll never forget this, Ralph!" He gave me a wave without turning around. A great athlete, yes. A great competitor. But he'll never get a Christmas card from me.

Following almost immediately came Crisis No. 3. Rick DeMont, a 16-year-old swimmer from San Rafael, Calif., had been stripped of his gold medal in the 400-meter freestyle and was suspended from further competition because he had taken Marax, an asthma medicine he had used since he was a child. It contained a banned substance, ephedrine. This was in the pre-steroid testing era. Ephedrine was listed as a stimulant.

We rushed through our stories about the missed heats of the 100, assigned blame, agonized, moralized, drew conclusions and wheeled 180 degrees to meet this new emergency. We had a one-page statement and little else. Where to turn? The American swimming federation was of little help. If you could find someone to quote, he'd generally shrug and say, "Let's not be too eager to assign blame," the same as the track people said, except for poor Stan Wright. It had become an American mantra. The most sensible statement of all came from a Belgian, and a royal one at that, Prince Alexandre de Merode, the chairman of the IOC's Medical Council. He laid the blame squarely on the U.S. doctors. DeMont had correctly listed Marax as a medication he took. It was up to the American medical staff to forward the information to the IOC for clearance. No one did.

"A 16-year-old boy is being made to pay for the sins of people who should know better," Prince de Merode said. "The medical authorities from other countries all submitted the names of drugs for clearance. Why didn't the Americans?"

Why indeed? Stories were being written and rewritten and filed and then rewritten again. Deadlines were being blown, nerves were fraying. We needed a quote from Dr. Winston Riehl, the head physician of the American Olympic team. Unavailable, of course. Never available for the entire Olympic period. His statement came a month later in a forum that allowed no questioning, a bylined article in the *American Medical News*, house organ for the AMA. Dr. Riehl's statement was that it was up to the boy himself to get information to the IOC. If he would have pulled a stunt like that at a press conference, he would have been laughed off the podium, but this was the friendly arena of a doctor talking to doctors.

Of course we didn't know this at the time. We were a thrashing mass of writers, trying to get the thing sorted out, fully unable to grasp the monumental incompetence of the American Olympic contingent. And it was all happening under deadline pressure and intense competition.

I saw a lot of good writers crack up that night — just too many crises on top of each other. Next to me in the press room, Stan Hochman, a tough columnist from Philadelphia, leaned back in his chair, stared at the ceiling and murmured, "I just can't go anymore. I can't do it. It's too much." I had seen this happen before ... hell, it had happened to me. I had been talked through more than one impossible story by an older colleague.

"Come on, Stan," I told him. "Lead with the Merode quote. Take a rip at the American doctors for not being here. Go get 'em." So he went back to his typewriter. So did I. And if someone were to tell us that this was just window dressing compared to what lay ahead, I wouldn't have believed him.

Since Munich, I must have read 100 reports of the events leading up to, and after, the killing of the 11 Israelis and five Palestinian terrorists and a German policeman. I have interviewed survivors. I sat through a phony Steven Spielberg movie about Israeli retribution based on the story of a self-proclaimed Mossad operative who actually had failed basic training in the Israeli defense force and was employed as a gate guard for El Al Airlines in New York. I cannot add anything by weighing in with my own version of what happened on September 5 or what went wrong. But I can tell you what I saw in the Olympic Village that day and what it was like during that period and afterward.

And I can tell you what it is like to have your spirit crushed by the realization that the bulk of the people you are there to write about have little conception of death or suffering or anything except their own limited sphere. Of course I knew all this already, that if someone claiming to be a reporter would try to pump his own set of values into other people, he'd be better off writing essays or addressing study groups. But the message in Munich was so dramatic that it startled me. They just don't care. It's all meaningless to them. Maybe the idea was more poignant because it involved the doomed Israelis whom they didn't care about, Jews, my own people. The us-against-them syndrome. But I had been through the army and a lifetime of organized sports, venues which at times were not particularly receptive to the chosen people without major mishap. This, however, was different.

When I woke up on Tuesday, Sept. 5, the takeover of the Israeli compound was all over the news. I went by the press center. TVs were on everywhere. Announcements would be forthcoming, we were told, when something new was learned. I've always hated the deadening atmosphere of the official press center at just about every major sports event, waiting for press conferences, the milling about, the interviewing of one other. Sometimes you can't avoid it. You're pinned, such as at the Super Bowls these days and, I would assume, at the recent Olympics, from what people have told me. But security was loose at Munich. That's how the Palestinians had managed to infiltrate the Israeli dorm with such apparent ease. It was still early on this Tuesday morning, maybe still time to get into the Olympic Village, to see for myself what was going on.

I had my rental car and my homemade parking pass, with an ABC-TV logo and all sorts of other colorful nonsense and a gray blurry picture of myself next to the lettering I had done with my own hand: *DURCHFAHRT*. "Drive Through." In previous days it had gotten me into the garage next to the village but not this time. They were in the process of firming up security. I parked in the street and approached the main gate. Two lines were being formed. The Olympic Organizing Committee had bragged that in honor of The Carefree Olympics they would arm their security people only with walkie-talkies, certainly not guns, but that bit of fluff was over.

I showed my press credential. I was waved away. I turned, took two steps, cut back and bolted for what looked like the least organized part of the phalanx. My God, I had gotten through. Whack! It was like running into a tree branch while you were looking behind you. I had been knocked to my knees by a rifle butt in the side of the head. I scrambled up and tried to keep running. People were shouting. They had a choice: break ranks and chase me, start shooting or just let this lunatic go. They chose the latter.

"Loony, loony, loony!" a couple of writers told me later. "They were ready for anything. Terrorists had gotten in. You could have gotten shot … SHOULD have gotten shot. What the hell were you thinking of?"

I was thinking of nothing except that my head hurt, and that's the truth.

I found the Israeli dorm at 31 Connollystrasse. Ropes had been stretched in front of it. The drama already was being played out, the masked terrorist negotiating with the police, the guy with the white hat. Across the street was the Italian dorm. I went up to the roof and found a vantage point. People were coming up there in twos and threes. Someone had a radio, news of the hostage crisis interspersed with music. We watched. Not a whole lot was happening. After a while a table was set up. Someone brought a couple of bottles. There were glasses, sandwiches. "My God," I thought. "It's turned into a cocktail party."

I went downstairs and took a look around the area. I heard music coming from the athletes' recreation area 300 yards away. Rock music, accompanied by the cling-cling of pinball machines. It was a pretty day. On a grassy patch nearby, you could see the slow gyrations of the athletes dancing to the music. The miniature golf course was getting plenty of action, the oversized checker board, the ping pong tables. Recreation as usual. Very few people showed an interest in the drama of life and death that was taking place down the street where nine bound Israelis stared into the mouths of Kalashnikov-47's ... they had less than 12 hours to live. It was a picture of widespread indifference.

I walked back to the roped off area in front of 31 Connollystrasse. Negotiations were still going on between the terrorists — at first thought to be members of a special group called Black September but later identified by Abu Daoud, who planned the attack, as Fatah agents of Yasser Arafat's Palestinian Liberation Organization — and the security forces. John Forster, an American rower whom I knew, stood alongside and watched with me.

"I walked around there, trying to find out how a guy could play a pinball machine when people were facing death a few hundred yards away," he said. "A couple of kayakers just walked by here. They were talking about their race. You wonder about people's order of priorities. Over there by the ping pong tables, everyone's still on vacation. They just don't know what a crisis is. For them all this is just the six o'clock news. Just part of the Disneyland they're living in."

I started writing and phoning it in to the *Post* in pieces. The *Post* was an afternoon paper that could do updates all day long, allowing for the six-hour time difference. I hunted down Shaul Ladany, a 50-kilometer race walker on the Israeli team whom I'd known when he competed indoors in New York. He'd been a professor in the Rutgers Business School. I found a little room where we could talk. There were no other writers around. The ABC-TV crew had gotten into the village that day, but no other reporters.

"Instead of coming to the room where I lived with the fencers and marksmen," he said, "the terrorists went to the strongmen's room, the wrestlers and weightlifters. And that's what saved my life. Weinberg, the wrestling coach, and Romano, the weightlifter, held them off at the door and gave us time to escape. They were both killed.

"You know," he said, "it was risky coming here into West Germany. The country is filled with little cell groups of Arab terrorist organizations. It was pointed out to the German authorities, but they chose to do nothing about it."

"What can you do now?" I asked him.

"One of the things is counter-measures of the same nature," he said. "Every country has hot-headed young men just waiting to be turned loose. Israel is no exception."

The actual revenge operation was carried out by loosely defined Mossad hit teams — not Yuval Aviv, the fraudulent operative who fooled Spielberg and his crew. But it was the underlings who were slain, not Abu Daoud, who planned the Munich killings. In 1999 he wrote a book called *Palestine: From Jerusalem to Munich*, which detailed the operation and won him 10,000 French francs and the Palestine Prize for Culture. Three years later the book was translated from French to English under the title, *Memoirs of a Palestinian Terrorist.*

Arafat, who authorized the operation, sending Daoud off with the words, "Allah be with you," was awarded one third of the Nobel Peace Prize in 1994. Six years later his official newspaper, *Al-Hayat Al-Jadida*, urged Arab nations to boycott the Olympic Games in Australia because a moment of silence had been planned in memory of the 11 slain Israelis.

As the day wore on, I kept returning to the site of the hostage operation and just before they were taken away by bus to the helicopters that would signal their ultimate death I saw a sight I will never forget. By some sort of unspoken communication, a gathering of some of the world's great Jewish athletes had formed outside the ropes. I recognized Abby Hoffman, the women's 800-meter champion of Canada, and Irena Szewinska, formerly Irena Kirszenstein, the great Polish Olympic sprint champion, and a few others. They stood in a group, silent, watching, held together in some sort of speechless bond.

At 11 o'clock that night, Conrad Ahlers, a government spokesman, said all the hostages were liberated. It went out on the wires. I was downtown, accompanied by a German newsman I knew who acted as translator. I wanted to find out how the people of Munich felt about what was happening at their Olympics. Basically indifferent, except for a few hours later, when the news of the deaths became official. Then there was resentment and a strong concern for all the deutschmarks the country stood to lose if the Olympics were canceled.

"Our mistake was having the Israelis and the Arabs both in the Olympics," was an opinion I heard more than once. "We should have kept them both out."

"So soon?" said Nissim Kivity, a London-based Israeli journalist when I mentioned it to him the next day. "I thought that kind of thinking wouldn't come for at least a week."

I had been working round the clock. On the morning of the 6th, I was battling waves of fatigue, but the news I heard brought some life to my step. *The New York Times* had decided to roll in the heavy artillery. David Binder, the head of their Bonn Bureau, and Flora Lewis, one of their leading op-ed columnists, had been called in to firm up their coverage. The village was accessible on that Wednesday. I had morning appointments set up with a couple more Israeli athletes. I was walking down the main street when I got the feeling I was being followed. Sure enough ... red face, dark business suit ... I recognized Binder. And the woman with him had to be Flora Lewis. I picked up the pace, entered the jewelry store that had been popular with the athletes, walked through it quickly and out the back door. "Two-dooring," we used to call it when I was in school. And proceeded to my interviews. It was one of the few uppers during a dismal period.

The official mourning ceremony was awful and it finally convinced me that I just couldn't stay there anymore. The older Israeli officials sat in the front row, their faces twisted in grief. How many times before? And over the amplifiers came the booming voice of Brundage, offering a final touch of inhumanity.

"Two savage attacks!" he said, lumping the 11 deaths with his own personal demon, the ouster of Rhodesia. "It was the first time in 20 years that the Committee has gone against me," he had said, his voice shaking with rage, when he first heard that the IOC had voted Rhodesia out. And in the face of a far greater tragedy, he still couldn't let go of it.

Some nations chose to respect Israel's sorrow. Some did not. After the mourning ceremony, I ran into Clifford Buck, the head of the American Olympic Committee. I asked him how he felt about what had happened.

"Wait till I've had my lunch first," he said.

"We didn't send any flowers, we didn't stop our practices for a minute of silent prayer," said Rod Milburn, an American gold medalist in the high hurdles. "Officially, we didn't do a thing."

The Russians, naturally, ducked the mourning ceremony. It made no sense to alienate the Arab nations, with whom the Soviets did business. "I believe we had our International Olympic Committee member at the ceremony," said Idar Valiachmetiv, the Soviet press chief, although he wasn't sure. The Russian athletes spent most of the day sunbathing and horsing around in front of their dorm. When the ceremony was ending, a group of them passed by, raucous, noisy, on their way to soccer practice.

Now in two days I'm supposed to go out and cover Russia vs. USA in basketball and sit down and write hard copy about the Soviet zone defense, I was thinking. Sorry, I can't do it.

At nine o'clock that night, after the ceremony, 70,000 fans, equipped with noisemakers and flags, filled the stadium to watch Hungary play Germany in soccer. A banner was hung in the stands: 17 DEAD, ALREADY FORGOTTEN? Security forces took down the sign. The offenders were expelled.

The games would go on, but not every heart was in them. Wilma Van Gool, a Dutch sprinter, had developed a friendship with Israeli sprinter and hurdler Esther Roth-Shahamorov, whose coach had been killed. The Israeli athletes were no longer competing. Van Gool dropped out of the semifinals of the 200 meters. She said she just couldn't compete any more. I heard other isolated stories. The Norwegian team handball contingent said they couldn't continue. The Handball Federation informed them that if they dropped out they would be expelled from the federation. So they competed.

On Thursday the 7th, I made one last visit to 31 Connollystrasse. There were notices on the bulletin board about an upcoming Rosh Hashanah party, a few personal messages. My sense of outrage that I'd felt for the last two days had turned into a heavy, deadening sadness. I was glad I was getting out of there. I had already written a signoff column for the *Post*. I didn't know how they'd take it.

Rupert Murdoch, who bought the *Post* five years later, probably would have fired me. But the paper in those days was the only liberal daily in the city. My editor told me that I had caught the mood of the paper's readership. Everyone had been numbed by what happened. Watch the rest of the games on TV, write a few overview pieces if I felt like it, then go back on the Jets beat. Oh yes, we've put you in for a Pulitzer. I didn't win it, but I was told that I'd been a finalist, whatever that meant.

America closed out the competition as the world's whiners. Stan Wright had filed an appeal, concerning the missed heats of the 100. The bus had been caught in traffic, he said. The appeals board laughed at him. Vince Matthews won the gold medal in the 400, and Wayne Collett took the silver, and on the victory stand, they staged some half-assed demonstration involving chatting with each other and shuffling their feet during the anthem. It was a poor imitation of the black gloves of Mexico City, and I guessed that it was Matthews' way of getting back at Bowerman as much as anyone for what he had put him through before the games started. Mount Olympus took it big, however, and both of them were barred for life.

Jim Ryun, America's star miler, panicked and tried to cut through traffic during his heat of the 1,500 and knocked himself out of the race. An American appeal, naturally. Another denial. Everyone's fault but ours. And, of course, America's first ever basketball loss, to Russia, after the Soviets had been given three chances to inbounds the pass leading to their winning basket, drew the loudest howls of all. So bitter was our reaction that to this day the team never has claimed its silver medal.

Only TV's Bill Russell pointed out that we were playing outdated, 1940-style basketball, and the reason for it was Hank Iba. Iba hadn't coached for almost a decade, but he had officially been appointed the U.S. coach for the last three Olympics. We never should have been that close to the Russians in the first place. We shot a miserable 19-for-57, but even so, when we pressed their backcourt, they came apart. But this was late in the game. When we freelanced and drove to the bucket, they couldn't keep up and they fouled us. But pressure was not Iba's style. He had taken a bunch of racehorses and put them in front of a wagon, but he was dearly beloved by our Olympic Committee.

Mark Spitz, the swimmer with his seven gold medals, was the closest thing America had to an Olympic superstar, but there was no joy in this young man, only public hostility and a mercenary tinge that turned off the newsmen attending his monosyllabic press conferences. David Wolper, the movie man, stood behind him at his last one, reminding him not to give away anything quotable, not when it could be profitably merchandized later on.

ABC's Chris Schenkel put a perfect ending on this sorry mess of an Olympic Games during the last major event, the marathon. The camera followed Frank Shorter through the Bavarian countryside, and Schenkel, his words as empty as his brain, intoned, "Bavaria, whose motto always has been live and let live. And that could well be the motto for this Olympics." Maybe no one had told him what had happened.

I went back to covering the Jets with a sense of relief. Only one of the players came over to me and spoke with understanding about what had gone on over in Munich and my desire to abandon my coverage. John Elliott, a defensive tackle from the University of Texas.

"I know just what you went through and why you left," he said. "I would have done the same thing."

It would be simplistic to say that set everything right in the world of sports, but it helped. It had come from an unexpected source. Maybe others had shared his feelings. Would I come back and cover another Olympics, Montreal in '76, Moscow in '80? Probably, once I had dried out from this one. I mean, I was a professional. I was getting paid.

Moscow 1980

When I left the *New York Post* and came to *Sports Illustrated* in August 1979, part of the deal was that the only event I would cover, aside from pro football, would be the Olympic Games. "So you can keep your streak intact," I was told.

So it was with some misgiving, but a sense of sticking to the bargain, that *SI* pulled me out of the NFL training camps and onto a Swissair flight to Moscow in 1980. What presented itself over the next three weeks was a writer's workshop of intrigue, politics, double-dealing, protest, all the elements of what I had come to expect from this great, quadrennial gathering of sporting nations and what I had written to the best of my ability and understanding in the four previous Olympics I had covered. OK, maybe not so much in Tokyo, which really was a "fun" Olympics, compared to what came afterward.

The first of three pieces I filed from Moscow, all with considerable fervor, involved three refuseniks who were undergoing a hunger strike to try to influence participating nations to put pressure on the Soviet government to ease restrictions on people trying to leave … just three young guys starving themselves on the floor of their apartment. The next piece was an in-depth look at one young man who had been trying to get out of Russia for more than five years. I thought the idea that we had to communicate by writing on one of those kid's erasable slates because everything in his apartment was bugged was an interesting touch. The third piece was about how the city had cleared out all the undesirables: drunks, troublemakers, Jews who had been particularly outspoken, etc., to provide the city with a cosmetic look for the Olympic period. "For their own safety," was the official version.

All were bounced back to me with the message, "Too political." The third one carried further instructions to cover Russia's opening basketball game against Czechoslovakia, with the notation, "Try to mention Misha Bear if you can ... Gil loves Misha Bear," Gil referring to managing editor Gil Rogin and Misha referring to Russia's Hallmark-cute logo to prove to the world what a sweet country it was that America and 64 other nations had chosen to boycott, imagine! The boycott, of course, took place because Russia had invaded Afghanistan.

SI, I was told, was downplaying any political angle during the games themselves, make that non-playing it, because the magazine had been afforded pretty good access to Russian athletes, and it was not in its best interest to jeopardize that relationship.

Well, this was a new one. If you live long enough, I guess you'll experience all sorts of variations on the art of existence. The stories I had rounded up involved personal forays, following up angles, some of which had been supplied by my trip to Moscow's synagogue on Arkhipova Street, within walking distance of our hotel, the Rossiya. Before I left for Moscow, *Time Magazine*'s bureau chief told me to make the synagogue my first stop.

"That's where you'll find out what's going on," he said. So I did ... and I did.

It was a lively Saturday afternoon scene, the action outside the building ... Jews, non-Jews, tourists, KGB operatives, everyone talking things over, swapping rumors and information, "hondeling," is the Yiddish word for it. At one point a young man in a neat business suit approached me and said, "They will not let me leave this country ... would you help me and take some papers to someone in the United States for me?"

Behind him, a few people were laughing and signaling to me with a thumbs down motion and mouthing the initials "KGB." But I really didn't need much help. He looked about as Jewish as Rosie O'Grady's father. I said, "Since I'm a guest in this country, I don't think it would be right to violate its laws." He snorted and moved on to someone else.

Walking back to the hotel after that opening session, I was followed to the very door itself by two similarly looking gentlemen whom I assume occupied the same role. Next day at the synagogue I asked a woman about it.

"Oh yes, they were KGB," she said. "They probably followed you because they had nothing better to do. They wanted to see if there was any 'rabbit' in you."

I asked her why everyone always was outside the synagogue and nobody ever seemed to go in it.

"See for yourself," she said.

So next day I did. It was large, majestic, actually. And totally deserted, except for two people, a youngster I assumed was a student, an acolyte of some kind, and a man who was perhaps in his 30s and introduced himself as the rabbi. Stocky, genial, wearing a little Van Dyke beard and a porkpie hat, he seemed quite ready to answer all questions. No, there was no prohibition on Jews leaving the country, as far as he knew. How about the refuseniks? "Troublemakers," he said. No, there was no truth to the rumor that troublemakers had been cleared out. At that point I thanked him and took my leave.

On the way out, the youngster, the student, who had listened to our conversation with his head bowed, murmured, "I'm sorry," and didn't look up.

I was getting stuff on my own, away from the official *SI* entourage, and that I learned was frowned upon. You were expected to be part of the team. Motion was severely limited. You traveled in a pack. "Are we ready to go now? Who, Jill? Oh, she forgot to make her phone call? How about Chris? Bathroom again, huh? Poor guy. Where's Jen? Yeah, I know, she said she'd be ready ... we'll give her another 20 minutes, and that's it." Maddening, frustrating, impossible if you wanted to get something done. But right there was the weakness of my argument. There was nothing I really had to get done in that first week of rejected stories unless you call Russia-Czechoslovakia basketball something. And that story never ran, as well it shouldn't have ... maybe because I didn't give Misha Bear his due.

Early in the games, I realized that there was a story to be written that nobody had been chasing, The Olympics Within the Olympics, Russia vs. East Germany. The fans gave me the first indication. The East Germans sat in a block, low on the backstretch of the massive Lenin Stadium, mostly businessmen and politicians and their families, off on a short holiday. They cheered their own athletes and were quick to whistle, the European equivalent of booing, when something went wrong but equally loud were the cheers for an athlete from another country who showed well against a Soviet competitor, cutting down the odds that Russia would add to its massive gold medal total. When a Russian athlete did well, the East German fans responded with silence.

The Russian fans were looser, less organized, Muscovites mainly, the privileged few who were lucky enough to be awarded tickets. They were a satisfied group; their athletes won two out of every five medals awarded in the entire games, thanks to the 65-nation boycott that reduced the competition to a kind of intramural tournament among Iron Curtain countries. They became even blasé about their triumphs except when the loser happened to be an East German. When Russia's Lyudmila Kondratyeva, for instance, beat East Germany's world record holder, Marlie Gohr, in the 100, a mighty roar rocked the stadium.

"Molodyets!" They yelled. *"Molodyets!"* Literally translated: "Good little boy." Actually, "Attaboy!"

I hunted down my best source on the Russian squad, Igor Ter-Ovanesyan, the famous Ter-O, whose long jump battles with Ralph Boston lit up the U.S. indoor track circuit for so many years, who liked the meets in New York so he'd go down to the Village afterward and party with the Americans and listen to some jazz. A good guy, clever, fluent in English and in 1980 one of the Soviet coaches.

"Do you know that the plaza of the Olympic Village is filled with observers?" he said. "Come, let's take a walk."

We walked out of the plaza area toward an open field bordering the practice track, away from all metal. "Never talk to someone here near anything metallic," he said.

"It's bugged? All of it's bugged? Everything?" I said, slow to catch on. He looked at me and raised his eyebrows.

"We can talk, but to be seen talking to GDR (German Democratic Republic) athletes or coaches is not a good thing," he said. "Yes, of course, they are our main rivals here. It's not so much one nation against another, it's the rivalry between athletic systems. The athletes know that if they talk to GDR athletes, they are observed, and that is not good. But even so, you are always thinking, *Is this man talking to me because he is friendly, or does he want to know something? About training methods, about medical things.* It is much safer just to avoid them, especially here, where we want to beat each other so badly."

I called the magazine. Its opening Olympic story had mentioned the pleasant face Moscow had adopted for its Olympics. I was told to write what I had, and then they'd see. I tried to sell it … not mentioning Ter-O's name, of course, but using his quotes and describing the scene, the avoidance of metal, the presence of observers. I felt that I needed one or two more people to quote and then I was in. The piece was never used.

In Montreal I had filed 49 pieces for the *Post*; every one printed. In Moscow my total would be two, although at this point it was zero. I tried to shake the depression that was gripping me like some slow-moving quicksand. Once I had talked to an AP guy who was stationed in Bucharest and I asked him what it was like.

"Don't ever spend any time there if you have the least little bit of a suicide tendency," he told me. I was beginning to feel that way about Moscow. The actual physical nature of the city contributed heavily to this feeling. The guidebooks described Moscow as dictated by "Stalinist architecture," meaning, if the book was being euphemistic, a reliance on Medieval forms. To me it meant something different, though. It meant something heavy and unyielding and gray, a lurking monster, a massive figure like something out of an H.P. Lovecraft science fiction fantasy. It was effective, it could crush your spirit. If it had been deliberately done, then the Soviet system never got enough credit for cleverly exploiting the powers of psychology. Or maybe they just liked size.

Take the Rossiya, our official press hotel … "The evil, Hideous Hotel Rossiya," the journalist and photographer, Declan McCullagh, had written. "Stalinist in architecture and demeanor. Try to stay anywhere else." At one time its 3,200 rooms made it the largest hotel in the world. One afternoon I decided to measure its circumference by stepping it off. I counted 1,075 steps, each one stretched to at least a yard. Three quarters of a mile around the Rossiya, hugging as close to the building as I could. Maybe that was a record, too. Passes, along with room keys, were always required. You couldn't even have a drink in the bar without a pass. In other words, a normal young Muscovite, who wasn't staying there, was prohibited from taking his girl for a drink at the Rossiya, such as a New Yorker could at the Plaza, for instance. I hadn't realized the restrictions Moscow put on its citizens. I mean, the country supposedly conceived in socialism was the most elitist I'd ever seen.

The size of things, my God, the size. Was this also part of a psychological master plan to show individuals how insignificant they were? Well, it worked on me. Buildings were massive, monuments, tombs, apartment complexes. There were huge, 14-lane highways that ran through the city with practically no traffic on them. Standing at the bottom of one of the escalators in a subway station, you seemed to be peering upward from a very deep mine. Never have I seen manmade caverns to match them. To enter the Olympic Village, you showed your press credential at a checkpoint. You got a pass. Then you took your pass half a mile away to the entrance to the village. Why couldn't it all have been in the same area? I could only guess that it represented a love of space, size, open plains, vast steppes, mournful balalaika music. When the Russians moved into Afghanistan, they didn't do it quietly or deftly; they rolled in with their tanks and armor as if it were World War III. And yes, it all started getting to me, the crushing weight of a city, a system, *Sports Illustrated*.

I started watching the early morning soaps on Russian TV. One in particular got my attention. It involved a weightlifter, a good-looking, dark haired guy with glasses, who was having trouble with his wife, and somehow that affected him in competition. My Russian wasn't good enough to keep me on top of the plot, but I had a general idea of what was going on. I began to really look forward to it each morning.

I was turning into a toad. I had to break out of it, show some spirit, do something! We had been told to watch ourselves, that the babushka ladies that manned the halls were KGB spies, that every hotel room would be bugged. Oh yeah? Well, bug this! I called the room of Kenny Moore, a former world class long distance runner who was doing our track coverage. He was kind of a nervous guy, a typically skittery marathoner.

"Herr Moore?" I said in my best Weber and Fields German accent. "This is Doktor Paulus Schrieber of the GDR team. Two of our runners want to defect to the vest, and I was told you could help arrange this." He began stammering ... "w-w-w-ell I d-d-don't know ..." and I figured I'd better cut it off before the poor guy had a heart attack. If he'd have been thinking clearly, he'd have figured out that the name was Paul the Writer, but I guess he had enough on his mind, with everything being bugged and both of us on our way to Lubyanka Prison or a mental hospital or worse.

Finally I connected on a story ... Americans who were competing under different banners, the basketball player with the obscure Italian grandfather, the flyweight boxer who'd been born in Puerto Rico, etc. And there was Rocky Crosswhite from Bethesda, Md., a former Davidson reserve center who had become Mr. Basketball. In Australia. He had married an Australian girl and gotten Australian citizenship, and this was his third Olympics for the Aussies. The government had left the decision whether or not to compete up to the athletes, and the team had voted 14-1 to play. His was the one negative vote, but as captain, he felt it was his duty to stick with his teammates.

"Let's face it," he said. "This isn't the Olympics, it's the Eastern European Games. Look at this … fences, security checks going in and out … I went through nine of them on one trip the other day.

"This is all supposed to be for friendship between athletes, right? The other night a bloke from Zimbabwe was visiting us in our quarters, and the guard made him leave. He said that athletes aren't allowed to go from block to block. At other Olympics you always were able to dance at the disco with some of the girls who worked as guides or translators, but they've forbidden them here. One night I went in there and saw blokes dancing with blokes."

As the competition progressed, I thought of something a Polish boxing coach had told me. "Don't get too ambitious about winning medals here. The Russians are unbeatable at home." He sounded like someone talking about playing Alabama in Tuscaloosa when Bear Bryant was coaching or playing the Broncos at Mile High. The Russians had organized a highly efficient Olympic package, but hanging over everything was the pervasive smell of home cooking. I began to keep a record of protest, of things that weren't exactly right, both in and out of the arena. I called my collection, "Olympic Outtakes," and although I knew they'd never see the light of day in *SI*, at least their compilation made me feel better.

Romania accused the Russians of rigging the scoring system and ganging up on their prize Olympian, little Nadia Comaneci, the gymnast, the star of Montreal. "It was an arrangement to ensure a Soviet winner," reported the Romanian Communist Party newspaper, *Scinteia*, under a headline that screamed, "They Stole Her Medal!" East Germany complained that a do-over gave Russian diver Aleksandr Portnov an extra attempt, whereas their own Falk Hoffmann was denied one under exactly the same circumstances. The track was where the strongest protests erupted.

Triple jumpers Juan Carlos de Oliveira of Brazil and Ian Campbell of Australia, who were expected to mount the most serious challenges to the Russians, were called for fouls on nine of their 12 final jumps. The Australians sent a letter of complaint to the IAAF after the Russian officials ruled that Campbell had dragged his foot on the step part on what would have been a winning effort. British track people viewed the videotape of the jump and rushed to his defense, saying there had been no foul at all, and besides, how could someone possibly drag his foot on the explosive thump that marks the step on a world class triple jump?

The Finns said the Russians opened the gates for their javelin man, creating a helpful updraft. The British press reviewed replays of Yuriy Sedykh's world record hammer throw and reported that they showed he clearly stepped over the line. The Cubans complained that phony measuring cost their discus man, Luis Delis, a gold medal. England's decathlon champion, Daley Thompson, laughed when he discussed how the deck had been stacked against him — wet circle to throw out of in the discus, the circle being scrupulously dried off when the Russians threw. Each Russian high jump and pole vault effort was replayed on the scoreboard screen, an on-the-spot coaching aid denied everyone else. Everyone questioned the curious seeding and lane assignments that awarded the Russians the inside lane three out of four times the 1,600-meter relay was run in heats and final. Complaints came pouring in after a qualifying throw by the eventual javelin winner, Russia's Dainis Kula, was allowed after it landed hindsight first.

International Amateur Athletics Association president, Adriaan Paulen, kept his inspectors off the track and left things solely up to the Russians. Privately, IAAF officials said Paulen was trying to wrap up the Russian vote for the day when he came up for reelection later in the year. The GDR amateur athletic head, George Wieczek, stormed out of one of Paulen's meetings.

"This is false, absolutely false," he said. Paulen broke down and sent his inspectors, himself included, out onto the track. The first cheater they caught was Russian pole vaulter Sergei Kulibaba, who was flashing signals to a teammate. And he was doing it in front of the 77-year-old Paulen himself.

"It wasn't only him — they all did it," said the winner Wladyslaw Kozakiewicz of Poland, and that accusation was backed up by Sweden's Miro Zalar. "The officials, too. They were holding up flags to show Russian vaulters how the wind was blowing." Kulibaba and the forty thieves.

Not since London in 1908, when anti-American sentiment overwhelmed the competition and caused British judges to practically carry Italian marathoner Dorando Pietri over the finish line in order to beat America's Johnny Hayes, had there been such sustained and widespread criticism of the officiating. But why should the Russians, who knew they'd dominate the games, with America and West Germany and so many other nations out of the competition, have to cheat to pile up even more medals? Their overall medal total was topped only once, when the United States ran the table in the backyard Olympics of 1904 in St. Louis. I can only repeat that these seemed to be an overwhelming love of things massive. More, we must have still more medals.

Maybe they felt that in some way it compensated for the $200 million the country lost in expected tourist revenue that never materialized. Or the cost of importing Beaujolais from France or butter and jam from Hungary for the press dining room, so we would all write about the glorious food and drink — which, of course, would disappear like a mirage once the games ended. Or the cost of making sure the city was sanitized and swept clean of undesirables. Who ever heard of taking a bus to a 103,000-seat stadium half an hour before the competition started and arriving in plenty of time? But that's what deserted streets will do for you. Which could be laid in part to the cost of bringing in elite security forces from all 11 time zones of the empire. One afternoon a photographer of ours who spoke Russian asked a security officer for directions to the boxing arena.

"I don't know. I'm not from here," he told him.

"Where are you from?"

"Siberia."

Muscovites, who were brave enough to talk freely, admitted that the loss of revenue was a very big concern, hardly justified by the harvest of medals.

"Very few of us care anything about the Olympic Games," said a professor's wife with whom I talked. "Tourists and journalists come here and they see clean streets and new paint and no traffic. They see all the gold medals the Russians have won. What they don't see is all the lies. The lies.

"We have heard that the funding for the games was taken from the budget, particularly the budget for hospitals. We watched the opening ceremonies on TV, and my friend said, 'There goes another wing on the children's ward, there goes an X-ray machine.'"

Western journalists were seduced by the pseudo-comfort, the special food, the precision with which the buses and subways ran and the events were organized, a direct contrast to the sloppiness of Montreal. But they couldn't help feeling the antiseptic quality of these games, a lack of spontaneity. Athletes who wanted to run a victory lap had to break away from security guards. And here and there, when you turned a wrong corner, you could run into something embarrassing. A wrong turn on the way to opening ceremonies would put you on a street where hundreds of policemen, stretching for miles, stood three feet apart from each other. Or when you came back you might run into a convoy of nearly 100 military trucks, each one packed with the soldiers who had put on a series of card stunts in the stadium half an hour previously. Toy soldiers back in their boxes.

If you wanted to get out of the journalists' E-Section, if you wanted to talk to someone in the stands, you met with polite but firm resistance. "Journalists are not permitted to leave their section." Athletes and coaches were similarly confined to their F-Section. A little Yugoslavian track coach named Daniel Korica began referring to himself as "The Prisoner of F." I overheard a conversation in which a couple of U.S. journalists, who had never covered an Olympics, were remarking about the efficiency and organization. An old timer overheard it, too, and interrupted the conversation with, "Yes, and Berlin ran a very efficient Olympics in 1936."

I remember something the dissident writer, Vasily Aksyonov, had to say before he was expelled from the country.

"Four years ago when Moscow was chosen for the Olympics, we thought there would be a fraud when the time came, but we expected a fraud of false liberty and false relaxation. We hoped the authorities would arrange a kind of 'Swinging Moscow' for three weeks. We never wanted the paramilitary curfew you see in the streets now, or this big clean up and Moscow artificially emptied."

By the time the games were in their second week, a sense of ennui was settling over the journalistic community. It seemed that every time you turned on a TV set Russia was playing Bulgaria in something. One day in the press lounge, a few of us were having a drink and in the background was the constant drone of the TV set with its daily Olympic coverage. Suddenly everyone's eyes became fixed on the screen. The bartender had switched channels, and now there was a children's program.

Pro Krasniyu Shapitschku. Little Red Riding Hood. We watched it to the end.

A week before the closing ceremony, I finally got a real, honest to goodness, serious assignment from *Sports Illustrated*. It ended up as something that has stayed with me for many years and even now sets off a whole spectrum of mixed emotions. Vasily Alekseyev, Russia's two-time super heavyweight lifting champion, the strongest man in history, was making a comeback at 38. Nobody knew how he would do. He had been out of competition for a while, supposedly nursing a bad hip. He hadn't been seen. But if he wanted to compete, he would have to lift the Olympic qualifying weight.

A few days before the Olympics began, he walked into the Izmailovo Sport Palace, lifted the qualifying weight rather easily and left the hall. He was enormous. He weighed 379 pounds, which would have made him the heaviest man to ever to step on the platform. He said, "I will be lighter for the competition."

Alekseyev had been a favorite subject for *Sports Illustrated* through the years. My assignment — cover Alekseyev on championship night. Win or lose, he would be my story. Fine with me.

I was told that the Russian weightlifting federation actually had a PR office, which was practically unheard of over there. Their idea of PR usually involved the phrase, "No one is permitted ..." But I found it, and it was nothing like what I had expected. Once upon a time, theatrical booking offices in Tin Pan Alley might have looked like that. It had a homey feel, pictures of famous wrestlers and lifters on the wall, a large cluttered desk, a few chairs, including an overstuffed one in the corner, a big couch, which contained, when I showed up, a British journalist fast asleep. Another one was in the big armchair, thumbing through a weightlifting magazine. He had the cauliflower ears of a wrestler. The sleeper showed a massive expanse of chest. They were typical of a certain breed of English writers, people who had once participated in the sport they covered. And they had made themselves right at home in the office of Aleksandr Gavrilovets, who was seated at the desk.

His official title was director of international sports writers commission of weight lifting. Actually he was more of an information director ... I hesitate to use the phrase PR man because he was more than that. He was a person who knew what was what. Late 30s, maybe early 40s, dark, good looking, he wore a navy blue pinstriped suit giving him a polished, Western look. I introduced myself and told him what my assignment was.

"The big guy, huh?" he said, in perfect English. I was thinking what an unexpected way it was for him to put it. The English writer/weightlifter who'd been sleeping, awoke and got up. "Be back later, Alex," he said, and Gavrilovets waved as he left. He blew out his breath.

"He's not going to do anything, you know." he said. "He's not in condition." I was surprised for the second time. This is not the way Russian federation directors talk about their world class athletes. I told him I had to write about Alekseyev, win or lose. He nodded.

"And I imagine you'll want to talk to him afterward." I said I would. He thought about it for a minute.

"All right, here's what you do," he said. "As soon as he's out of the competition, come down to the entrance to the dressing room. Don't wait to see who wins. Come right away. I'll meet you there and I'll see what I can do." I thanked him.

I don't know how weightlifting fans are the world over, but the ones in the gray concrete hall called the Izmailovo Palace of Sport that Wednesday night were rough. Weightlifters, if you don't know it, just don't come back. The last superheavyweight lifter to make a successful comeback was Samson. The training is too intense. The muscles must be in a constant state of awareness. They don't just retire to their dacha for a couple of years, say, "Now it's time to regain my title," and pick up where they left off.

When Alekseyev, lighter, as he had predicted at 357, walked out onto the platform, rubbing his hands in front of him — his heavy brows drawn together like those of the famed Cossack chieftan, Stenka Razin — the crown let out a cheer, broken by occasional shouts of *"My s'toboi!"* We're with you!

Twelve minutes later he was finished, the jeers and whistles growing louder and more raucous on each of the three times he failed to get the weight above his head. At one time a shout was heard above the others, and our Russian-speaking photographer shook his head.

"Brutal, just brutal," he said.

"What did the guy yell, Jerry?" I asked him.

"He yelled, 'You'll make a lot of sausages, Alekseyev!'"

I watched Alekseyev leave the arena to the jeering and I was out of the stands and down to the dressing room entrance. Aleksandr Gavrilovets was already there. "Not now," he said. "The brass is in there."

Again I was struck by his unusual terminology — unusual for a Russian. The door opened, and two serious-faced, middle-aged men walked out. "Now," said Gavrilovets.

Alekseyev was slumped against the wall, the sweat pouring off him. Gavrilovets translated for me.

"The world has not seen the end of Alekseyev," he said. "You will see. Let them whistle. I'm not finished." He went on in this vein for a while and then excused himself to take a shower. Then it dawned on me ... I had gotten him by myself. I had everything I needed. I was finished. It was a wrap. Write the scene, the jeers, the big guy and his quotes, watch the end to see who wins. All I had to do was get it down. My God, this guy had done everything for me, set everything up, and it was a negative angle at that. How could I thank him? I started to.

"That's all right," he said. "You'll excuse me ... I have to be back out there."

So I wrote my story, and it got decent play, and I couldn't get Aleksandr Gavrilovets out of my mind. Who ever heard of getting that kind of help at those Olympics? A couple of days later, I spotted him in the bar at the Rossiya. He was having a drink with a couple of writers. I waited until he was finished. I had to thank him properly this time. I watched him. There was just something ... my antennae were tingling. He's not one of them. I just knew it. Not one of them.

I had felt that way on rare occasions in the past. I had felt it with Jack Kent Cooke, the owner of the Redskins. He isn't what he pretends to be. I looked at him carefully. Gavrilovets, Gavrilovets. That wasn't a Russian name. The writers said good bye, and he got up to leave and I went over.

"Can I talk to you for a minute?" I said. He said, sure.

"I want to thank you for what you did for me," I said. He waved it away.

"It was nothing," he said.

"You didn't have to do it ... it was very kind of you," I said.

"That's all right."

I was delaying what I wanted to ask him. I knew it. He was NOT one of them.

Gavrilovets ... Gavrilovets ... he looked, well, could be Russian, could be anything.

"Are you Jewish?" I asked him. He let his breath out slowly and looked down at his hands. I hadn't asked Cooke that question, but after interviewing him one afternoon, I asked Mo Siegel, the Washington columnist and a friend of Cooke.

"Now why would you ever ask that?" Siegel said in his Atlanta drawl.

"I just feel it, Mo," I told him. "My antennae are telling me."

"Well, you're very perceptive," he said. "His mother was Jewish. Name of Jacobs. From South Africa."

Finally Aleksandr Gavrilovets looked up at me. "You would not be helping me if you pursue this topic," he said slowly. I told him it was already forgotten. I could feel a deep, overwhelming sadness coming over me. I feel it again right now.

"Some day, someplace else," I said, "maybe we could sit down and have a long talk."

"I'd like that very much," he said.

It hasn't happened. Maybe some day it will. I think about him quite often.

The coda to this final Olympic odyssey of mine came at the Moscow airport. I had a bunch of confidential papers, addresses of refuseniks I had met, things they had given me to give to different organizations in the U.S., the kind of stuff I assumed would be of interest to Russian customs officials at the airport. And there would be no way they would find them. I was taking back one large suitcase that would be checked through and an open carry-bag that had my Olympic stuff, statistics, notes I had taken on various events. I mixed the papers in with my notes on the swimming results that were next to the track and boxing statistics.

The customs official was a woman in her late 30s perhaps, attractive but cold looking with intelligent blue eyes. I put both bags on the counter for her to inspect. She checked the big one and pushed it along without opening it. She stared at the carry bag for a moment, looked me in the eyes and pointed to the pile of event statistics, signaling me to bring them out. I did. She ruffled the pages, stopping at the swimming. She looked at each one of my carefully hidden secret notes, studied them, stared at me again and signaled me to return them to the bag and move along. She had told me without wasting a single word:

"You can hide nothing. I can find whatever I want. What's more, I don't care about any of it."

A fitting farewell to my 16-year career as an Olympic journalist.

Chapter 10

Quarterbacks

SIX QUARTERBACKS WHO CHANGED THE GAME
This article appeared in the Aug. 17, 1998 issue of Sports Illustrated.

Good quarterbacks leave indelible stamps on the game, but a few of them go a step further. They change the game, through a style that gives life to a new offensive system, by force of personality or simply by coming along at the right time.

Here are the six NFL quarterbacks I believe effected the most profound changes. Sid Luckman was the first to run the modern T formation with a man in motion, which bore a striking resemblance to today's basic set. Otto Graham, innovative and a deadly accurate passer, will nevertheless be remembered as the first man for whom his coach called all the plays. John Unitas was a tough, snarling veteran of the semipro ranks who clawed his way to the top; once he got there he battled to do things his way, no matter how his coach felt about it. Joe Namath became the standard-bearer for a league. He gave the AFL respectability, changed the salary structure of pro football and captivated fans with his brashness and flair. Joe Montana was the master of a system that swept the game, with its reliance on quick reads and short, precision passing. Finally, there was Doug Williams, who with one brilliant performance opened the way for today's generation of black quarterbacks — make that quarterbacks who happen to be black — to multiply and flourish.

Many great quarterbacks — Sammy Baugh, Bobby Layne, Norm Van Brocklin and Dan Marino, for instance — were not included, not because of any lack of ability but because they didn't have the impact the select half-dozen did.

When Sid Luckman died in July, at 81, the last originator of the oldest offensive formation still in use was gone. The T with a man in motion was the brain work of a coaching triumvirate of George Halas, Clark Shaughnessy and Ralph Jones, and Luckman, a 22-year-old Chicago Bears rookie out of Columbia, was the man chosen to implement it on the field. That was in 1939, and the basic set remains.

"I'd been a single-wing tailback," Luckman said when I visited him at his Fort Lauderdale suburban apartment in May. "You're set deep, the ball comes to you, and you either pass, run or spin. When I came to the Bears, we worked for hours on my spinning, on hiding the ball, only this time it was as a T quarterback. They brought in the old Bears quarterback, Carl Brumbaugh, to work with me. We spent endless time just going over my footwork, faking, spinning, setting up as fast as I could, running to my left and throwing right, days and days of it."

Luckman seemed frail as we talked. All the charm that I remembered from the dozen or so times I had interviewed him through the years was there, but he'd occasionally stop to gather himself, to get things just right. Seated with him at a table heaped with charts and memorabilia and the scrapbooks of a lifetime in the game, I felt as if I were listening to Orville Wright describing the origins of the flying machine.

"Ralph Jones had coached the T with the Bears in the early 1930s," Luckman said, "but it was the old T, with everyone bunched in there. Shaughnessy was coaching at the University of Chicago, and they were about to drop football, so he spent a lot of time with us. I'd be up in Shaughnessy's room every night in training camp, going over every aspect of the thing. The whole idea was to spread the field and give the defense more area to cover.

"We had an 11 o'clock curfew, and Halas would drop by around 1 a.m. and say, 'That's enough, Sid. Go to bed.'"

The system was still experimental in 1939, and Luckman was a backup tailback in the Bears' basic offense, the single wing. But on Oct. 22, with Chicago trailing the New York Giants 16-0 at the Polo Grounds, Halas told Luckman, "Get in at quarterback and run the T."

"Bob MacLeod, our right halfback, went in motion and ran straight down the field on a stop-and-go," Luckman said. "I was so nervous I threw a duck, end over end. The defensive back had the interception, but MacLeod took the ball away from him and went all the way. Then I threw a little swing pass to Bob Swisher, and he shook a couple of tackles and went 60 yards for another score. We lost the game 16-13, and we used the T off and on for the rest of the season, but no one made a big thing about it."

The T explosion came one year later. While the Bears were using the formation to go 8-3 on the way to the NFL Championship Game, in which they would annihilate the Washington Redskins 73-0, Shaughnessy, who had moved on to coach Stanford, was dazzling the college world with the T. Stanford went 9-0, then beat Nebraska 21-13 in the Rose Bowl. The rush was on. "I went back to Columbia to help Lou Little put in the T," Luckman said. "I went to Holy Cross, to Army when Red Blaik called me, to Notre Dame to work with Johnny Lujack and George Ratterman."

The Bears won four NFL titles in the 1940s, and other teams gradually switched to the new formation. Luckman, who in 10 games in 1943 threw 28 touchdown passes en route to winning league MVP honors, was the first T master, a gifted passer, long and short, a skilled faker and ball handler. He was there when it all began.

Otto Graham played for 10 years with the Cleveland Browns beginning in 1946, and the Browns were in a league championship game every one of those seasons. If you're looking for a record that never will be matched, that's a good place to start.

He played for a club that outrecruited everyone else (the heart of the post-World War II Browns was a group of service vets who still had college eligibility left), outcoached everyone else and was years ahead of the rest of pro football in organization and innovation. He played for the only coach to have an NFL team named after him, Paul Brown. Brown's ego reached such a peak that he decided that he, not Graham, would call the plays. That became Brown's system.

The messenger-guard rotation was introduced in the early '50s. Brown's bold move changed the game, even though the innovation didn't immediately catch on. Many stories of that era mentioned how unhappy Graham was with the arrangement, but he says it wasn't true. "A lot of people in this world have great egos, but on the Browns there was room for only one ego, and it wasn't mine," says Graham, who's 76 and living in Sarasota, Fla. "I never openly criticized the coach. We had a checkoff system, and occasionally I'd change one of his plays, but as for his calling the game, we never talked about it. He was the admiral, the general, the CEO.

"I'm sure that some quarterbacks couldn't have played in that system," says Graham, who twice led the NFL in passing yardage and was the top-rated passer of his time. "I don't think Bobby Layne could have. But what I loved was that we were a passing team in an era of the run. In the morning we'd work on the run, in the afternoon the pass. What were my talents? I could throw hard if I had to, I could lay it up soft, I could drill the sideline pass. God-given ability. The rest was practice, practice, practice. I had the luxury of having the same receivers for almost my entire career. We developed the timed sideline attack, the comeback route where the receiver goes to the sideline, stops and comes back to the ball, with everything thrown on rhythm."

In their NFL debut in 1950, the Browns, four-time champs of the rival All-America Football Conference, crushed the defending NFL champion Philadelphia Eagles 35-10. Philly's 5-2 defense couldn't cover the sideline comebacks. The Giants scouted that game and, dropping the ends in their 6-1 alignment into linebacker positions, stopped the Browns when the teams met two weeks later. The 4-3, today's standard defensive set, was born.

"After the game against the Eagles," says Graham, "their coach, Greasy Neale, said we were nothing but a basketball team. Pretty good basketball team, huh?"

In 1955, after completing an unremarkable career at Louisville, getting drafted in the ninth round by the Pittsburgh Steelers and being released near the end of training camp, 22-year-old John Unitas was the quarterback for the Bloomfield Rams in western Pennsylvania. He made six bucks a game. "They called it semipro football," he says. "Actually it was just sandlot, a bunch of guys knocking the hell out of each other on an oil-soaked field under the Bloomfield Bridge."

Five years later, after Unitas had led the Baltimore Colts to two NFL championships, Eagles quarterback Norm Van Brocklin was asked what made Unitas so great. "He knows what it's like to eat potato soup seven days a week," the Dutchman replied.

Unitas became synonymous with toughness on the field, for stepping up in the teeth of the rush and delivering the ball. "I often thought that sometimes he'd hold the ball one count longer than he had to," Los Angeles

Rams defensive tackle Merlin Olsen once said, "just so he could take the hit and laugh in your face."

"I kept a picture of Johnny U over my bed," Namath once said. "To me he meant one thing — toughness."

How did Unitas change the game? He was the antithesis of the highly drafted, highly publicized young quarterback. He developed a swagger, a willingness to gamble. He showed that anyone with basic skills could beat the odds if he wanted to succeed badly enough and was willing to work.

He's 65 now, vice president of sales for a computer electronics firm and chairman of Unitas Management Corp., a sports management firm, and the Johnny Unitas Golden Arm Educational Foundation, which awards scholarships. On a sunny day in May, we sat on the porch that overlooks his 19 acres of pastureland in Baldwin, Md., and I mentioned my favorite quote of his: "You don't arrive as a quarterback until you can tell the coach to go to hell."

"Once you've got (the game) down, you've got a better feel on the field than a coach has," Unitas said. "My first year I was learning. By the end of the second year, it was like a complete revelation, like a cloud had moved away. I'd get a feel for how to move the defense into coverages that I wanted. I'd keep a chart on every defensive back, on his tendencies.

"Weeb Ewbank, our coach, used to be scared to death of (Detroit Lions Hall of Fame cornerback) Night Train Lane. He'd tell me to stay away from him. I thought, Hell, I'm not going to give him the day off. But Weeb was the perfect coach for me because he'd always get players' input."

How about the system today with, for instance, the radio receivers that have become standard in quarterbacks' helmets so coaches can send in plays from the sidelines? "I'd be very deaf," said Unitas, a three-time league MVP and 10-time Pro Bowl player who still ranks third in career touchdown passes. "Mine would be out of service."

Unitas thought for a moment. "One of the greatest compliments I've ever had," he said, "came against the Green Bay Packers on a fourth-and-one in a tight game. Before we huddled, I was checking the line of scrimmage to see where the ball was and I heard one of their guys say to Henry Jordan, their defensive tackle, 'What do you think he's going to do?' Jordan said, 'Damned if I know. I've been playing against him for five years, and I haven't figured his ass out yet.' That's what quarterbacks today are missing."

The hit had been a brutal one, helmet to rib cage, and it had come just as New York Jets quarterback Joe Namath released the ball. Namath was stretched out on the turf of Denver's Mile High Stadium for a couple of minutes. This was September 1969, a little more than eight months after the Jets had stunned the Colts in Super Bowl III. After the game, no one was more worried about Namath's condition than Dave Costa, the Broncos' defensive tackle who had delivered the blow.

As Namath was getting his sore ribs treated, Costa stood in the New York locker room in civvies, just outside the trainers' room, practically wringing his hands. "Is he all right?" He asked. "Honest to God, I didn't mean to hurt him."

I asked him why he was so upset.

"Are you kidding?" he said. "All that Joe has meant to us, to our league, whipping the Colts' ass the way he did. He's the reason a lot of us are making decent money."

In 1965 Namath, then a rookie out of Alabama, spurned the St. Louis Cardinals and signed a three-year, $427,000 deal with the Jets. At that time the contract was the biggest for a pro football rookie. The signing was a public relations bonanza for the struggling AFL. "Ridiculous," Packers coach and general manager Vince Lombardi said at the time, but the signing war was on. The following year Lombardi topped Namath's big deal with a $1 million package for a pair of rookie running backs: Donny Anderson ($600,000) and Jim Grabowski ($400,000). Also, the Atlanta Falcons came up with more than $300,000 for linebacker Tommy Nobis, the first player picked in the '66 draft.

The brash Namath was a shot in the arm for the AFL. In his first season, Jets home attendance increased by more than 12,000 per game. The Houston Oilers set a single-game franchise home-attendance record that would stand for 14 years when 52,680 turned out to see Namath ride the bench in his pro debut. In June 1966 the AFL and the NFL merged.

Then came the Super Bowl, with Namath guaranteeing a victory and then meticulously picking apart a Colts team that was favored by 19½ points. After having been whipped by Lombardi's Packers in the first two Super Bowls, the AFL now could look the NFL in the eye. "A bunch of guys from the Chiefs — Buck Buchanan, Emmitt Thomas, Willie Lanier — were waiting at the hotel to meet us after the game," Namath says. "They just wanted to shake our hands. John Hadl, the Chargers' quarterback, told me he was sitting in the stands at the game, taking abuse from Baltimore fans, and when we won, he just started crying. Couldn't help it, he said, and John's a pretty tough guy."

Looking back on that Super Bowl almost 30 years later, what did it all mean? "I got letters from a lot of high school coaches who told me they used the game as a motivator," says Namath, who, in 1967, became the first player to pass for more than 4,000 yards in a season. "Maybe it motivated some other people, too. There are a lot of underdogs in the world. Maybe it meant something to the underdogs in life."

It was a system built out of desperation, the Bill Walsh system, also known as the Cincinnati system and popularly mislabeled the West Coast offense, whose true architect was Sid Gillman. It was a system that Walsh, the Cincinnati Bengals' quarterbacks and receivers coach, had installed to accommodate Virgil Carter, a quick-thinking, short-to medium-range passer who became the starter during the 1970 season after Greg Cook went down with an injury.

"I didn't think of it as a system; it had no name," Walsh says. "It's just what we did. Keep the sticks moving with high-percentage passes, get through your progression of reads quickly, make the guy underneath, the guy closest to the passer, your final read."

The system worked for Carter and his successor, Ken Anderson, and also for Steve DeBerg, the quarterback for the San Francisco 49ers in 1979, when Walsh took over as coach. But when Joe Montana arrived that year, Walsh knew he had something special. "He took the system to a new level," Walsh says. "His gracefulness on the move, his skill, his resourcefulness, all of that blended into the system.

"We'd have what we called bad-situation practices where I'd take Joe aside and tell him, 'OK, I want you to go to the third read on every play.' Then in a game he'd do it, but what made him extraordinary was his innate ability to concentrate downfield with all hell breaking loose around him and then to put the ball in exactly the right spot on perfect timing. It would be like a guy standing on the Speedway in Indianapolis, looking past the cars and throwing his pass."

"The coolest quarterback I've ever seen," Luckman said of Montana. "Nothing ever seemed to bother him."

"I'd been throwing on the move ever since high school," says Montana, who still lives life on the go, traveling the country making speeches and endorsements, and checking out the California wine country for investments. "The beauty of Bill's system was that there was always a place to go with the ball. I was the mailman, just delivering people's mail, and there were all kinds of houses to go to."

The Montana-Walsh legacy in San Francisco is three Super Bowl victories, and Montana would add a fourth under George Seifert. Walsh's disciples spread the system throughout the NFL, sometimes in modified form but always recognizable. Mike Holmgren took it to Green Bay, where it was perfect for Brett Favre, another quarterback who was gifted on the move. Steve Young, nimble and creative, kept it alive in San Francisco and brought the 49ers one more NFL title. It's no wonder Young (97.0) and Montana (92.3) have the top two career quarterback ratings in NFL history. No one, however, took the system to a higher level than Montana.

On one glorious January afternoon in 1988 Doug Williams changed the perception of a nation, changed it for all time. He removed an adjective. "When I came into the league," he says, "I was never Doug Williams, quarterback. It was always Doug Williams, black quarterback. Nowadays you don't hear that when people talk about Jeff Blake or Kordell Stewart or Steve McNair. They're just quarterbacks. I like to think I had a hand in that."

On a hunch, Redskins coach Joe Gibbs had benched Jay Schroeder for the playoffs and started Williams in his place, and now Super Sunday had arrived and Williams would go against John Elway and the Broncos, who were favored by 3 1/2 points. The first quarter ended with Denver leading 10-0. The second ended with Washington in front 35-10. For all intents and purposes, the game was over.

Williams put up eye-popping single-quarter numbers: 228 yards passing, four touchdowns. The struggles of a career — two division championships in five years with the Tampa Bay Buccaneers (still the only titles in that franchise's history) without much recognition; a two-year stopover in the USFL; a couple of seasons as an off-and-on starter in Washington — had crystallized in one inspired quarter. He finished with four touchdown passes and a Super Bowl-record 340 total yards in the 42-10 triumph and, of course, he was voted the game's MVP, but what he remembers best is what someone asked him during an interview in the week leading up to the game: "How long have you been a black quarterback?"

"Everyone laughed at the question," he says, "but I knew what the guy meant. I answered, 'Since I've been in the NFL.' At Grambling I'd just been a quarterback."

He's back at Grambling this season as the successor to Eddie Robinson, the Tigers' retired coaching legend. In May he was working out of a temporary office in a converted trailer. There was no secretary on duty when we talked. He took all phone calls himself.

"Did I change history?" he said. "Well, I'm not going to the Hall of Fame. I like to think that I was part of history. But maybe I changed the way people looked at things. Maybe I changed things for the black quarterbacks who followed me."

He wasn't the first black quarterback in the NFL. In the dawn of pro football, there was Fritz Pollard, a run-and-pass tailback in the 1920s. In the '50s there were Willie Thrower and Charlie (Choo Choo) Brackins, mere blips on the screen. Marlin (the Magician) Briscoe was a one-year wonder for the '68 Broncos before he was converted to wideout. Joe Gilliam once started ahead of Terry Bradshaw in Pittsburgh, but drugs cut his career short, and James (Shack) Harris had productive years with the Buffalo Bills and the Rams, although he never achieved stardom.

"When I left Grambling (in 1969)," says Harris, who's now the pro personnel director for the Baltimore Ravens, "Coach Robinson told me, 'Don't expect things to be fair in the NFL. You're going to have to be better than anyone else just to survive.' There was a lot of pressure, and that's what I tried to tell Doug when he came into the league."

"I was a one-week holdout after I was drafted," says Williams, who was the Buccaneers' first-round pick in 1978. "I guess that didn't sit right with some people. They must have figured I should have felt lucky to have been drafted at all. Then after five years and two division titles, I was only the 43rd-highest-paid quarterback in the league.

"I held out again and eventually went to the USFL. My wife had just died of a brain tumor. There was a three-month-old baby girl to take care of. You couldn't believe some of the letters I'd gotten in Tampa. Everyone heard about the package I got with the watermelon inside and the note, 'Throw this, nigger. They might be able to catch it.' It got so that every time I got a letter with no return address, I wouldn't open it."

A rough career, but one Super Sunday put a grace note on it — for all time.

"A very special moment for a very special person," Harris says. "A special moment for all of us."

* * *

TALKING FOOTBALL WITH JOHNNY U

This article appeared in the Sept. 23, 2002 issue of Sports Illustrated.

Almost 40 years later it still bothered John Unitas, the idea that people had accused him of gambling at the end of the overtime drive that beat the Giants in the most famous of all pro football games, the 1958 NFL Championship. Sitting on the porch of his home in Baldwin, Md., on a spring day in 1998, Johnny U was off on one of his favorite topics — the way a quarterback can influence a defense, almost bend it to his will. "Gambling?" he snorted. "Some gamble."

The play was the seven-yard pass to tight end Jim Mutscheller that put the Baltimore Colts on the one-yard line, setting up Alan Ameche's game-winning plunge. The thinking was, Why did Unitas throw the ball and risk an interception when all the Colts needed was a field goal to win?

"It wasn't a gamble," Unitas said. "They didn't see what I saw. Nine times out of 10 Emlen Tunnell, the strong safety, would be on Mutscheller. This time it was Cliff Livingston, the linebacker, trying to take away the inside. So I checked off to a diagonal outside. Who's there to cover him? Lindon Crow, the cornerback, and he's got to worry about Lenny Moore. Not a gamble. An educated move."

The quarterback's ability to set up a defense, to craft his own sequence of plays, was a big part of the game then. Very little came in from the sideline. It was his show, and Unitas was determined that we should understand this element of pro football, which has been lost in today's era.

"Look, you're the strong safety," he said. "I'm going to overload, put three men in a two-man area, then go back weakside. What do you do? If I want you to come up and play the run, I split the guard out farther. If I want the cornerback to play the run, I tighten the splits. You see, I've got you doing what I want you to do."

Throughout his career Unitas maintained this dogged adherence to the idea of control. His message: Don't mess with me. I'm running the show.

Physically he had it all — the whiplike delivery, the athletic ability, the great sense of timing and, oh, man, the courage. He had to do it the hard way. The NFL hadn't liberalized the passing rules. His receivers could get mugged downfield. Defensive linemen could head-slap their way into the backfield, and when they homed in on a quarterback they could hit him any way they wanted. None of today's cellophane-wrapper protection from the officials.

And Unitas got hit plenty. He'd snarl and wipe the blood off his face and lead his team down the field on another of his great scoring drives, operating in that hunch-shouldered way of his, with the herky-jerky setup and deadly accuracy. Eighteen years of that.

"I weigh 270 pounds," Merlin Olsen, the Los Angeles Rams' great defensive tackle, once said, "and I don't know if I could absorb the punishment he takes. I wonder if I could stand there, week after week, and say, 'Here I am. Take your best shot.'"

Yes, Unitas was the best I ever saw. He got the gameplan on Wednesday, but once the whistle blew, it was his game to run in whatever way he chose. "I charted the tendencies of every defensive back in the league," he said. "I could tell you how Lem Barney would react to a certain pattern, or how Jesse Whittenton would play a certain zone coverage. Raymond Berry and I put in our own set of audibles based on the tendencies of the coverage guys."

Coaches were an annoyance to Unitas. He'd get a little help from the press box "just to let me know about the other team's blitz tendencies," he said. "Otherwise, just leave me alone." How would he feel having a radio in his helmet, getting messages from the sideline before every play? "I'd get very deaf all of a sudden," he said. "My radio would be permanently out of service."

Unitas had the good fortune to play much of his career for Weeb Ewbank, one of the few coaches who had a great feel for the quarterback position and knew enough not to mess too much with the exceptional young man he had playing for him. But the two did have their occasional disagreements, and I reminded Unitas about a famous quote of his, one that stuck with me for years: "You don't become a real quarterback until you can tell the coach to go to hell."

"Oh, sure, I remember that," Unitas said, laughing. "I loved playing for Weeb, but sometimes I'd just ignore what he told me. Early in my career he'd try to limit where I could throw against certain people. He had tremendous respect for Night Train Lane. He'd tell me, 'Don't throw the ball in his area.' Well, hell, I wasn't going to give him the day off. So I'd throw at him, and maybe he'd pick one off, but we could do things against him, too.

"Jack Butler of the Steelers was another guy Weeb had deep respect for. We played them in an exhibition game, and Weeb told me to stay away from him. Lenny Moore said, 'Weeb, I can get open in the deep middle.' Weeb said, 'There's no way you'll get behind him.' So next time we're in the huddle, I tell Lenny, 'Damn, let's do it.' We hit the deep post for six points two times. It proved one thing to me: I could do what I wanted out there. After the game Weeb came over to me and said, 'John, I'm never going to tell you what to do again.'"

The end came in 1973, 15 years after that great championship game. Unitas was 40, his body wracked by injuries, playing out the string on a hopeless San Diego Chargers team that had one major asset, a fine rookie quarterback named Dan Fouts.

"The coach, Harland Svare, asked me to work with Danny," Unitas said, "and Dan was all excited about it. Then after five or six games, the offensive coach, Bob Schnelker, came over to me and said, 'The coaches had a meeting last night, and we'd rather you didn't work with him anymore.' Who knows why? Anyway, I told Fouts, and oh, boy, he was hot. So I said, 'What the hell, we'll keep doing it. They're not smart enough to know what's going on anyway.'"

I didn't want the afternoon with Unitas to end. When it was time to say goodbye, the hand he extended was crippled and twisted. "Carpal tunnel," he said. "When they operated on it, they cut a nerve. Now I can't rotate the thumb to pick up anything."

How many more things like that were there? "In '68 I tore muscles in my arm," he said. "Two nerves were dead. I lost feeling in my fingers and I haven't completely regained it. Let's see, two knee replacements, and then the triple bypass."

That's what finally got him, the heart, the one that had been the biggest and most spirited in the game.

* * *

GOODBYE TO ALL THAT, ROGER
This article appeared in the April 14, 1980 issue of Sports Illustrated.

So long, Roger, we gave you a bum deal, kid. For openers, we never picked you All-Pro. That's we, the writers, the pickers, the guys who vote on the AP and Pro Football Writers ballots. Now that's a bad call right away, because all you did was end up as the NFL's top-rated passer — in history, the whole 59 years. Higher than Unitas, than Tarkenton or Jurgensen, than Tittle or Baugh. And you quarterbacked the Cowboys in four of their five Super Bowls, winning twice. And brought the team from behind to victory 14 times in the last two minutes or in overtime, 23 times in the fourth quarter. Hey, what does a guy have to do?

Oh, you made the all-division team a few times. But never the big one, the starting 11, AFC and NFC combined. "You look back on it and it seems amazing, doesn't it?" says one selector. "But it just worked out that when he had his greatest years, someone had a slightly better one. And then you felt that Roger would always be around, and he'd be great for the next 10 years or so, and his time would come. So you went with the hot hand ... and Staubach got stiffed."

And now he's gone. Staubach made it official last week at a press conference in the Texas Stadium Club room. There were 200 witnesses, some from as far away as New Jersey, 42 of them with microphones. With the metronomic click-click-click of the cameras in the background, Staubach spoke for 18 minutes.

He wore an open-neck shirt and a dark blue sweater. He looked a very youthful 38. A few gray hairs, a few lines in the face, but not the image of the old pro saying farewell. He looked youthful until you saw film clips of him in his rookie year of '69. Flattop haircut, baby face — a child, really. And the guy was 27 with a year of Vietnam behind him.

The book on Staubach was always that his four years of naval service didn't count when you figured his NFL age, that being in Nam doesn't age you as quickly as ducking forearms. It's an argument that probably would have been projected into his 50th year: "He's not really a 50-year-old quarterback, you see; his actual NFL age is only 46."

But last week Staubach put an end to it, joining a very small fraternity of NFL stars who quit when they could still command a big salary — Jimmy Brown, Fran Tarkenton, Whizzer White if you want to go way back. His announcement overshadowed two other major Cowboy retirements, each of which could have commanded a major press conference of its own. Offensive Tackle Rayfield Wright, 34, and Free Safety Cliff Harris, 31, with nine years of combined All-Pro behind them, each called it a career. With Wright it was a forced decision. Tom Landry decided that 13 seasons was enough. But Harris, the definitive safetyman of the '70s and an almost certain Hall of Famer, caught the Cowboys by surprise when he told them he had a good opportunity with a young and energetic oil company, and there comes a time in every man's life ...

Gone, too, is Hollywood Henderson, the strongside linebacker. No, his reinstatement is not being considered, nor will it be. That holds true whatever happens to his replacement, Mike Hegman, who is facing possible prosecution on a charge of theft for allegedly forging a friend's name on $10,534 worth of checks.

So all of a sudden there are holes all over the Cowboys' depth chart as well as in the roof of their stadium. It is hoped that Too Tall Jones will return from his one-year boxing career. Underline hope; so far he hasn't said anything about it. Charlie Waters, the All-Pro strong safety, is coming back from major knee surgery. And the Cowboys won't be drafting until the third round, Nos. 1 and 2 having gone to the Colts for Defensive End John Dutton.

So last week Landry, who hasn't experienced such a severe case of the shorts since the early expansion years in Dallas, watched his quarterback say goodbye, and he was wondering where he'd find another one like him.

"He hadn't indicated anything during the season," he said later. "He'd had such a good year, one of his best ever. But things weren't encouraging during the off-season. Right after the playoffs, he told me he was considering the possibility of retiring. He said he wanted to tell me early, so I could get ready for it."

Staubach might have decided already. After the 21-19 loss to the Rams in the playoffs, he was driving home with his wife, Marianne, and he told her he'd had it. "That's it," he said. "Can you believe that the last pass I completed in the NFL was to Herbert Scott?"

Every official in Texas Stadium reached for his flag on that play. Guards aren't eligible receivers in the NFL. Staubach had been trying to throw the ball away, throw it into the ground, but he'd gotten too much on it, and it hit Scott in the belly and he reflexively grabbed it. Staubach had been zapped earlier in the game when Jack Reynolds bounced his head off the Tartan Turf, giving Roger his fifth concussion of the season.

He was tired and his head hurt and his team had just been eliminated from the playoffs. December talk, his wife figured. She'd heard it before. But Lord knows, it wouldn't be such a bad idea. Five concussions, two of them serious. He'd experienced some numbness after the Pittsburgh game.

Twenty concussions, total, including high school. A few weeks after the Rams game, a New York neurologist told Staubach that, yes, there was some cumulative damage, a slight slowing of some of the reflexes.

He had paid his dues. His left shoulder was dislocated 17 times before he underwent surgery to have the ligaments tightened. When Staubach tries to move his left arm backward, the motion is markedly limited. The little finger on his throwing hand doesn't look like a finger at all. It's a perfect Z, discounting a big round knot in the middle. The index finger is swollen and off-line.

"I was hoping he meant it that day in the car, that he'd really retire," his wife says. "If he'd have played again this year and he'd have been knocked out again, my heart would have stopped. But I wasn't going to tell him that. The decision had to be his. Usually I could see his enthusiasm coming back in the off-season. This year I didn't."

The idea of his retiring had taken hold, although in Dallas, Staubach had become an institution. His secretary, Roz Cole, was sending out 10,000 pictures a season. He would write a personal message on 300 a week; he'd answer 3,000 letters a year. His life had become an inspiration to the country, but it had its price. He'd get requests for 70 to 80 speaking engagements a week. Church groups, prisons, hospitals. It's not in Staubach's nature to stiff anybody. You've never heard any stories about him brushing off a kid with an autograph book. Sonny Jurgensen used to duck out on the writers, through a back door, after his games; Joe Namath had one set of writers he'd talk to and another he wouldn't, but no journalist ever said Staubach had given him a hard time.

What could he do? He had a life to live. He has five children at home. "They need quality time from me," he concluded. "Not just time, but quality time. I'd be watching films and my daughter would come in to tell me about something that happened in school, and I'd say, 'Not now, can't you see I'm busy?' and she'd go away. And then an hour later, I'd think, 'What the heck have I done?' and I'd go and find her up in her bedroom and try to tell her how sorry I was."

He added up the pluses and minuses of life in the NFL. And outside: he is president of a real-estate company, Holloway-Staubach, that is branching out. In that league he was known as a "young executive." The decision became clear to Staubach. It was time.

A press conference was announced. The next day Gil Brandt, the Cowboys' Vice-President for Personnel Development, was stopped by a patrolman for making an improper turn on the North Central Expressway in Dallas. He had left his wallet and driver's license in the office.

"I'll tell you what," the cop said. "You tell me what Roger's gonna do, and I'll let you go."

"Buddy, I just wish I knew," Brandt said. The cop let him go anyway.

On Monday morning Staubach drove to the practice field to say goodbye to his teammates. He wanted to keep it light.

"I felt it was only fitting that Herb Scott caught my last pass," he said. "He's worked hard during his career, and he never got to catch one. And he did such a good job getting open on the play."

It was nice and loose — for a while. One more oversight in Staubach's career is that he never got the recognition he deserved as a comic. He's got a genuine zany streak and he should have been born looking like Woody Allen, but when you're president of the student body in high school and prom king and a star in three sports — well, those credentials don't break 'em up.

A few days before the press conference, the Cowboys' receptionist got a call from a cactus-voiced fan who told her, "If Roger's leaving, you can just cancel my season tickets right now." She hung up. Then came another call, nastier than the first. Then another. Then Staubach called. "I want to find out how many fans have canceled their season tickets," he said.

"Dammit, Roger," she said. "They were all you!"

When it came time for Staubach to thank his teammates for the 11 years, things got a little heavy. You don't just snappy-patter out of a career.

But the toughest time came in the press conference when Staubach had to speak of Landry. "Of course the nuts and bolts of the Dallas Cowboys," he said, and there was a pause of 10 seconds or so while he got himself together, "was the man who wears the funny hat on the sidelines."

"I don't know why, but I just couldn't say his name," Staubach said later. "I didn't want to get too emotional, but when I came to his name — well, I knew if I said it I'd probably lose control."

The press conference over, Staubach drove home with Marianne. Danny White and Glenn Carano, who will line up for the quarterback job next season, dropped by, along with Middle Linebacker Bob Breunig, and they played some two-on-two half-court basketball in the backyard. Staubach and White took two of three games.

When sundown came, Staubach and his family went to a friend's house for a first night of Passover seder. "I wore a yarmulke," he said. "The kids got a tremendous kick out of the hiding of the matzo and then ransoming it; the food was terrific. It was a good way to end a very tough day."

For the Cowboys the tough days are only beginning. Landry will spend more time coaching the defense this season, and former Cowboy Halfback Danny Reeves will have more responsibility for the offense. It's not hard to figure out why Landry is so interested in his defense. The Cowboys gave up 313 points last year, the most since 1963, when Don Meredith and Eddie LeBaron were battling to quarterback a 4-10 team. The rushing defense was 11th in the league, and the Cowboys had the fewest interceptions (13) in the NFL. Staubach pulled out four games in the last two minutes. "He was the difference between a good year and an average year," Landry says. And now there's no Staubach to carry the Cowboys anymore.

Everyone says White has the potential to produce points, but what about the defense? "It's the kind of challenge that Landry handles best," Harris says. "Somehow I get the feeling he'll find exactly the right pieces to fit into the puzzle. I think his genius will really come out next season."

Landry still isn't convinced Harris will stay retired. "He's impulsive," the coach says. "He does things the way he plays. He gives so much, just like Roger, that he needs the spark, and if he doesn't think it's there ... well, then he just doesn't feel he can give what's needed. I think he might get the spark back."

Harris likes to talk about the oil firm he works for, U.S. Companies Inc., which acquires property, makes tests, then drills. He gets excited when he tells you about the chances of hitting a big one. Staubach has already become an investor in U.S. Companies. Harris doesn't sound as if he really wants to drill receivers anymore.

"Listen to this," he says. "One of the guys who called me when I retired was Lynn Swann. Can you imagine? Swann, of all people. Such a bitter rival, for so long. He said, 'I don't mind your leaving. It'll extend my career.'"

Harris was one of four players, along with Staubach, Breunig and Tony Dorsett, who came up with $2,000 apiece to help Hegman cover those checks. Hegman himself covered the rest, and the bank, Republic National of Dallas, is supposedly satisfied, but the Dallas DA's office has not yet decided what to do about the case.

Henderson is gone. "Landry has had it up to here with him, and so have a lot of us," one player says. "The guy would always pick defensive day to come up with a sore back or something. When he pulled that sideline stunt in the Washington game (Henderson was fooling with a bandanna for a TV camera) it was the last straw. We were getting blown out, and he wasn't making any tackles — that's the wrong time to clown."

"The offers we've had on a trade for him are embarrassing," says Brandt. "Nothing as high as a first- or second-round draft, which we need. I don't know, Butch Johnson (a backup wide receiver) keeps talking about wanting to be traded. Maybe we can put together a package with him and Thomas."

Pat Thomas, L.A.'s left cornerback, is mad at the Rams and wants to play for Dallas. He's visited the Cowboys' office, which is only a short trip from his home in Plano. But not many people seriously expect the Rams to trade their best defensive back to a traditional playoff rival.

Then there's talk about Patriot Cornerback Mike Haynes, who has played out his option and wouldn't mind wearing silver and blue. But if the Cowboys pick him up, it would cost them two years' worth of first-round picks, based on Haynes' salary, which would mean going in hock until 1982. It's a risky way to travel, and it's never been their style.

The reality is that Staubach is gone and so is Harris, and the defense shows patches. For the first time in years, the Cowboys are going into a season shorthanded. Landry has been there before. He didn't lose all that hair for nothing.

* * *

BORN TO BE A QUARTERBACK
This article appeared in the Aug. 6, 1990 issue of Sports Illustrated.

It's a normal minicamp lunch break at the San Francisco 49ers' training facility. The players are unwrapping their sandwiches in the locker room, and Joe Montana is giving an interview upstairs in p.r. director Jerry Walker's office. Well, most of Joe Montana is concentrating on the interview. His right hand is busy with something else, as if it has a life of its own, a mechanized life of autograph production.

A steady stream of objects appears on the table in front of him — hats, jerseys, photos, posters — and Montana's right hand automatically rises, then lowers, producing a large sweeping J and tailing off to an almost illegible ana. Then his hand rises again, and another item is moved into place. Secretaries, p.r. people, coaches, players all come to present offerings at this ritual.

"A book to sign," says Walker. "Two pictures," says tight end Jamie Williams. "A ball," says p.r. assistant Dave Rahn. "Make this one out to 'a Nevada sports fan,'" says defensive coordinator Bill McPherson, sliding in a picture.

Rise and fall, rise and fall; the big J, the scribbled ana. Most of the time Montana doesn't even look at what he's signing. You get the feeling that someone could slip in a small child, a hamburger bun, a fish. It's all the same. At 34, the world's most famous quarterback has turned into an autograph machine.

Secretary Darla Maeda brings a hat. Walker is back with a toy rabbit. Guard Guy McIntyre is next with a jersey.

"Oh, no, not you too," Montana says, rolling his eyes.

"Yeah, me." It's Norb Hecker, the team's senior administrator, and he has a poster showing a glowering Montana. "A beauty, huh?" he says.

"They name animals after him," Rahn says, producing a picture of a German shepherd. "They send in every piece of football equipment you can think of. The office is cluttered with stuff." There is a children's book from a woman in Hillsborough, Calif. "To Joe Montana, for your kids … let me know if you need extra copies," reads the accompanying letter. There are eight mail cartons filled with letters going back four months, letters from France, Ireland, Tokyo.

"He'll come up here once or twice a week to sign stuff," says p.r. assistant Al Barba. We use the real Joe pictures until they run out, then we send the ones with the printed autograph. Everyone will get something — eventually."

Since he blistered the Denver Broncos in last January's Super Bowl, Montana is hot again, just as he was after the 49ers' Super Bowl victory in '82 and the one in '85, having been voted the game's Most Valuable Player each time. The first success represented the thrill of discovery, the potential star who blossomed, and it carried a healthy round of commercial endorsements with it. The second one reestablished him after Miami Dolphins quarterback Dan Marino had captured most of the headlines in '84. But then, in the 1985 season, the adulation for Montana cooled.

There were drug rumors, all unsubstantiated. Montana in his Ferrari reportedly stopped by police, even though the car was in his garage at the time. Montana seen in a bar, when he happened to be in a team meeting. In '86 there was the back operation two weeks into the season. Doctors said Montana might never play again. He was back in 55 days. The '87 season was his best statistically at that time, but the year ended with a disastrous loss to the Vikings in an NFC divisional playoff. When Montana was lifted for Steve Young in that game, it was the first time since he had reached football maturity that San Francisco coach Bill Walsh had given him the hook. The fans cheered when Young entered the game. Trade Joe now, they said, while you can still get something for him.

Walsh started Young a few times in '88, saying he was giving Montana time to get over nagging injuries and "general fatigue." Montana says it was a lack of confidence, tracing back to the end of '87. "It's tearing my guts out," Montana told his wife, Jennifer. But the exclamation point on the '88 season was the terrific 92-yard drive in the final minutes to beat Cincinnati in Super Bowl XXIII, and Montana came into '89 riding the crest. He put together a remarkable season, the best any quarterback has ever had, according to the NFL's rating system. And he was even better in the playoffs and Super Bowl XXIV, reaching a level of brilliance that had never been seen in postseason football. Which leaves only one question to ask about this remarkable 11-year veteran: Is he the greatest quarterback ever to play the game?

Wait, let's back off from that one for a minute. Greatest ever? What about Unitas, Baugh, Luckman, Graham? History's a serious business. Van Brocklin, Bradshaw, Tittle? When, in the long history of the NFL, was a quarterback in his prime called the greatest ever? The man in the most glamorous position in football going against the most famous names of the past? Does anyone point to a surgeon in Houston and say, "Yep, there's the greatest doctor ever?" How about Albert Schweitzer? It's rare ground we're treading on.

Montana's roots are in western Pennsylvania, the cradle of quarterbacks. Soft coal and quarterbacks. Steel mills and quarterbacks. Johnny Lujack from Connellsville, Joe Namath from Beaver Falls, George Blanda from Youngwood, Dan Marino from Pittsburgh, Montana from Monongahela, Tom Clements and Chuck Fusina from McKees Rocks, Arnold Galiffa from Donora, Terry Hanratty from Butler — he was Montana's idol as a kid. Terry Hanratty of Notre Dame, the Golden Domer. Montana would throw footballs through a swinging tire in the backyard, just like Terry did. Why? Why do so many of them come from western Pennsylvania? "Toughness, dedication, hard work and competitiveness; a no-nonsense, blue-collar background," says John Unitas, from Pittsburgh.

But there are a lot of no-nonsense, blue-collar places in the country. Why not Georgia or Texas, where the great running backs come from? Why not Michigan or Ohio, with all those fine linemen? What is it about western Pennsylvania and quarterbacks?

"Maybe it's the Iron City beer," says Montana.

The most logical answer is tradition — and focus. If you're a kid with athletic ability in western Pennsylvania, you've probably got a picture of Montana or Marino on your wall. Montana had the athletic gift. You could see it right away.

"He used to wreck his crib by standing up and rocking," his mother, Theresa, says. "Then he'd climb up on the side and jump to our bed. You'd hear a thump in the middle of the night and know he hit the bed and went on the floor."

And he had the focus, supplied by his father, Joseph Sr., who put a ball in his son's hands when the kid was big enough to walk and said, "Throw it."

"I played all sports in the service, but when I was a kid I never had anyone to take me in the backyard and throw a ball to me," says Joe Sr., who moved to California with his wife in '86. "Maybe that's why I got Joe started in sports. Once he got started, he was always waiting at the door with a ball when I came home from work. What I really wanted to do was make it fun for him. And I wanted to make sure he got the right fundamentals. I read books. You watch some quarterbacks, sometimes they need two steps to get away from the line of scrimmage. I felt the first step should be straight back, not to the side. We worked on techniques, sprint out, run right, run left, pivot and throw the ball.

"You know, I've been accused of pushing him. I don't think that's right. It's just that he loved it so much, and I loved watching him. And I wanted to make sure he learned the right way."

Joe Jr. was an only child, a pampered child, perhaps, but he didn't see it that way. The family lived in a two-story frame house in a middle-class neighborhood on Park Ave., a house no better than the neighbors' and no worse. To Montana, his home was his strength, his support system. He was shy with strangers, outgoing at home. He had a few friends, neighborhood kids mostly, but no one was as close to him as his father — and his mother. His fondest childhood memory? Playing ball in the backyard with his dad, then coming into the kitchen, where his mother would have a steaming pot of ravioli on the stove. That was the best.

Montana started playing peewee football when he was eight, one year younger than the legal limit. His father listed his age as nine. His first coach on the Little Wildcats was Carl Crawley, a defensive lineman in college and now an NCAA referee.

"We ran a pro offense, with a lot of the stuff he's doing now, the underneath stuff," Crawley says. "Joe would roll out. If the cornerback came off, he'd dump it off; if he stayed back, he'd keep going and pick up five or six yards. He was an amazingly accurate passer for a kid."

Montana's favorite receiver was Mike Brantley, who caught his passes through junior high and high school. Brantley eventually made it as far as the Pittsburgh Steelers' training camp. "Joe throwing to Mike was like the right hand throwing to the left hand," Crawley says.

Crawley remembers Montana as an "exuberant kid who had stardom written all over him, but nobody ever resented it because it came so naturally. And there was no show-off in him. He wanted to win and he'd do whatever it took, and that's another thing the kids liked about him. With Joe on the field, they knew they were never out of any game."

In the spring it was baseball, and Montana played all the positions. As a pitcher in Little League, he threw three perfect games. In the winter it was basketball, for which there was no organized program for kids until Joe Sr. started one. The team practiced and played in the local armory, and the kids paid a dollar a piece for a janitor to clean up after them. The practices were five nights a week, and there were always tournaments to play in. "Those were the most fun," Montana says. "The trips. We'd go anywhere. One night we played in a tournament in Bethel Park, Pennsylvania, then drove up to Niagara Falls for another one, then back to Bethel Park for the finals."

Montana has always said that his favorite sport, through Waverly Elementary and Finleyville Junior High and finally Ringgold High, was basketball. He loved the practices. "I could practice basketball all day," he says. Practicing football was work.

He came to Ringgold with a reputation for being something of a wunderkind. When coach Chuck Abramski took his first look at Montana on the football field, he saw an agile, 6-foot, 165-pound sophomore with a nice touch on the ball, but a kid who was too skinny and too immature to stand up to the rigors of western Pennsylvania Class AAA football. Abramski gave Montana a seat on the bench and told him to watch and learn. And to be sure to report to the summer weight program before his junior year. Montana had other ideas.

"For me, competing in sports was a 365-day-a-year thing," he says. "I was playing American Legion baseball, summer basketball. It was hard for Coach Abramski to accept that."

Last January, a week before the Super Bowl, a story appeared in *The Baltimore Sun* saying that, in Monongahela, Montana was regarded as a lesser god, a fact the rest of the world was dimly aware of. A number of old resentments surfaced in the story, but the worst quotes of all were from Abramski. "A lot of people in Monongahela hate Joe," was one of them. "If I was in a war, I wouldn't want Joe on my side … his dad would have to carry his gun for him," was another, and it was the one that bothered Montana most because it hit him where he lived. No one connected with football had ever questioned his courage.

"I called him about it," Montana says. "Three times now, I've seen those Abramski quotes around Super Bowl time, about why people hate me. I asked him why he kept saying those things, and he said, 'Well, you never sent me a picture, and you sent one to Jeff Petrucci, the quarterback coach.'

I said, 'You never asked.' I mean, I don't send my picture around everywhere. We ended up yelling at each other. We had to put our wives on.

"Of course, I know what it was really about … that summer weight program. Chuck was a great coach in a lot of ways. He always tried to get the kids good equipment, he was always helping them get into college. I even wrote a letter of recommendation for him to go to another school after he left Ringgold. He was a fired-up, gung-ho coach, but he never got over the fact that I didn't take part in his summer weight program before my junior year. The man's all football."

Abramski, hard and wiry at 58, still lives in Monongahela, but he's out of football now. He sells real estate, just as Joe Montana Sr. does in the Bay Area. Abramski bounced around the western Pennsylvania high school circuit and held one college coaching job, at California University of Pennsylvania, under his old assistant at Ringgold, Petrucci. The problem was always the same: He was a great guy for developing a program, but school administrators found him impossible to deal with.

"I came from the south side of New Castle, the poor side," Abramski says. "My father was an alcoholic. My mother died of tuberculosis when I was 10. My grandmother raised me. There have been coaches with more brains, but nobody in the world worked harder at football than me. The year before I came to Ringgold, they lost every game and scored two touchdowns. They left me 14 players in uniform. Two years later, we had 100 kids out for football and we dressed 60, home and away. Three years later, Joe's senior year, we had one of the best teams in the eastern United States. We went 8-1 and then lost to Mt. Lebanon in the playoffs on a miserable, sleety night with three starters out. Before the season we scrimmaged South Moreland and scored 19 touchdowns. Nineteen touchdowns!"

The weight program was Abramski's baby, his joy. It was part of the toughening-up process. According to Abramski, Montana and only one other player, a halfback, didn't participate in his summer program. Petrucci says that about 20 percent to 30 percent of the squad didn't take part. Some former players say the number was higher. But here was Abramski's junior quarterback, a guy who had superstar written all over him — hell, everyone knew it — and he wasn't there. It ate Abramski up. When the season started, Montana was on the bench. "It's very painful now, when people say I harbored this hatred for Joe," Abramski says. "Hell, I loved the kid. I was doing what I thought was right for my squad."

"It's just an unfortunate thing," says Petrucci. "Here's a kid who never did anything wrong, never smoked or drank or broke curfew, never gave anyone a hard time, just a terrific kid. And on the other side, you've got a good coach who's stubborn."

People who were close to the situation feel that the real source of Abramski's resentment was not Joe but his father, who had worked with Joe for so long and taught him all the right habits. It was a matter of control, the fact that the father, not the coach, had had more to do with making a star out of the boy.

And now Abramski had benched that potential star, and his quarterback was 6-3, 215-pound Paul Timko, a big, rough youngster who splattered defenders when he ran the option play but had a throwing arm like a tackle's. In the scrimmages, Timko would line up at defensive end and take dead aim at Montana, the guy who was trying to take his job away. "Every day he just beat the hell out of me," Montana said. "I'd be dead when I came home. Football wasn't much fun at that point."

The Ringgold Rams were blown out by Elizabeth Forward 34-6 in the 1972 opener. They won the next two games by forfeit because of a teachers' strike, but lost the two practice games that were played to fill in the schedule. Timko wasn't the answer, obviously, especially with an away game coming up against mighty Monessen, the favorite to win the Big Ten league title. During the time of the forfeits, Montana had moved up to become the starter. Timko was shifted to tight end. "Hell, I wanted to play there anyway," Timko says.

Keith Bassi, who was the Ringgold fullback, says the scene that night at Monessen was like nothing he has ever seen before or since. "You had to be there," he says. "I mean, Monessen had some players — Bubba Holmes, who went to Minnesota; Tony Benjamin, who went to Duke. The rumor was that guys there had been held back a year in nursery school so they'd be more mature when they hit high school. We were doing our calisthenics, and there was this big roar, and here they came, 120 of them, in single file from the top of that concrete stadium, biggest stadium in the (Monongahela) Valley. It was like Custer's Last Stand."

The final score was 34-34, Holmes scoring for Monessen in the last moments. "We call it our 34-34 win," Bassi says. Montana's passing numbers read 12 for 22, 223 yards and four touchdowns, three of them to Timko, the new tight end.

Last April, Ringgold threw a welcome-home dinner for Montana at the New Eagle Fire Hall. The 1,000 tickets were sold out in three hours. Among the gifts presented to Montana was a set of videotapes of all his high school games. A month later Joe Ravasio, the current football coach at Ringgold, showed me the original game films in a store room off the boys' locker room.

The first pass Montana threw against Monessen was on a scramble to his right; he pulled up and hit Brantley, crossing underneath. The second was a sideline completion to Timko, neatly plunked between two defenders. The show was on. "They played a three-deep, where they give you the short stuff," said Frank Lawrence, who had been the offensive line coach. "Joe just killed 'em with timed patterns." It was an eerie feeling, watching Montana drop back from center, set and throw. All his 49er mechanics were there, the quick setup, the nifty glide to the outside, scrambling but under control, buying time, looking for a receiver underneath. It seemed as if he had been doing it all his life, and this was a kid in his first high school start. "Watch Joe now," Lawrence said as Ringgold scored on a one-yard plunge. "See that? He backpedals after the touchdown and throws his hands up. Same mannerisms as now."

There were some amazing athletic plays by Montana — a 10-yard bootleg to the one, having faked everyone; a 35-yard touchdown pass to Timko, a play on which he rolled left, corkscrewed his body, dodged a rusher and laid the ball into the hands of the tight end, who was surrounded by three defenders.

We watched it all, junior year and senior year. The somewhat slender kid was gradually filling out, standing taller in the pocket, almost 6-2 now, up to 180 pounds — the makings of a superstar. In the Laurel Highlands game his senior year (won by Ringgold 44-0), Montana rolled to his right, went up on his toes and pump-faked two defensive players out of position before he hit his receiver on a crossing pattern. But the most interesting thing was that the cameraman wasn't fooled. He kept the camera right on Montana. By then everyone knew what he was capable of.

He was all-everything his senior year — including Parade All-America as a quarterback — a gifted athlete who starred on a league championship basketball team ("He could stand flat-footed and dunk with two hands," says Fran Lamendola, his basketball coach), a baseball player good enough to get invited back to a major league tryout camp, a potential standout in sports in which he merely filled in — a victory in his only tennis match, an informal 6-9 high jump, a junior high record in his only attempt at the discus. He was a B student who could have done better if someone had figured out a way to get him indoors, in front of a book, a little longer. He was popular in school, easy to get to know, hard to get close to. His classmates elected him class vice-president his senior year; the Ringgold yearbook, Flame 74, lists him as a member of the choir as a senior. The photo that appears under "Sports Personalities" in the yearbook shows a thin kid with blond, floppy hair that is almost girlish-looking. He is leaning on the wall next to a trophy case; no waist or hips, string-bean legs in long bell-bottoms. "Joe Banana" was one of Abramski's nicknames for Montana.

North Carolina State offered him a basketball scholarship. Notre Dame basketball coach Digger Phelps said he would try to arrange it so Montana could play football and basketball. A few dozen college offers came in. Georgia assistant coach Sam Mrvos stood next to Montana's dad at one practice session, watched Joe throw a bullet while sprinting to his left and told Joe Sr., "We'll give him a scholarship right now." Georgia was one of the schools Montana visited, along with Boston College, Minnesota and Notre Dame. His parents had taken him for a look around Penn State, and he had been to Pitt many times to watch the Panthers play.

It was all window dressing. His mind was already made up. It would be Notre Dame, where his idol, Hanratty, had played.

"In his senior year, the games at Legion Field were a happening," said Bob Osleger, the golf coach at Ringgold. "There was this flat bit of ground above the stadium, and Joe's father would stand there and watch the game, and all these college coaches and scouts would vie for position to stand near him. The whispers would start, about which college coaches were there that night, and I can see it so clearly now. Joe's dad would be standing there with his hands in his pockets and all these guys jockeying for position around him."

Sixteen and a half years later, Montana was back, sitting on the dais at the dinner in the New Eagle Fire Hall, facing a roomful of people who had paid the cut rate of $20 a head, same price they paid for his first welcome-home dinner in '79. Earlier in the day he had given four speeches to a few thousand school kids — elementary, middle and high school — and there was a gleeful moment when six-year-old Anthony Vaccaro asked him, "Do you know who's living in your house?"

"No," Montana said.

"I am," Anthony said, "512 Park Avenue."

"Do you sleep in my bedroom?"

"Yes."

But there was also an edge to Montana's return that some kids couldn't quite understand. That day the *Pittsburgh Post-Gazette* ran a story that dredged up all the old resentments. Some people felt Montana had turned his back on the Mon Valley when he moved to San Francisco, and that his parents had done likewise when they followed him west. There was mention in the *Post-Gazette* of his infrequent visits home and how his name had been rejected in a newspaper phone-in poll on the naming of Ringgold's new stadium. Once again there was an old Abramski quote about all the people who hated him.

Montana read the piece on his way to Monongahela from the Pittsburgh airport, and his opening remarks to the Ringgold middle school students left a few kids scratching their heads. "What you hear about me, about my feelings, are totally false," he said. "When they say Joe Montana doesn't think of the Mon Valley as his home, well, you can tell whoever's saying it that he's full of it." It was a sentiment he would repeat to the high school kids, and at the dinner. His relatives in town knew only too well what he was talking about.

"My 14-year-old granddaughter, Jamie, was afraid to go to school that day," says Montana's aunt, Elinor Johnson. "She was afraid the kids were going to boo him."

"The kids were telling me he doesn't really care about Monongahela," Jamie says. "There's a picture of Joe on a locker in school that says, 'My Hero — Joke!' They don't know him. They hear what some people say. Sometimes I'll get upset, sometimes I'll walk away."

"You grew up working in a mill or a factory," says Pam Giordenango, Jamie's mother. "Now the mill's closed, the factory's closed. Heavy industry moved out of the Valley. People lost their jobs, lost their homes, lost their families. They're bitter. Whatever they read in the news gives them something to bitch about, other than the fact that they can't make their house payments, can't afford to put food on the table. Now here comes Joe, who's made a lot of money playing football. He's an easy target."

I am standing in front of the armory, the old place where Montana practiced basketball at night. It seems small, much too small to hold a basketball court. A blue Chevy pulls up and stops. "If you want to get inside, you have to get the key from the minister down the street," the woman in the car says. She seems friendly. On an impulse I ask her, "What do you think of Joe Montana?"

"I don't like him," she says.

"Why not?"

"Stillers," she says.

Stillers? A bitter family in town?

"Stillers, Pittsburgh Stillers," she says. "Joe should be a Stiller."

A youngster asked Montana the same question earlier in the day. How come you aren't a Steeler, if you like this town so much?

"The football draft is like the draft in the Army," Montana had said. "When they call you, you go."

"Hey, you're in Steeler country," Elinor Johnson says. "They don't want Joe to beat Terry Bradshaw's record. You can get your man in the street, your man in the bar, he'll tell you that."

There's more, of course, like the fact that Montana's parents worked for Civic Finance — his father was the manager, his mother a secretary — while the area was going through a financial crisis. "One person who defaulted on a loan can spread more bad news around town than 50 people can spread good news," says Carl Crawley. And then the fact that the Montanas left for California, to be with Joe and Jennifer. Joe Jr. had instigated the move in 1986. He had always been close to his parents, but how could you be close when you were 2,500 miles apart? "Joe said, 'Quit and come out here with Jennifer and me,'" his father says. "It's hard, though, when you've lived somewhere all your life, when your roots are there."

There had also been a newspaper story about a financial mix-up, an accusation that Montana had billed a Monongahela group for speaking at a dinner held to honor him for being the '82 Super Bowl MVP. It was a bum rap. Montana was an infrequent public speaker in those days, and the few appearances he made were mostly unpaid charity work. There was no fee for his Monongahela appearance, only a guarantee of airfare, but when he put in an appearance at a second affair, in nearby Washington, Pa., there was a tap dance about who would pick up the expense for Montana's trip home. "I never knew a thing about it until I read all that stuff in the paper," Montana says.

As for the stadium that does not bear his name, the newspaper poll drew on a wide area, feeding on neighborhood rivalries and jealousies. None of the other local heroes was acceptable either, not Stan Musial, not Ken Griffey.

Perhaps the main cause of conflict is that Montana has always guarded his privacy. "We've come back to Monongahela four or five times in the last few years to visit relatives," Jennifer Montana says, "but people don't know that. What is he supposed to do, go down to the corner drugstore and hang out?"

That's probably what the people of Monongahela wanted. They wanted a superstar to act like one. But Montana's public persona had become a nightmare for him. "I love to eat out," he says, "but it's just no fun anymore. There's always a group of people coming by your table, always some guy just pulling up a chair and lighting a cigarette and starting to talk football."

He did what he had to do publicly — sign autographs and give interviews — but his privacy was his, and that included trips back home. In Monongahela, it was hard to understand. He was still Joey, the local kid. It's a complex area, the Mon Valley, fiercely loyal at times, but a place where it's easy to form resentments. And it's the area that Montana left in the fall of 1974 for a strange sojourn at Notre Dame that mirrored his entire athletic career — lows, moments of despair, followed by glorious highs.

He was 18 when he arrived in South Bend, still skinny, still shy with people he didn't know, a bit at sea so far away from his hometown and his parents. He had become engaged to his high school sweetheart, Kim Moses, from Monongahela Valley Catholic High. They would be married in the second semester of his freshman year and divorced less than three years later.

At Notre Dame he found himself amid an incredible collection of talent. He was a high school hotshot who was surrounded by hotshots, a hatchery fish in the deep ocean. Forty-six players who played for Notre Dame during the Montana years would be drafted by the NFL, eight in the first round. The Irish won a national championship under Ara Parseghian the year before Montana arrived in South Bend, and they would win another one, under Dan Devine, in '77, Montana's junior year.

Montana saw no varsity action his first year and got only minimal playing time in the freshman games. The eye-catching recruit was Gary Forystek, a big, strong, rocket-armed kid from Livonia, Mich. Montana?

Well, he had that sleepy look about him. He missed home. He would call his dad three, four times a week. Joe Sr. told him to hang in. On a whim Montana once drove home in the middle of the night. Joe Sr. occasionally would make the eight-hour drive from Monongahela to watch Joe Jr. in an afternoon scrimmage, grab a bite to eat with his son, and then drive home to be at work the next day.

"His dad would sometimes show up in the middle of the night, and we'd all go out at 1 a.m. for a stack of pancakes," says Montana's freshman roommate, Nick DeCicco. "It was crazy."

"The fact is, his father was his best friend," says Steve Orsini, Montana's former teammate at Notre Dame. "The person Joe felt closest to was back in Monongahela."

Parseghian resigned suddenly, for health reasons, on Dec. 15, 1974, and the new coach was Devine, from the Green Bay Packers. "I asked the coaches about my quarterbacks when I first got there," Devine says. "No one said much about Joe. He'd been something like the seventh or eighth quarterback. Then he had a fine spring practice, really outstanding. I came home and told my wife, 'I'm gonna start Joe Montana in the final spring game,' and she said, 'Who's Joe Montana?' I said, 'He's the guy who's going to feed our family for the next few years.'"

It took a while in coming, until Montana came off the bench as a sophomore to pull out two games in the fourth quarter, and then did it again as a junior. The players couldn't figure out why it was taking the coach so long to grasp something they already knew, that this skinny, sleepy-eyed kid from Monongahela was the man, the guy who could get it done when he had to.

"Whenever he came on the field," says L.A. Raider nose guard Bob Golic, who played at Notre Dame with Montana, "the players knew they had a friend coming in."

"When the pressure came," says 49er free safety Dave Waymer, who started his Notre Dame career as a wideout, "we knew he was the guy who wouldn't overheat."

Montana started the season behind Rick Slager as a sophomore in '75, and behind Rusty Lisch in '77, Joe's year of junior eligibility after he had separated his shoulder and missed all of '76. The time Montana spent on the bench still bothers him; the resentment of Devine is still there. Waymer says the reason was that Montana was a Parseghian recruit, and Devine favored his own guys, which really doesn't figure because Montana went nowhere under Parseghian.

Walsh, the former 49ers coach, says there's something about Montana when you first see him on the practice field, "an almost blasè look, although actually he's anything but that. I could see a college coach being put off by the fact that he's not responding overtly, so he'd say, 'Well, this guy's not motivated, he's not with the program.'"

Devine says Montana simply wasn't ready to start at the beginning of his sophomore year. He said that he got him in "as soon as he had medical clearance to play" as a junior. Montana feels that there was something about him that Devine just didn't like.

The interesting thing is that Montana, who has been called extremely coachable by whoever has worked with him, has had three major coaches in his life — Abramski at Ringgold, Devine at Notre Dame and Walsh with the 49ers — and at one time he has held bitter feelings toward each one. And for the same reason: Why won't he play me?

"Yeah, I guess it's true ... I never thought of it," Montana says, "although with Bill it wasn't a major problem; it only lasted a few games. With Abramski I guess it was because no player had ever challenged him like I did. The Devine situation was a mystery to me. I mean, I'd been demoted to third string the year after I got hurt. Other guys had gotten their positions back. I couldn't understand it. It hurt me."

Montana carried a B- over C+ average and eventually graduated with a degree in business administration and marketing. Dave Huffman, Montana's center at Notre Dame and currently a guard with the Vikings, remembers him as "just a regular guy who wanted to play hoops, go drink a beer. We called him Joe Montanalow because he was the spitting image of Barry Manilow. In his senior year, he moved into an apartment above a bar. When the bar closed down, we'd go upstairs to Joe's place. It was our after-hours joint."

There is a stat sheet compiled by the Notre Dame sports information department entitled "Joe Montana's Comeback Statistics," which lists six games. The Irish won five of those games in the fourth quarter, and they almost won the sixth — the 1978 game at Southern Cal in which Montana brought the Irish back from a 24-6 deficit to a 25-24 lead before USC pulled it out with a field goal at the end. At the top of the list is a game at North Carolina in his sophomore season. The Irish were down 14-6 with 5:11 to play, when Montana came off the bench and pulled out a 21-14 win with 129 yards passing in his minute and two seconds on the field. That's the kind of list it is, and there probably isn't another one like it.

"(Athletic director) Moose Krause grabbed my hand in the locker room after the North Carolina game," Devine says, "and said, 'Fantastic. Greatest comeback I've ever seen. Better than the Ohio State game in '35.' Then Joe does it again next week against Air Force; comes off the bench and brings us back from 30-10 down in the fourth quarter to a 31-30 win. In the locker room, Moose said, 'This one's better than last week.'"

The legend was born; Montana was the Comeback Kid. Then, kaboom! The big slide. Montana was hurt before his junior season, and when he returned a year later it was as the third-string quarterback, behind Lisch and Forystek.

"When we lost to Mississippi (20-13 in the second game of the season) with Joe on the bench, I thought, 'What a weird deal,'" says Ken MacAfee, an All-America tight end at Notre Dame who went on to play for the 49ers. "I mean, we all knew he could do it, he knew he could do it, but he wasn't playing. He was really down. I remember going to his apartment one night and he said, 'I'm just sick of this crap, sick of the whole thing.'"

Devine says, "Joe probably doesn't remember this, but he hadn't been given medical clearance to play in those first two games." Montana says it's news to him. Devine says that on the following Wednesday he told him to be ready to play at Purdue. Lisch started, then he was yanked for Forystek. When Forystek tried to scramble on one play, Purdue linebacker Fred Arrington met him with a ferocious blow. Forystek went down with a broken vertebra, a broken collarbone and a severe concussion. His football career was over.

Devine came back with Lisch ("I didn't want to bring Joe in until he had the wind at his back"), and then finally Montana trotted onto the field. The Notre Dame players began waving their fists and cheering. The fans went crazy.

In the press box, Purdue sports information director Tom Shupe turned to Notre Dame's S.I.D., Roger Valdiserri, and said, "What's everybody yelling for?"

"Because Joe Montana's in the game," Valdiserri said, "and you're in trouble."

It became comeback No. 3 on the list. Down 24-14 with 11 minutes to go, Montana threw for 154 yards and a touchdown, and the Irish won 31-24. The following year there were comebacks against Pitt and Southern Cal ("I have nightmares about Montana in that game," says L.A. Rams coach John Robinson, who coached the Trojans. "I remember thinking, Isn't this guy ever gonna miss on one?"), and the famous Cotton Bowl win over Houston on Jan. 1, 1979.

But the game Devine has special memories of is the one at Clemson in 1977, one that didn't make the list. "I remember Joe driving us down the field to win it in the fourth quarter," he says, "and I remember him having something like a second-and-52 at one point and getting a first down out of it. But best of all, I remember him taking off down the sidelines with two linebackers closing in on him, and I was yelling, 'Go out of bounds, Joe! Go out of bounds!' And there was this tremendous collision, and they went down in a heap, and only one guy got up, and it was Joe. I said, 'My God, he's taking on the whole Clemson team.'"

It's strange, and maybe it's partly because of guilt feelings, but Devine has become one of Montana's biggest boosters. Montana still resents the fact that Devine didn't give him what he feels was his rightfully earned playing time, but the resentment has softened, and they have gotten together socially since their Notre Dame days. Devine says he handled Montana the best way he knew how, right or wrong, but he adds that there's no question in his mind that Montana is the greatest ever to play the game. Devine describes a scene in the 1989 Super Bowl, during which he was in the stands, when Cincinnati kicked a field goal to make the score 16-13 with 3:20 to go. Devine turned to the man next to him and said, "I'd have thought twice about kicking it. They've given Joe a shot."

The 1979 Cotton Bowl against Houston, the famous Chicken Soup game, was, of course, the one that put the capper on the Comeback Kid's collegiate career. A freak ice storm had hit Dallas, and "all you heard as you came in was, bam, bam, bam, people knocking ice off the seats," Waymer says. By the fourth quarter, Montana was in the locker room with hypothermia, his temperature down to 96 degrees, and the medical staff was pumping bouillon into him (no, not chicken soup, bouillon; the team kept it on hand for cold-weather emergencies) to warm him up. Houston was building a 34-12 lead, while Montana lay in the locker room covered with blankets. Oh, yes, it's a story, all right.

"Rick Slager was in law school then, and he was a graduate assistant coach on the sidelines with me," Devine says. "His job was to run into the locker room every five minutes to see what Joe's temperature was. He'd come back and say, 'It's up to 97 degrees,' and five minutes later I'd tell him to run in and find out again."

With 7:37 to go, Montana came running onto the field, and a mighty roar went up. "Uh, no, not exactly a mighty roar," recalls Huffman, the Notre Dame center. "More like a feeble, frozen roar, since there were only a few people left in the stands, and ice was falling out of their mouths. Actually, I didn't even know Joe was out there until I felt his hands taking the snap. I thought, Wait a minute, these are different hands."

With six seconds left, the Irish were down by six points. "I told Joe to run a 91, a quick out," Devine says, "and if it wasn't there, to throw it away. Kris Haines, our wideout, slipped, and Joe threw it away. Now there were two seconds left. I turned my back on the field. That meant Joe could call his own play. He called the 91 again, the noseguard came through, Haines broke to the flag, and with the noseguard staring him in the face, Joe threw a perfect pass, low and outside, a bullet — under all that pressure, with terrible conditions. He was so calm. I swear to God he was no different than he would have been in practice."

Final score, 35-34, and six months later Notre Dame was marketing a promotional film called *Seven and a Half Minutes to Destiny*, "which," Devine says, "was really a Joe Montana film."

So you look for hints, for clues to help you understand Montana's ability to bring his team back from the brink. It would become his trademark in the NFL, too. Montana says that right until the end of his Notre Dame career he was filled with doubts about his ability. Even after the Houston game, he says, "I remained a skeptic, maybe because of the mind games Devine had been playing with me." Did any of his Notre Dame teammates have a feeling that Montana's career would take off the way it did, that they were in the presence of royalty?

"If I'd have known how famous he'd get, I'd have stayed in closer contact with him," Huffman says. "To us, he was just Joe Montanalow, a regular guy. If he wasn't so skinny, we'd have made him a lineman."

"Well, I knew he was going to be good, but I never knew he'd be that good," says MacAfee, now a dentist in the Philadelphia area. "The thing is, I don't think the guy ever feels pressure. The people around him feel it more than he does. I don't think he knows what it is. When he walks onto the field, he could be throwing to Dwight Clark or Jerry Rice or Kris Haines. He could be playing Navy, or the Jets in September, or Denver in the Super Bowl. I don't think there's any difference in his mind. To him it's just football. He doesn't change, it's just the aura that changes. At Notre Dame, I can't remember Joe ever missing a read. Even watching him on TV now, he knows the system so perfectly, he knows so well where everything's going to go. He could call everything himself, call it on the line. I don't even know why they send in plays for him."

When the 1979 draft was approaching and the Cotton Bowl glow had worn off, the NFL scouts got together and started putting down numbers for Montana. One combine gave him a grade of 6½ with 9 being the top of the scale and 1 the bottom. Washington State's Jack Thompson got the highest grade among the quarterbacks — 8. Montana's arm was rated a 6, or average. "He can thread the needle," the report said, "but usually goes with his primary receiver and forces the ball to him even when he's in a crowd. He's a gutty, gambling, cocky type. Doesn't have great tools but could eventually start."

The dumb teams believed the report. The smart one has won four Super Bowls.

Chapter 11

Wine

When my divorce was heading into its final stages, I made a resolution. I will not be a cliché older bachelor, chasing around after young women, making a fool of himself, working out, pulling my belly in, pretending. The resolution lasted until I met my divorce lawyer's legal secretary. Her name was Jana. She was 29.

I was waiting for my appointment with the lawyer in her reception area. I asked to use her copier and I set up a pile of work to get through. I always tried to find something useful to do while I was burning off waiting time. OK, it wasn't real work, actually. It was copying wine tasting notes. I still wrote a wine column, but I wasn't what you'd call making a living at it. All of a sudden, I was aware of someone looking over my shoulder. She was big, and blonde, and young.

"Wine, huh?" she said. Now I was in an ugly mood in those days and normally I'd have said without thinking, "Congratulations, you pass the test." But something told me to keep it buttoned up and see what happened. Maybe it was the smell of her perfume. Or the look of her, that attractive, tough look you'd see in actresses of the 1940s, the kind of women who always seemed to have a cigarette hanging out of their mouth, except that she had the added dimension of size. I always was a sucker for big women, and she was about 5-10 and a solid 175 or so.

So I told her I was working on my wine tasting notes and I think that got her, the idea of a guy turning such a frivolous pastime into actual work, and when she asked me how I judged wines, I went into this matter of fact explanation about how you first looked at the color, then you entered a note for the bouquet, which you listed under "nose," and then the taste. And then you arrived at a final grade. And moved on to the next wine.

"Fascinating," she said, and before I knew it, I took the fatal step. I knew this would be the one to sink me and would blow my resolution all to hell, but I did it anyway.

"Would you like to go to a wine tasting sometime?" I asked her.

"I'd love to," she said, and I was off on the idiot, old bachelor merry-go-round. A big, brawley Jersey chick, rough around the edges … she'd pronounce all right as "aright," and straight as "shtraight." But smart, too, and acute in her judgments, particularly about people.

And we met them, boy did we. Waiters in restaurants, sommeliers, fellow wine writers, fellow judges in the tasting competitions, all areas in which I felt I had a little bit of an edge, where my age wouldn't be an embarrassment. We became a twosome. She lived with her parents. Nice people, who never gave me the narrow-eyed treatment, not even when I was first introduced to them. One night, when her mother said goodbye as we were walking out the door, she added, "Have fun, kids." Kids! I had her by about five years.

I thought about that, and it almost broke it, between Jana and me, but I just liked the idea too much, the idea of what was happening. It was flattering, and then there was that, how can I say it better? That animal magnetism, at least on my part. I really don't know what she felt. I was in a kind of dippy whirl. I was acting stupid. Hard edges were being replaced by Jell-O. I didn't know what I really was anymore.

Pretty soon she began telling me about her life, or at least one aspect of it, and it was something I didn't want to hear. He was one of the chefs at Le Cirque in New York. He promised to marry her. He strung her along. He had four kids. She'd go over to his house and they'd take care of the kids together, for a day. She'd devote day after to day to this. You'd think that he'd be so grateful that he'd make good on his promise and he'd divorce his wife, now estranged … uh, she thought, maybe, hopefully. Confusing was what it was. Also repetitive.

"He ruined my life," she'd say, staring out a misty window, if one were available. "Just ruined it."

"All right already," I'd tell her. "It's enough. I've got it. Bad deal all around. Time to move on."

"Just ruined it."

I was sick of it.

Coming up was the big wine event, A View from the Vineyards, the grand California wine tasting at the Hotel Pierre on 5th Ave., next to the park. A hundred or so vineyards bring some of their best entries. The wines are paired with original creations from a dozen or so specially chosen restaurants. I checked the list when I got the invitation. Le Cirque was one of the restaurants mentioned. I was beginning to get menacing feelings. I wasn't sure how much wine I'd taste that night.

I got there early, as I usually do at these affairs. Before I tasted a single wine, I checked out the Le Cirque table. I saw an old friend, Bernard, a Swiss waiter I'd known for years, a gossip, a person who knew everything. We said hello. "Who's the chef who was going with Jana?" I asked him.

"Daniel," he said. "Daniel Boulud." The name didn't mean anything then, but now it's a big name in culinary matters. He has his own restaurant. It always gets multiple stars, etc.

"Is he here tonight?" I asked Bernard.

"He's in charge of our display," he said.

I was feeling my brain beginning to cloud over. When I was young, I'd had a maniac temper, helpful when channeled in the right direction, such as the ring or the football field or the buffet line, harmful most of the other times. I could feel things coming back, little buttons popping inside my head.

"Where is he now?" I said, straining to keep my tone level.

"In the kitchen, I think."

I went in the kitchen. Some guy in a white apron approached and said, "No one allowed in here."

"Well, YOU'RE in here!" He faded. I guess I must have looked a little crazy. I looked around. I didn't really know what I'd do when I found him, but it would be something, I knew that. I saw two guys in purple uniforms heading toward me. Hotel security. I got out of the kitchen. It was a wine tasting. I'd taste some wine. I tried a little Grgich Hills chardonnay. The wine tasted like ashes. Once I had been a judge at Craig Goldwyn's Champagne Shootout, and a fellow judge was Bill, a veteran wine writer. He brought some notes in with him, but he went to the bathroom at the beginning of the event, and while he was there, one of Goldwyn's assistants threw the notes out. Clifford never found them. He walked out of the judging, quit.

"You can never taste wines when you're mad," he told me a few weeks later. "The anger sends strange enzymes through your taste buds, and the wine tastes bitter."

I'd never believed him until I tried to taste that Grgich chardonnay. I checked a couple of other tables, said hello to a few people. The evening was moving on. I was a rudderless ship, lurching aimlessly. Then I saw a guy at the Le Cirque table and I knew it was my man. I walked over, slowly so as not to attract attention. He had his back turned. He was bending over the table, messing with some crepes or something. I stood there and waited. The Le Cirque table was getting a lot of action, but finally he saw me.

"Yes?" he said. He wasn't what I thought he'd be. I expected some Romeo type, darkly good looking in a continental way. This guy was kind of zany looking, with glasses. But what the hell. He was the guy who had stiffed her, who had ruined her life. My bete noire.

"I know Jana," I said.

"That's good," he said.

"I'm going with her," I said. I imagine my voice must have come out in some kind of a snarl.

"You'll excuse me, please. I'm very busy," he said, turning back to his table. That broke it.

"Why you cool-assed mother ..." and I was about to go over the table, but now I saw a little posse of security forces headed my way, and one of them was pointing at me. I melted into the crowd and made for an adjoining room. My brain was buzzing. What to do? What to do? I couldn't think of anything. I took off my jacket, headed over to the Ridge Vineyards table, swiped a glass and a bottle of their Montebello Cabernet, draped my jacket over it, walked out of the hotel, over to Central Park. I found a bench in a secluded spot, drank the bottle of Ridge, got into my car and drove home.

I was a careful, erratic driver, never exceeding 55, selecting the middle lane out of the cluster and adhering to it. It was close to 2 a.m. when I got home. I sat in the dark with unformed thoughts racing.

I knew I wouldn't sleep. My brain was on fire. Finally I called her. Rinnggg, rinnggg, ANSWER THE DAMN PHONE! She answered. To her credit, she didn't give me the "Do you know what time it is?" bit.

"Well, I saw him," I said in a voice that was close to breaking.

"Saw who?"

"Daniel. I saw Daniel."

"Daniel? Daniel who?"

"Daniel!" I hollered. "Your goddamn boyfriend at the goddamn Le Cirque!"

"Le Cirque?" she said. "Jean hasn't worked at Le Cirque in two years."

I was being wrapped in a ball of fuzz, of cotton candy. Comprehension was slow in coming.

"Huh? Jean? Jean? The writer said ..."

The romance ended shortly thereafter. Self-preservation kicked in. That idiot drive home ... I mean I could have ...

I saw her once a few years later. She had married a guy with a double problem, gambling and drinking. It was a scenario I'd heard repeated by half the waitresses in half the diners in New Jersey. "Well, I love him, but ..."

Anyway, by then a Flaming Redhead had entered my life. But that's another story.

* * *

EATING AND DRINKING IN SPAIN
This column appeared on SI.com *on March 11, 2005.*

Who was it who wanted to know what Barcelona was like, especially in the food and wines department? Andrew swears that he had an e-mail or two on the subject. Which will reap a harvest of a more complete reply than anyone dreamed of.

Spanish wines officially have been "discovered." Actually they were discovered before I was writing the wine column for the *New York Post*, and that was 30 years ago, but what they have discovered now is how to put a fancy price tag on them. In this country, that is. In Barcelona and the Costa Brava, the Catalan wines and Riojas, and that's mostly what we drank, are pretty cheap.

For instance, in an intimate little restaurant called El Salon we ordered the most expensive red wine on the list, a beautiful, silky Rioja called Contino, the '99 Reserva, which cost 23 euros, or $30. The second time we ate there we had one of the high-end whites, a complex, delicate blend of muscat, sauvignon blanc and Gewurztraminer, the 2001 Gessani Gramonae, which cost 16 euros, or $21.

At least twice we had the most expensive Catalan sparkling wine on the list for $29 and $28. We were drinking gorgeous Burgundian-tasting whites, a blend of chardonnay and a beautiful, deeply colored Catalan grape called xarel-lo (pronounced "shar-ail-yo") for about the same price, if that much.

We made one winery trip, to Torres, the hub of the company's gigantic wine empire, in Vilafranca del Penedes, about 50 miles southwest of Barcelona. It's a 45 million-bottle operation, and I've known their wines for many, many years. The quality never has gone down. At one time, my house red was their Sangre de Toro at around $4 a bottle. I used to write about it whenever anyone asked for my favorite bargain wine.

Now I can afford to go a little on the higher end, but if anyone asks me what's really good in the $12-20 range, I'll tell them the 2000 Torres' Gran Coronas Reserva — an aristocratic, Bordeaux-tasting blend of 85 percent cabernet sauvignon, 15 percent tempranillo, the classic red grape of Spain. Or for a white, their 2003 Fransola, a sauvignon blanc with real punch and spice.

The Flaming Redhead and I have a complex way of ranking restaurants, and yes, there's a chart involved. I just compared the grades with those of the wines we drank in Rome, which we visited a couple of years ago. Barcelona, a seven-point underdog, came up with the victory. So I'll give you our top half dozen or so, in order, and call it a wrap:

1) **Tragaluz**: One of the most artistic places I've ever eaten in — no, not because of what was on the walls but on the plate. Everything was a creation, a little masterpiece. For instance the fish chowder, probably the best I've ever eaten, was set off by a pair of clams in its center, intricately wrapped around each other and propped up like a pair of old pals.

2) **El Salon**: Very serious in the old sauce department, very innovative.

3) **Torres**: Yes, the wines swung that election.

4) **Café Marabu in San Feliu**: A seaside town on the way north, up the Costa Brava. We just walked in, cold. The show stopper there was a fresh, perfectly cooked lenguada, the local fish.

5) **El Quim**: A tapas bar in the mercat de la bouqueria, the big market off the Ramblas. You sit at a counter in the middle of this gigantic temple of food and choose one, choose two, three, four, name it,

from a fascinating assortment of dishes of sausage, fresh octopus, potato frittata, blood pudding, all the things I love.

6) **Euskal Extea**: A Basque place with knock-'em-dead steaks. For some reason Spain, or at least Barcelona, seems to have the kind of beef you just don't see on the continent. Linda had a delicious filet the size of a sirloin. I had a prime sirloin so big that … I'm ashamed to admit this … for the first time in my life I could not finish a steak served in a restaurant.

Do me one favor. If you're going to Barcelona, please avoid a place much favored by the tourist publications. The name is Cal Pep. Nasty, miserable folk who refused to honor a reservation or even admit we made one and just about threw us out. Actually the only genuinely nasty people we met in the eight days we were there.

* * *

NEW ZEALAND FOOD AND WINE REPORT
This column appeared on SI.com *on June 3, 2005.*

Best wine I tasted, as previously mentioned: 2003 Neudorf pinot noir, Home Block. This is a small property in the Moutere hills outside the arts and crafts city of Nelson. It's pinot noir and chardonnay country, just like in the Cote d'Or. Both Neudorf Pinot and Chardonnay are fine wines, but those with a little extra class carry the Moutere designation.

The Moutere Pinot I tasted, the 2003, was exotic, with anise and clove and spices. New Zealand is capable of pinots like this, especially in the Central Otago mountains in the south, but none are this good. But then, as a topper to the topper, there was the 2003 Home Block.

Put it in front of me on a blind tasting, and I'd guess it's from Burgundy's Domaine de la Romanee-Conti, which is marked by an almost Oriental kind of opulence. It was a little deeper than the 2003 Moutrere, a bit longer in the finish, the same exotics. I'd have to go back through 35 years of tasting notes, but off the top of my head, I'd say this is the best pinot noir, outside of Burgundy, that I've ever tasted.

So we were there on that particular day with the *San Francisco Chronicle* columnist, Ira Miller, and his wife, Sharon. Ira is a collector. I mean, he brought back enough New Zealand wine to service half the British Navy, and he immediately asked Neudorf's owner, Tim Finn, if he could buy three bottles ($43 apiece). I almost slammed him in the ribs. Ugly American ... I mean, they make about 10 bottles for the whole country (actually 100 cases, which is little enough). Mr. Finn, being a gentleman, said yes, and as they were wrapping up these treasures, I'm standing there with my finger up my ... uh, I mean feeling really out of it. So I finally piped up, "Excuse me, comma, but do you think I could also buy a bottle?" Yes. So now I have one. When do I drink it? Whom do I drink it with? Such problems.

Pegasus Bay in Waipara, north of Christchurch: The first of their wines that I tasted, their 2004 Riesling ($32 in the restaurant, around $15 retail), was in a restaurant. Linda and I stared at each other. We're in the Rheingau. A Spatlese, beautifully made, clean as a whistle bearing the fine Germanic fruit and acidity. The second one, the '03 Riesling (same price) was at the winery, and it was different, more new world, with a higher, more piercing acidity, but again, beautifully made.

The young co-owner and winemaker, Matthew Donaldson, is passionate about his wines. Please, would you just taste this one ... hasn't been released yet ... and I want to know what you think of this ... and here are some pinot noir barrel samples, just pulled them ... won't take you long to get through them. Thirteen to be exact. Lovely fruit, for the most part. Velvety racehorse style. Passion in the winemaking, a desire for elegance. Bottled pinots we tasted carry those same trademarks.

Did someone say that New Zealand can't make red wines? They're more elegant now than the ones we tasted on our last trip, three years ago, and we thought they were pretty impressive.

Most of their sauvignon blancs, which are usually what you see over here, are not my style. More of the citrus, grapefruit character I'm not nuts about. But the Pegasus Sauvignon ($12) made up for it in intensity, in a richness and floral quality. Right up and down the line, you saw nothing but quality ... their merlots, their rieslings, especially their late harvest dessert chardonnay, of which we bought four bottles.

This is a place you must visit if you're ever in New Zealand, and plan to have lunch there because right now there is a tremendous competition among the wineries to hire great chefs and put a fine lunch on the table. And at Pegasus, we had the best of all the winery lunches.

The number one meal we had in the entire month, though, was on our last day, and it was at Harbourside in Auckland. It's not cheap, but it's a seafood paradise. Two things jumped out at me (I beat 'em back with a spoon). The seafood chowder was loaded with good things, fish, prawns, mussels, etc. And it had neither of the two elements I can't stand, that thickener stuff that turns chowder into white sludge, and those tasteless, blanded out potatoes.

It was a French-style chowder, on the thinner side with great flavor. Saffron and orange zest in the recipe, both of which worked beautifully. The second was the seafood platter itself, which blended a few things and baked them into a quenelle, or large seafood sausage. Just terrific.

I ate a lot of fish and chips, and the standout was a well-known waterside place high up on the North Island called the Mangonui Fish Shop. And our sleeper find, actually it was the Redhead's ... she saw one of their recipes reprinted in a food magazine ... was the Lime Caffeteria in Rotorua, where they have the mineral baths. Just a little lunch place, but everything was done with a deft hand and a light touch.

* * *

MORE OVERSEAS ADVENTURE
This column appeared on SI.com *on June 9, 2006.*

I was asked the following: "Did you see anything on your vacation except the inside of wineries?" Yes. We saw vineyards and tasting rooms.

It's the unexpected that leaves the sharpest memories, as we drove through Germany and Alsace and the Alto Adige in Italy's far north. Lindau Island in Germany, in Lake Constance, was an unexpected pleasure, an easygoing vacation town sprinkled with surprising grace notes.

St. Peter's, a modest little alabaster church at one end of the island, is one of Lindau's grace notes. Plain, just about deserted on the evening when we stepped inside, you were immediately struck by the spirituality of the place. And then near the altar you saw them, twelve 16th century wall murals by Hans Holbein, some fading, totally unprotected, just … well, just there. The 12 stations of the cross.

I thought of them a couple of days later when, foolishly, we followed the hype and signed up for the tour of Linderhof, Mad King Ludwig of Bavaria's rococo pleasure castle, with its ornate sculpted peacocks and lavish bed embroidery. The place was mobbed. You waited over an hour for a castle tour, which went off every 10 minutes or so. All that for one man's self-indulgence, while in St. Peter's, a place of true meaning, nothing but solitude.

The Hotel Turm in the northern Italian town of Fie was a grace note. "You are an artist, is that correct?" The owner, Stefan Pramstrahler, asked Linda. Yes, correct. "So you would like to see what we have in the hotel?"

It was a trip through an art gallery. Original paintings by such as Dali, Klimt, Otto Dix, Picasso, lined the halls, the rooms, the health spa, even the garage. Ancient Russian icons, medieval wood carvings. How many? Maybe 250 pieces, maybe 300. Everything was done with style and exquisite taste, even the ironwork on the railings, the areas of rough marble flooring. We saw doors that went back to the very beginnings of the building, to the 11th or 12th century, doors that almost seemed built in miniature, to accommodate the smaller people of that era. It was a hotel that took your breath away, and the rate sheet was modest. This was no Trump Castle.

I decided that we would drive out of our way to visit my old post in Landstuhl, where the big army hospital is, where I was stationed 50 years ago. Then we would drive the seven or eight K's up the road to Vogelweh, where our team, the WACOM (Western Area Command) Rhinos, played its home games, and I'd show Linda the field where we played, the gym where I boxed (TKO by LeRoy, Ezekual, Roker at 2:38 of the first).

A big mistake. I had visited my post one time in the last 50 years and seen my barracks without too much hassle, but that was before the word "security" entered the vocabulary. This time I didn't recognize it. There used to be one gate; now there were five. A German security firm called Pond had been hired by the U.S. Army to handle things. We needed a "sponsor" to get us on the post. I finally got one through the Public Affairs Office, a corporal who couldn't figure out which building had been my old barracks, even though it was the one in which he was currently billeted. It looked totally unfamiliar. It had had a paint job to get it to conform with the rows of similar buildings. I didn't even take Linda inside.

OK, let's look at the field, at the gym. The Public Affairs lady had called ahead to get someone to come down to the security office and get us in. She had spoken to the NCO at the gym, who went by the name of Sergeant Fred. I called him when we got down to Vogelweh, which now goes by the name of Pulaski Barracks. He said he couldn't spare anybody and hung up. No sense getting mad ... look, I lived in the temporary duty barracks here ... I just want to show my wife where I ... etc.

"Try me in half an hour," he said. I called in half an hour. Nobody home. I kept trying. The German security guards weren't happy about my using their phone. Finally I reached him.

"Look, I told you there's nobody here." Gosh, what's a sponsor, anyway? Just grab a guy who has five minutes to kill, who can come down and sign us in.

"No is no, see?" And then it all started coming back. The Army. The tight, stupid faces. The denials — just to show they could do it. The barracks sergeant who cleaned out my locker the day the football season ended and threw out, among other things, draft cards I'd gotten from the Colts and the Browns.

"Let's get the hell out of this place," I said to Linda.

I haven't mentioned restaurants yet. Every trip we make we rate them on a 10-point system that's too complicated to go into right now. Then we rank them all from one to whatever. Before I give you our top 10, let me say that the only Michelin French three-star establishment that Linda and I ever ate in together was ranked tied for 22nd of 29 restaurants.

Now I know you want to say, aha, reverse snobbishness, but let me explain. We are rating not only the quality of food, and there's no question that the chefs at our three-star place could put away those of the modest restaurants that got higher rankings. We're judging the quality of the whole experience. And when you look back at something and groan, then it has fallen short.

The Auberge de L'Ill in Illhaeusern is Alsace's only three-star. It has proudly carried that banner for as long as anyone can remember. Everyone speaks of it fondly. Less stuffy, less pricey, a really friendly feeling, and so forth. I ate there 31 years ago, all by myself, a very modest little meal, mainly because of the funds situation. It was delicious.

I don't know if the place has changed that much, or maybe I have or perhaps just the times. The first thing that happens, on setting foot upon the threshold, is that you are instantly made aware of your status, not only as a diner but as a human being. This is established by where you are placed in the room or rooms.

Thus the Japanese gentleman and his female companion (wife?), both of them beautifully and expensively dressed, got the table overlooking not one, but two of the carefully maintained gardens. Next rung belonged to those who got the table looking out on one garden. They had the look of spenders. Then came those who were placed in the center of the room because, I would assume, they wanted to be seen. Then came Linda and me, not at the lowest rung. That was reserved for the loud German fella (actually a pretty funny guy; we engaged him in conversation for most of the evening) in the shaggy sweater, accompanied by his tootsie girlfriend.

I was dressed neatly if not expensively. Tweed jacket and black turtleneck, my Gerard Depardieu look. No, not a shirt and tie, but acceptable, if not prosperous looking. Looks a little crazy, actually. Might get a bit troublesome when into the old vino. We got the seat adjoining a window, but a window leading to nothing … a yard, some nondescript machinery, you know, nothing you'd want to look at, but still … glass!

The fifth-rung German and his ladyfriend got the seat under some wall decoration thing that looked like a huge pan. God forbid it should have come loose. Both of them would have been crushed to death.

Well, like idiots we fell into the trap, the 142-euro tasting menu. That's per person, and it wasn't served unless both of us got it. (The Redhead made the sacrifice.) And as these meals usually go, the amuse bouche was lovely, the next course was light and friendly, and then boom, boom, boom, here they came, the cream sauce specials, three straight courses, each heavily creamed.

And your system rebels. Getting the bites down becomes a struggle. The third one was a trio of little veal medallions and some mushy green gnocchi. I was finished. I realized that if I took one more bite of either of those things I was in danger of throwing up. There should have been a photographer there to take a picture of me leaving a piece of meat on the plate. The last time that happened was, I believe, in 1958.

I kind of got interested in the timing of the service. They'd bring you a course. It would take you about a minute and a half to eat it. Thirty minutes later you'd get another course. I began timing it. Almost 30 minutes to the dot. Yes, this was *planned*. Thus, if you had a five course meal, there was no way you'd get out in less than two and a half hours, three hours for six course, etc. Our meal took three and a half.

And what were you doing when you weren't eating? Sweating. The heat in the room became unbearable. Linda said she was getting dizzy. Me, too. When we finally emerged from the place, we were like miners who had been trapped underground for 10 days, gasping and clutching at the cool night air.

I won't get into the rest of it, the cheese platter, followed by four, count 'em, separate desserts. "Who can eat all those?" I asked Linda. "She can," she said, motioning to a lady at the center table whose mouth was opening like an alligator's. Oh yes, the bill. No, I won't get into that, not at all. I'm too ashamed.

People we spoke to continued to rave about the Auberge. But some of the restaurant people we got to know told a different story.

"At one time that style was fashionable, but they haven't changed with the times," said a chef at a small restaurant where we ate a couple of times. "It's a style the Michelin people can understand." Well, not us.

Here, then, are our top 10 in Germany, Alsace, Luxembourg and Italy's Alto Adige:

1. **Hotel Turm, Fie, Grade 9.22**
   Highest grade we've ever given. Best restaurant in Italy we've ever eaten in. Herr Prahmstrahler is also the chef. His cooking is light and delicate and unforgettable. Huge, natural wine cellar with rarities from the region at modest prices.
2. **Tie between Luc Brendel, LaTable du Gourmet in Riquewihr, Alsace, and Wald Hotel Sonorra, Dreis, Germany, 8.17**
   Magnificent French cooking with an Alsatian twist at La Table. Best sweetbreads I've ever eaten. The Wald Sonorra is one of those countrified landmarks people flock to. Very fancy. Considered one of Germany's keynote restaurants, but we didn't know it. We just stumbled in late on a Sunday afternoon and had a marvelous meal.
4. **Rotisserie Ardennaise, Luxembourg, 8.06**
   Another of those Sunday "got lucky" meals. Fresh escargots and steak au poivre.

5. **Three-way tie among Auberge Le Bouc Bleu in Beblenheim, Alsace; Zum Treppchen in Beilstein on the Mosel in Germany and the café at Schloss Johannissberg vineyard in the Rheingau, 8.0**

Bouc Bleu, a pretty little place, became a real favorite. Husband-wife team. He's the chef, she's from the Southwest of France and supervises the wines, notably Cadillacs and Madirans. Zum Treppchen bowled Linda over with its selection of giant baked potatoes stuffed with all manner of wonderful things and a dessert that the owner, Rita Schneider, explained was from her home in the Tirol. It's called Kaiserschmarm and it consists of shredded pancakes and raisins in vanilla ice cream. "You're not doing it justice," Linda says. "Light and delicate, still warm when we got it ..." OK, OK already. Our lunch at the Schloss was very light, but everything was perfect, including a fresh trout. You can't get that in restaurants in the U.S.

8. **St. Michael-Eppan, Alto Adige, 7.835**

An inexpensive workingman's place a few K's from the inn where we always stay. Of the five or six times we've eaten there, Linda has had the turkey in pepper sauce, I'd say four times.

9. **Weinhotel Landsknecht, St. Goar, Germany, 7.56**

Perfect white asparagus in Holandaise sauce, terrific wines of the Mittelrhein from the owner's vineyard.

10. **Hotel Uhrerhof Deur, Bulla, Alto Adige, Italy, 7.5**

We've stayed here for years. Owned by the Zemmer family, and the papa, Walter, formerly the head chef at the Greif Hotel in Bolzano, does the cooking. Dinners are included in the very modest hotel bill, which is just fine with us because his menu is full of surprises, everything done with the lightest possible touch.

Chapter 12

Collecting

You either have the collecting instinct or you don't. There is very little middle ground. I have had it from the age of five, when I got my first look at the model soldiers of W. Britain, Ltd. It has never left me; it has only grown and spread horizontally, threatening to devour the house in a mass of cartons and boxes and objects still to be classified and arranged. It has reached the point at which only small objects can still be collected.

Briefly, my collecting interests encompass the following, and I'm sure I'm leaving off a few:

- Books
- Football programs
- Military miniatures, also known as toy soldiers
- Coins
- Cigar box labels
- Menus (only restaurants in which I've eaten and liked the food)
- Wine labels and metal Champagne capsules (only things that I've drunk)
- Casino chips, worldwide (Collection now defunct, having been stolen by neighbor who came by to take my mail in while I was on trips. She took a lot more, too, including a basic coin collection I started as a youngster. Coins made a comeback, the chips project was abandoned after setback.)
- Stamps (I think the old albums I had as a child are around somewhere. Still three old storage boxes to look through.)

The most important thing a collector can have is a wife who understands. She doesn't even have to have the instinct herself, she just has to be tolerant and avoid, at all costs, the deadly, "Why do you need another ... ?" My wife, Linda Bailey Zimmerman, known to my readers as The Flaming Redhead, has been a collector all her life, the purest kind, the one who is not backed up by huge sums with which to snap up entire aggregations. As a child in a modest household, she gathered rocks, bits of paper, fabric, anything that didn't require cash outlay. Later, as an artist, she became fascinated by the Bohemian lifestyle of Paris in the 1920s and '30s. One thing led to another, and it was only a matter of time until the books in our house formed an amalgamation with that earlier, Parisian way of life, and it found expression in the works and life of Anais Nin.

So unlike my rather sloppy, undisciplined collecting habits, the Redhead narrowed her focus and in time built up a serious Nin archive helped immeasurably by the dealer, Peter Howard of Serendipity Books in Berkeley. I've known Peter for years, having been drawn to his interesting trove of radical literature, but something about the Redhead sent a message to him that this is a person who is really serious. So when Anais Nin's brother, Joaquin Nin-Culmell, died in Berkeley in 2004, and Peter was entrusted with the sale of his archive, he called Linda and invited her out to have first crack at the material, an unquestioned act of kindness. The items she picked up became the cornerstone of a worthwhile collection.

And now we must contrast that with the obverse side of the collecting picture. The sad literature of divorce is filled with tales of spouses who either destroyed their mate's collection or dumped it off at the Salvation Army or Goodwill, as a pointed and painfully effective act of malice. I've heard my share of these stories and I take them the way I take all such chronicles of marital battles. I won't pass judgment until I've heard the other side, until I can figure out what brought this on? Assault, extreme public embarrassment, a straight right cross? It had to be something.

But I have my own little story about the stormy confluence of the collecting and non-collecting instincts, with no malice involved, except that generated by people who have to listen to this tale. No true collector ever has let me finish it; it becomes only too obvious what is coming. It's always hand on the forehead, and then the entreaty, "Stop ... please ... don't tell me any more."

In the early days of my first marriage, I returned home from work one evening, intending to devote some quality time to that most enjoyable of pastimes, cataloguing and rearranging a collectible, in this case coins.

"Honey!" I shouted. "Have you seen my silver dollars?"

"You know you were supposed to give me money for the supermarket this morning," I heard from the next room, "and you didn't, so I ..." That's as far as I've ever gotten. It would have been interesting, sociologically, to have seen what the result ... check that ... it wouldn't have been interesting at all. It would have been horrible.

When I was five, and right up the time until I was 11 or 12, I got almost no allowance from my parents. I was paid off in "sets." Sets were the toy soldiers of the English firm of W. Britain, Ltd. Eight foot soldiers, or five mounted, or in the case of exotics such as camels (Bikaner Camel Corps, for instance), three formed a set. Each set cost 79 cents. If I did something particularly noteworthy, I'd get to pick one out. Generally this happened once or twice a month, but I distinctly recall one glorious stretch when I was on a once-a-week pace for at least a month and a half.

They were beautiful little things. On most pieces the arms were hinged and they could move. The best were the figures on which both arms moved, such as the kneeling Coldstream Guard officer, holding a pair of binoculars. Up, down, up, down, his arms went, as he lined up the distant target for the seven kneeling riflemen, with their high bearskin hats, alongside him. I loved that set, but anything on horseback that bore the designation "Guards" was good too. Life Guards, Horse Guards, Queens' Own, Prince Albert's Own ... I was exceptionally taken by anything designated as someone's "Own."

I could get modern metal soldiers at Woolworth's for a nickel apiece on the off times when my parents would send me a nickel or dime my way, and these were the rough pieces for playing with. With the British sets, never. You lined them up in formation and put them back in their box, which incidentally, had, written in script, the name of the battles in which that unit had distinguished itself. You treated them with respect. I knew this even as a wee lad. A born collector. That's why those early sets still exists today ... somewhere ... maybe in the garage ... maybe in the big box in the attic ... I swear they're around somewhere.

I couldn't sleep the night before a trip was scheduled to Macy's, or even better, FAO Schwarz on 59th and 5th, to buy a set. On the trip down to

Schwarz, riding the old 5th Ave. bus with the open top, I'd be on my feet, practically dancing up and down. Central Park, the zoo, oh my God, we're coming to it!

This might come as a surprise, but the price of 79 cents per set did not hold, but as I traced the course of my toy soldier collecting through the years and replaced the original term, "toy soldiers" with the somewhat fancier "military miniatures," I never have felt that the prices for wonderful figures seemed out of line.

I graduated to the more elegant handmades. I became a habitué of the soldier shows, but for years my favorite place to buy soldiers was Le Petit Soldier Shop on Royal and St. Peter in New Orleans. The owner, Dave Dugas, employed local artists to paint the figures, and I got to the point where I could actually begin to tell the work of different people. The prices, somewhere between $15 and $20 apiece, actually seemed low, considering the painstaking effort that went into painting what my wife calls, "Your little people." I would spend hours in that shop, going through hundreds of figures, piece by piece, gradually finding the absolute gems.

Well one day in the late summer of 1970, I was in New Orleans covering a Jets-Saints exhibition game and the first place I headed was to Dave's shop in the Quarter.

"I've got something to show you," he said. "It's way outside your price range, but you ought to look at it."

He reached in a drawer and pulled out the finest individual piece of military miniature art I had ever seen. It was totally outside my collecting interest, which, at that time was Napoleonic. It was an oversized Baluchi, a turn of the century Pakistani, when the troops were part of the British forces, in green fatigue dress, carrying sergeant's insignia. He wore a peaked turban, his hair was long, his mouth was turned down in an expression of pure merciless cruelty, and setting it all off were the coldest, deadest, murderer's eyes.

"It's a competition piece," Dave said. "Took a bronze at Lancaster, Pa. I'd like to see what won the gold."

I was barely hearing him. To have that figure … to have it … how much, Dave, how much, Dave, how much, Dave, how much … ?

"It's $250," he said, and my heart went clunk because I knew it would be something like that. As he had said, way beyond my price range. Don't forget this was 1970.

"I want to thank you, Dave, for breaking my heart," I said and stormed out of his shop, into the sultry New Orleans heat, striding blindly, past Bourbon, past Chartres, the eyes, they were burning a hole in my brain, those eyes. I had to have that piece. I stopped short. I knew exactly what would happen. He'd have the piece out. Some rich collector would arrive, take one look at it and it would be gone. Gone forever. I turned and started trotting back, then sprinting. People stared at a crazy man running by them. I burst into the shop, the sweat running down my face, just in time to see Dave wrapping up the piece, the Baluchi.

For me.

"I knew you'd be back," he said.

There's a very happy kicker to this story. A week later my parents were at our house. Now my mother was the kind of old world mama who could spot a new object in the house wherever it resided, and she would immediately point to it and say, "How much?"

And no matter how much you told her, she'd clutch her heart and gasp, "Oh my God."

How much? A dollar forty nine, ma. Oh my God. How about this? Eighty-nine cents, Ma. Oh my God. I think you've got the picture. Like an idiot, I forgot to hide the Baluchi before she came. She barely said hello to everyone before she was standing in front of it.

"How much?" It wouldn't do to lie. She could always tell when I was lying.

I drew a deep breath, closed my eyes and said, "Two hundred and fifty dollars." She continued studying the figure.

"That's all?" she said. "It's a real work of art."

Yeah! Yeah! I almost let out a yell. That's what it is all right.

The moral of the story is that if you really love something, if it speaks to you, buy it, even if it means going without lunches for a month or so, as I did to pay for the Baluchi. This is especially true at auctions, although it's easy to get caught up in what they call "auction madness" and lose all perspective. I don't remember any of those lunches that I missed ... (uh, how can you if you missed them? All right, all right already, there's a point to be made here.) Lunches are overrated anyway. It's a matter of priorities. And you never forget the ones that get away. It haunts you. If only I'd have thrown in that one last bid.

There's a joy in collecting things that were fantastically cheap, in retrospect, especially when you had a feeling at the time that they were absolute steals. I started picking up football programs when I was in high school. I kept, of course, the ones from the games I had seen, all annotated and marked up, but these were from the games involving teams with a certain level of history attached to them. I haunted a store on 44th and 6th Ave. called Midtown Magazines that featured mostly girlie magazines. It was kind of an unhealthy place. You never wanted to lock your gaze onto any of the regular customers, or you might hear some suggestions that might not appeal to you. But for some reason, Midtown had a huge supply of old football programs, dirt cheap because few people other than me were interested in them.

Thus I was picking up Fordham in the 1930s with Vince Lombardi and the Seven Blocks of Granite, plus Army and Navy when they were powerhouses, plus any number of professional programs with Sammy Baugh and Sid Luckman and Don Hutson, for a dime apiece. Bowl games were more expensive, maybe a quarter, but when I bought in bulk, which I always did, they'd give me a negotiated price.

My father was furious. "More magazines ... you mean he's bringing more magazines into the house?" And I lived in fear that one day he'd go through some sort of clean-up pogrom, and there they'd go, so I'd try to find exotic places to hide them, which wasn't easy in a four-room apartment. But they were absolute gems in those days, featuring long articles by the leading sportswriters of the day, cartoons by Willard Mullin and others, strategic think pieces that were invaluable as reference points when I started writing about the sport.

When I went out to Stanford, I discovered, on my first trip to Los Angeles, the Adco Sports Exchange on Wilshire, run by an odd little birdlike character named Goodwin Goldfaden. His prices were high, compared to what I was used to, but he had real quality items, such as Carlisle with Jim Thorpe and Ivy League programs from the 19th century. His asking price was $5 apiece, but since I was the only one really interested in them, I could generally do OK via discounts, even on my college boy funds.

Ivy League programs of the 1890s interestingly were sold at the time for a dollar apiece compared to the standard 25-cent rate 50 years later. But Ivy numbers were mini-hard cover books, and only rich folk went to those games anyway. But a dollar then ... gosh, you could have a meal at Delmonico's for that.

Wine labels and champagne capsules are nice things to collect because they're free, if you know how to boil and then scrape off a label. (They use some iron glue type of stuff now.) So are menus, uh, sometimes. My method always was to slide it under the left armpit, lower the arm, and the jacket covered all. It wouldn't work, of course, if it was an informal type of place, with no jackets required, but a lot of times I'd wear one anyway, anticipating the fact that there might be a menu worth having.

My wife, Lady Law and Order, put a stop to this, at least temporarily. "Just ask them for it," she'd say. "I'm sure they'll let you have it."

This advice was correct about 60 percent of the time. A few restaurants actually sold them to us.

The most expensive was $35 at The Blue Duck in Prague, but that was such a terrific restaurant that I didn't begrudge them the sale. Besides, the thing was too heavy to slip under the arm, and I liked the people there too much to do a number on them. I've now gone back to the old way, which is tougher than ever because not only do I have to be on the lookout for waiters and maître d's but Linda as well.

I know people who use menus as decorative art, who have a whole gallery of framed covers lining the walls of their house, but to me, that's like keeping the wrapper and throwing away the candy. The cover is nice, of course, but it's the inside that makes for the fun reading, especially when you compare prices. I'm lucky enough to have had this menu instinct for a long time. Thus I can boast of such now defunct rarities as Le Chapon Fin in Bordeaux, when I had lunch there as a GI on leave in 1957 and could afford only one fancy meal, or Henri Soule's famous Le Pavillon in New York in 1964. *(Editor's note: Indiana University purchased Paul's menu collection.)*

Cigar box labels are the late entry. Almost 30 years ago, when my children were six and seven, they attended a summer camp called Appel Farm in the heat belt of southern New Jersey, inland, next to a town called Elmer. One Sunday we were visiting and we took the kids for ice cream at an old fashioned soda shop in town. It was an interesting place, with an old fashioned antiquely look to it, and sure enough, there were collectibles on sale. A few advertising posters, the usual chipped World War II Coca-Cola tray, nothing very special. And then I spotted a few loose leaf notebooks.

In them was a form of art I had never seen before, cigar box label art. The labels, the larger, 6 x 9 inner labels, or those that went inside the box, and the 4 1/2 x 4 1/2 outer labels, were neatly enclosed in plastic sheets, and some were stunningly beautiful. From the high gilt style of the 19th century to art deco or even the German Bauhaus style of some of the foreign labels, they represented innumerable themes. And they were cheap.

I started thumbing through each book. Prices started at 35 cents apiece and topped out at about a dollar for an 1872 label called Strawberry, which remains the oldest I have. There were three loose leaf books full of them; all were in mint condition. The kids had finished their ice cream sodas, and their attention span was running out. My ex-wife gave one of those pseudo-cheery, sarcastic, "Time to go now" calls, the implication being there he is, as usual, making us wait for him while indulges in some foolishness.

I had to move quickly. I asked the lady at the store how much for all the labels, all three books?

"I'll have to ask my husband," she said, showing no surprise, or actually much of anything. Emotion was not a big thing in Elmer.

"Look, I have to go," I said. "Just give me a fair price."

"Cash only," she said, answering a question but not the one I asked. "No checks, no credit cards. Cash."

Note to collector junkies. Always carry cash. You never know when you'll run into something, and cash opens many doors because then the transaction will be off the books, and they can stiff the government out of the taxes it needs to equip a highly trained military presence. Even so, I didn't know whether I had enough for all those labels and I didn't have time to pick and choose and I knew she wouldn't hold them for me, even with a deposit, not really being up for complicated transactions.

I've had a persistent nightmare that I'm sure collectors have shared. I've discovered the find of a lifetime, an antique gallery or perhaps an old bookstore or coin shop with priceless treasures to be had at knockdown prices, but I didn't have enough cash, or a vehicle in which to transport the goods. There was always some impediment. This time there wasn't. There were about 200 labels in those books, a few dupes, but most of them different, and the price she quoted me was, if I remember correctly, something like $100. Average 50 cents per label. I could cover it, and that bunch became the start of a most interesting collecting avenue.

In any new collecting venture, your interest gradually settles down, but you're on fire at first. I found catalogues, a few books that mentioned the cigar box labels, a beautifully illustrated article in an old *Fortune Magazine* complete with reproductions. I found a labels-only dealer, Cerebro in Lancaster, Pa., whose prices were reasonable ... it was always let's make a deal ... but then grew quite serious when the collecting interest began to grow. I would search for labels at ephemera book fairs and shows, hunt them up in old bookstores or secondhand shops while I was on the road. The fun of it was that they remained unknown commodities for many years, hence cheap.

They've had a curious history. Once upon a time, late in the 19th century, going into the early 20th, there were many different kinds of them. They were actually proud examples of the engraver's art, both in this country and Europe. But in later years, the factories began closing, and when they were sold, their new owners often found rolls of these labels left behind. Rather than being dumped on the market in huge quantities, the ones that weren't actually thrown out were released judiciously, but there were still plenty to go round with very little demand. And that's the market that I stepped into that day in Elmer.

They were marvelous things to devote evenings to, sorting them, classifying, assigning places in notebooks according to theme — pretty girls, foreign labels, 19th century heavy gilt, sports themes, romance, Greek mythology, animals. They were a sorter and cataloguer's dream. Prices have climbed, though ... actually to where they should be based on their quality. Collecting them is now an expensive pastime. So, personally, they're in what I call a passive, rather than an active phase. I'm happy with what I have, I won't be actively pursuing too many more, but if a few good ones come along at decent prices ... well, you never know.

And that brings us to the most serious collecting habit of all — books. You start by being a reader, which I was ever since, well, ever since I learned how to read. And since I never threw anything out, my library has a section of stained and worn and torn volumes, some still bearing faint food smells, that formed my childhood reading ... *Junket Is Nice, Here and Now Stories, Japanese Fairy Tales, Indian Fairy Tales, The Five Chinese Brothers*, and best of all, a book that I've re-ordered from an antiquarian shop because my daughter, Sarah, loved it so much, *Professor Peckham's Adventures in a Drop of Water*.

When I reached high school and then college, I learned about another way to build a library. Book clubs. Especially the ones whose ads bore the notation to be checked off, Bill Me Later. Those were before the days of rampant credit cards, and I'd say Bill Me Laters formed a huge part of what was a significant teenage library, leaning heavily toward the classics.

I developed a gang of aliases, each one a dedicated Bill Me Later devotee. There was Ralph Weaver and Warren Fleming, who like sports books, and Rabbi Nathan Feinberg, who specialized in pre-19th century classics, and Dr. Jurgen Buhl, whose tastes were mostly Thomas Mann and the heavier European volumes, plus a few others. Except that sometimes I would get them mixed up, or lose track, since, let's face it, I was too young to paralyze myself with intricate record keeping. Thus my house was a beehive of books arriving, bills, dunning notices, threats and still more books. My parents both worked, so I could get to the mail before they did, thus embarrassing questions generally were avoided.

I concentrated mostly on two clubs, The Heritage Club and The Classics Club, since they were the most persistent advertisers. Instinct kept me away from the Book of the Month Club. Too mainstream.

I was worried that they might have more sophisticated methods for dealing with the Warren Flemings and Jurgen Buhls of this world. The other two clubs, though, seemed to be more into flailing blindly, without too much care whom they struck. I remember vividly one afternoon when a very stern letter arrived from the Heritage Club for Dr. Buhl, c/o P. Zimmerman:

"You have persistently ignored every letter we have sent you requesting payment. The next correspondence you receive will be on, and this was underlined in red, for emphasis, (drum roll, please) Lawyer's Stationery."

And in the very same mailing, from the same Heritage Club, a nicely illustrated copy of The Vicar of Wakefield, addressed to Warren Fleming, c/o P/Zimmerman, with the salutation, "Welcome New Member!" (Damn two-faced Heritage Club ... the very idea.)

You'd think that someone might have wondered about this gang of thieves all sharing residence with poor Zimmerman, but the matter never came up.

When adulthood came, I put away, as Paul the Apostle said, childish things and began to learn about something that became a lifelong drive, the collecting of books. Not catfish collecting, as much of my early assemblages represented, but collecting with a point of view. What is catfish collecting?

Well, at one time I took my children, Sarah, and her younger brother, Michael, down to the Malcolm Forbes Galleries on 5th Ave. and 12th St. to get a look at the million dollar Faberge eggs from Czarist Russia, not really knowing what the rest of the museum held.

What we saw were some interesting examples of scatter-shot collecting of all manner of Americana, plus large glass cabinets filled with rank upon rank of military miniatures, mostly hand painted, jammed together in close order. Taken individually, some of the pieces would be interesting, but as a horde they lost all meaning. This, I explained to my children, is catfish collecting. Everything gets swallowed. Then we turned a corner, and I saw displayed something that represented exactly the opposite of what I had just told them about.

It was a diorama of the gun deck of Lord Nelson's HMS Victory during the battle of Trafalgar, the figures shockingly lifelike, puffs coming from the guns, blood-stained swaths around the gunners' heads, tiny mirrors fitted into the walls to expand the aspect of the scene. Never have I seen a more beautiful one.

Years later, Lane Stewart, a *Sports Illustrated* photographer who specialized in military miniatures, explained to me that the famous diorama had been done by the Chicago artist, Shep Haines. So highly regarded was he that when the captain of the HMS Victory — yes, Nelson's Victory is still a fully staffed flagship — comes to Chicago, he stays overnight on the couch in Shep Haines' living room.

It was all a lesson in catfish versus focused collecting designed to make collectors out of my children, a project I've essentially abandoned. Oh, they'll show an interest in things, but the true madness is not there, lucky for them. But there came a point when I progressed from catfish to collector, and one blessing was that it required less room in the house.

I focused on authors who were meaningful to me, or had been at one stage of my life — B. Traven, Ring Lardner, H. P. Lovecraft, George Orwell and especially Rudyard Kipling. Then there was a second tier, such as Vladimir Nabokov, Graham Greene, Ambrose Bierce, Joyce Cary, etc., plus individual books that had enough of an impact that I wanted them in first edition — some of Larry McMurtry's early works, here and there a Henry Miller or an H.G. Wells. Luckily, I began when most authors I liked were fairly affordable. Some never were, at least on my budget. Hemingway, for instance. Choice works were always out of sight, except for *For Whom the*

Bell Tolls, a regular $10 item at the auction galleries when I first started frequenting them in the late 1960s, but you can add a couple of zeros to that now.

If you're interested in books, not necessarily as collectibles, but just as, well, nice things to read, I'm sure you're aware of what I'm going to tell you now. Never lend books. For some reason there's something about them that leads people to feel that they don't have to be returned. The last time I made this mistake was, oh, about 25 years ago, and the result was a near disaster.

I had an old friend who lived in Bethesda, Md., a Redskins fan, naturally. One evening he and his wife were at our house for dinner. Before we sat down, he was browsing through the library and he picked out a first edition of Charles G. Finney's *Circus of Dr. Lao*, with the dreamlike Boris Artzybasheff illustrations.

"Hmmm, never read this," he said. "I'll just borrow it." I felt sick.

"You can read it before we sit down," I said, as the waves of panic rose. "It's a short book."

Everyone looked at me as if I were nuts. I had no allies in the room. He borrowed the book. And it remained borrowed. A year, two years went by. I'd call him up on some pretext or other. Oh by the way, comma, do you think you could send me that book? I'll send it, don't worry, I'll send it. The thing was obsessing me, keeping me awake at night.

Finally during the football season of the third year ML, Minus Lao, I talked my editor at *Sports Illustrated* into letting me cover a Redskins game in Washington. I called my friend and told him I'd be down his way.

"Oh, you've got to stay with us," he said. Damn right I've got to stay with you. Why do you think I'm coming there? So we had dinner. I mentioned the book as casually as I could, given my twisted expression. Oh, it's around somewhere, don't worry. Has anyone ever stopped worrying because someone said, "Don't worry?" Or taken it easy when someone said, "Take it easy?"

In the meantime I gave the living room bookcase a careful search. No Lao. Where could it be? Could he have gotten rid of it? We went to bed, after casual mention that it would be looked for the next day. I couldn't sleep. Could it be that there was a bookcase in their bedroom? Instinct told me yes. It was 3 a.m. I turned on the hall light and opened the bedroom door just enough to let me squeeze in and to provide a bit of meager light. There was a bookcase. They were asleep. His wife was naked from the waist up and uncovered. For God's sake, don't wake up. I mean, we were friends and all, but I could still see the headlines: Bedroom Freak Caught in Bethesda.

And then God finally decided to smile on his humble servant. There on the top shelf … easy while you're reaching up, now … was the off-white spine of the jacket, with the spidery red script writing, *The Circus of Doctor Lao*, and out of the bookcase it came, into my bag and home to its dear place, alphabetized between Faulkner and Fitzgerald.

I was at a party once and a woman asked me, "How can you be an author and a book collector, too?" The question sounds a bit daffy, but there's really some sense to it. How can you be involved in the big picture, the act of creation, the entire artistic impulse and still pin yourself down to the minutiae of collecting, the identification of obscure first edition points, the glorification of the unopened, unread volume? I told her to ask Larry McMurtry. He's a better example of it than me.

He is a dealer, and I, assume, a collector, as well, since the two go together. I had visited his shop in Georgetown, Booked Up, and spent a very pleasant afternoon there, talking about books we collect. I bought a couple of modern fiction works and then, and I expected him to groan at this, but he didn't … he was a complete gentleman … brought out a few of his old ones to inscribe: *Horseman, Pass By*; *Leaving Cheyenne*; *The Last Picture Show*.

I used to enjoy covering the Cowboys' training camp in Wichita Falls, Texas, because it was only 25 miles away from Archer City, the town depicted in *The Last Picture Show* and the new locale of McMurtry's Booked Ups, four of them, each with a different theme. I thought Linda would enjoy going down there, and we did a few times, but enjoy? Well, there's this thing called heat, and she knows all about it, having grown up in Phoenix.

The first Archer City Booked Up trip we made was on a day in which the thermometer in the center of town registered 116 degrees. None of the stores had air conditioning. They had fans, which were like dropping ice cubes into a furnace. In the first store, a poor old mongrel dog lay stretched out by the front counter, panting desperately. He had been bitten by a rattlesnake the day before. A few days later, we called up and found out that he made it, just barely. I got a tremendous kick out of watching Linda and Larry McMurtry, puzzling over the price of a book … is that a three or a five there? But it was a pretty tough day all around. The next two trips were better.

As for my combined authorship (seven books, all about football) and collecting ... well, the two actually did come into some sort of congruence on one occasion. I was in Miami in 1973, covering Jets-Dolphins. I was browsing a bookstore and I saw something I had to have. A slim volume, *Debs and the Poets*, a collection of writing from different sources, all expressing indignation about the jailing of Eugene V. Debs, the left-wing labor leader and a hero of mine, for anti-government statements. And laid in was a letter, written in prison, from Debs to a young follower. The price was $100, as well it should have been, because it was a choice item. But this was 1973, don't forget.

I tried to get the dealer to come down. He wouldn't budge. I told him I was an author myself. He took the news calmly. I told him I had a book on the shelves at the time, my revised *Thinking Man's Guide to Football*. He shrugged. Then I got a brilliant idea.

In collecting circles there's something known as an Association Copy, a book inscribed by the author to a well-known person, perhaps even more famous than the author; it's the association between the two that gives the book added value. I told him I'd trade him, straight up, the *Debs* for 10 *Thinking Man's Guides*; each one would be a "fascinating association copy," as they say in the catalogues.

"Like this," I said. "'To my pal, Fidel Castro. Remember that night in the Hotel Teresa, buddy?' Or, 'To Nikki Khruschchev. Still trying to hold your breath three minutes?' Ten like that. Waddya say?"

He actually thought it over for a good 30 seconds. I could hear the heavy chains of deep breathing. Finally he said, "That's absolutely ridiculous," but I did get the guy to give it some real thought. The story does not have a happy ending. He was a Dolphins fan. He was of the opinion that the eventual Super Bowl champs were going to blow the Jets out the next day. I thought New York would make it close. He gave me the Jets and 14, double or nothing on the Debs.

Miami scored four times in the first half and coasted in. Final score, 30-3. So I had to scrape up two yards for the Debs. It took me almost six months to pay it off.

I mentioned before that my kids were very sporadic collectors. Well, occasionally something would kick in. I went through a period when they were in the sixth, seventh grade when I was trying to teach them what really good writing was, as distinguished from pretense. My example of good writing was the quotation at the beginning of one of my favorite books, John O'Hara's *Appointment in Samarra*. It was a quotation from the play, *Sheppey*, by William Somerset Maugham, that begins, "Death Speaks," and goes on to mention the servant trying to flee, when in reality he and death have an appointment in Samara.

I got to like that quote so much that I became curious about what the play itself was like, so I started looking for it, and naturally it had to be in first edition. A hard title to find, but not impossible. Well, Michael and Sarah and I were in England one summer after I had laid my Death Speaks oration on them. They were about 13 and 14 at the time. We took a drive up to Oxford. We looked at things for while, then I gave them an allotment of cash and a couple of hours free time to do what they wanted, buy what they could afford. Meet you back right here. And off they went. And off I went to check out the bookstores.

The first one I went to had a basement level. Down I went, with no clear idea of what I was looking for. And then I heard a girl's voice from upstairs, "Do you have *Sheppey* by Somerset Maugham?" Damn! Why hadn't I asked for that right away? It would be just my luck that it would turn up, and that young woman would get it. Up the stairs I went. And what did I see but my 13-year old, my Mikey, with his squeaky little voice, trying to buy the book as a surprise for daddy. Oh my good heavens!

Well, I found the book, first edition, dust jacket, nice condition, a few years later in the catalogue of Nigel Williams in London, one of my favorite dealers. Not very expensive, either. I sent a note to Michael, who was away at school, reminding him of the time he tried to get it for me in Oxford, and how extra special it now had become. Yes, they take on a life of their own, these books complete with their own stories and memories. And that's something people who have not fallen prey to the collecting fever never will understand.

Chapter 13

Authority

I guess you could say that I'm the kind of person who never hit it off with the officiating branch of sports. I never could figure out why someone would want to be in a position to control the destinies of other people. When we used to see those training films in the army, in basic, you know, *Venereal Disease and You* or *The Evils of Going AWOL*, I immediately was locked onto the side of the poor miscreant (usually played by Jack Lemmon, who got his earliest start in movies by acting in training films for the armed services). I could always feel the heavy hand on my shoulder. "We're on to you, m'lad."

Once I was fixed up on a blind date with a young Cuban woman who happened to be a psychiatrist. She was a rare breed in this profession. She actually offered opinions, rather than the standard, "How do YOU feel about it?" or "What do YOU think it means?" Her opinions of me were not good. Among them, after we had spent about two tedious hours in each other's company, was, "You know you have a real problem with authority?"

Of course I knew it. Authority on both ends. I didn't like others to boss me around and I didn't like having to do the same, although the occasions in which I was in a position of authority were very infrequent in my life. But she took a bit of time to make sure I understood every unpleasant nuance of this pronouncement, and actually, if I remember right, and it was a long time ago, this served as a prelude to my closing out the evening. How does one close out an evening? By treating every topic of conversation in the most outlandish fashion I could think of.

She asked me about my family, and I created this fiction involving eight sisters and brothers, among which I was the youngest, and what it was like trying to survive in a situation such as this, and so forth. She looked bored.

"What's the matter?" I said.

"You've got only child written all over you," she said, only slightly covering her yawn. Yep, that cruel jet of truth closed out the evening all right.

I'm getting far off the subject, as usual.

Growing up as a New York kid, occasionally dealing with the authority figures known as the police, you learn two things. Run like hell and never give your right name. My neighborhood in Washington Heights, which is upper Manhattan, bordered on Fort Tryon Park, accessible by something we called The Big Lot, which actually were woods, eventually leading to the Medieval monastery, The Cloisters. Along the way, you'd pass a terraced overlook of the Henry Hudson Parkway we called The Fort. It afforded a spectacular sight line of the uptown lane of traffic, and in winter we'd make a supply of snowballs and bomb the cars as they headed north. Never did it occur to us that this activity could well lead to all manner of accidents. Thank God it never did.

Well, one day that word must have reached the police in the area because one of their cars stopped right underneath us, on the shoulder, and one of the officers stepped out of his vehicle and we could see him talking. And it was at this point that Clipper Goodman decided to bomb him with an ice ball, which hit him on the foot, and off we went in full flight.

Being idiots, we naturally headed for the area's main exit, and that's exactly where the law was waiting for us. First they told us what harm we could cause, then there was the roundup, with all names being taken, followed by the promises that this incident would be reported at school, and our parents would be summoned, and all hell would break loose. We were all crying ... and all giving fake names. Mine was Elliott Davidson. I remember one officer's final words to me, as he pointed a finger at my chest.

"Elliott, you're in trouble!"

In the army my natural aversion to authority presented its set of problems, although not as many as you'd think, once I'd gotten through basic training. The ability to make a deal, to broker the mutually advantageous tradeoff, generally could cover the initial problem. But I always did find it embarrassing when I found myself in the unusual position of actually having to exert some authority.

Not that I had any rank. I came out almost as clean as I went in, Private E-3, having been awarded a stripe on two occasions and being busted, losing it, in other words, both times. But on one occasion, late in basic, I found myself working a night KP, my assignment being to load the used food trays into a giant, wheeled, rack-holding contraption and then wheeling this monster over to the area where the washing took place. The hardest part was getting the thing moving after it had been loaded. Inertia was a formidable enemy. But I looked at the exercise as similar to driving a gigantic blocking sled, building leg muscles of steel.

Of course another problem was the heat generated by all the hot water. We worked in a perpetual cover of steam. Sweat obliterated my glasses, essentially rendering me sightless, so I was pushing that thing blind, aiming in a general direction at the start and then re-starting and re-directing it every time I hit a wall or a mess table. And that's what I was doing, straining, heaving, getting it rolling, then bonk! Into the wall. Then getting it going again, the sweat pouring off me. All of a sudden I heard, "Hey," which had the unmistakable sound of an officer, and sure enough, it was me he was signaling.

So I stopped and squinted in the direction of a young lieutenant who had been watching me.

"You're a pretty good worker," he said.

"Thank you, sir," I answered, figuring this was noncommittal enough. He explained that the mess hall was turning into a consolidated mess, taking in one whole other area, which happened to be in a rather primitive state at the time, and he would like me to "take charge of a detail" and get the place swept up and cleaned and generally prepared for the evening meal. It was a chilling announcement. Take charge of a detail? Who, me? A Private E-2?

"You'll find your detail in there," he said, pointing to the cavernous room next door and a pile of brooms nearby.

My detail consisted of seven short-timers, guys who had served their time and were waiting to rotate out in a few days and weren't at all happy about getting stuck on a sucker's gig like a night KP so close to their discharge date. Seven rough looking guys. How'd they feel about a nebbish such as myself actually trying to execute a command or two in their direction? Looking back on my own outlook on life when I became a short-timer myself, I'm sure they felt nothing more than annoyance, just another pain in the ass, courtesy of Uncle.

They were sitting on the floor, leaning against a wall, the usual position when you're waiting for your detail to begin. A few were sleeping, which happened in the army when you were off your feet for any period longer than two or three minutes. Some were smoking. I announced that the lieutenant had ordered me to get them to clean up the big room. I pointed to the brooms. A couple stared at me without changing their expression. The others who were awake didn't bother. There was only one course open to me, as I saw it, and I took it.

I grabbed a broom, turned and faced them and announced, "Look, I'm going to try to get as much of the cleaned up as I can. Anyone who wants to help me, fine. I'd appreciate it." And I pitched into a vigorous sweeping operation.

Maybe it was a feeling of pity for my sweat-soaked figure, and that did it, maybe just a sense of boredom, but eventually three guys hauled themselves up and found brooms and joined into a desultory sweeping activity. The others continued to sleep, or smoke, or whatever they were doing. Frankly, I didn't care. But the last thing on my mind was actually ordering any of them to do something. Not totally impossible, but very difficult for a person such as me. How did the episode end? Our shift ended at noon, and we stacked our brooms and reported back to our outfits. I never saw the lieutenant again.

The desire to regulate the activity of others, to enforce rules, to exert authority is a powerful incentive, I'm sure. Being a military history buff, of sorts, I could understand how a normal, even aesthetic, person could get caught up in the smell of battle and command a force. Just look at the Civil War general, Joshua Lawrence Chamberlain, the Bowdoin theology professor who led the famous bayonet charge at Little Round Top and earned a Congressional Medal of Honor. I could understand the idealism and even thirst for danger that would lead a young person into becoming a police officer. My wife, Linda's daughter, Heather, for instance, was a member of the Phoenix PD, and her husband, Steve, an FBI operative. I've talked to my share of cops, while on assignment, and once they felt they could trust you, they turned out to be incredible storytellers, great yarn-spinners, the best.

Actually I had two minor police work experiences. Once, in Germany, I pulled duty as a stockade guard. My job was to escort a prisoner to a dental appointment. "No talking to the prisoners," I was told. "And they all want to stop at the PX and give you money so you can buy stuff for them, and that's absolutely forbidden." There was no truth to it.

In the day room of the stockade, listening to the inmates and waiting to pick up my charge, I found myself liking these guys more than I liked the ones in my own outfit. The fellow I escorted turned out to be a young redheaded kid who'd been guilty of extended AWOL, which officially became "desertion," the No. 1 offense in the compound. Usually it involved seeing a girl. Yeah, we talked a bit on the way over, but every time he asked me something, he prefaced it with, "Guard," which I guess they were instructed to do, but it set my teeth on edge. I still hate it when I think about it. When we approached the PX, he handed me a few coins and said, "Guard, would you get some toothpaste for me?" so I left him outside, shlepped my carbine into the store with me and bought him his toothpaste, no big deal. And that was my prison guard experience.

And then, on the troopship home, they took the dozen or so biggest guys, myself among them, and made us MPs. My assignment was the deck area outside the cabins for the officer's dependents heading home, basically to stop the kids from running along the slippery surface. Now this was just a wonderful gig because 1) the worst facet of troopship life was boredom. There was absolutely nothing to do, which normally would have dictated five days of serious reading, except that the constant noise level was so great ... screaming, shrieking, singing, shouting ... that you simply couldn't concentrate, and 2) there was no place to get by yourself. Even staking out a piece of a hatch to sit on was difficult. You were always crowded. Your bunk, which actually was a hammock, was no good because down below you were always confronted by the heat and the lingering smell of vomit. My assignment provided me with space, with freedom to read at undisturbed moments, with conversation with the kids, their moms, anyone else who came along. A terrific deal.

Sometimes, in the buttoned up world of corporate sports, my built-in loony streak has backfired. When I reported to the office of Donald Trump for a previously set-up interview concerning Trump's team in the USFL, the Jersey Generals, I first had to face Trump's PR man.

He told me, "Mr. Trump wants to know the tenor of your questioning."

"I said, 'Tell Mr. Trump it's not a tenor, it's a baritone.'" I waited for the laugh that never came.

He said, "Just a minute, please," and disappeared. Two minutes later he's back out.

"Mr. Trump says he can't do the interview at this time."

As far as the other form of authority, that of a referee or umpire, uh uh. Definitely not for me, and I couldn't understand its attraction for others. There was an occasion once when both officials failed to make it to one of my son, Mike's, Pee Wee games for the Denville (N.J.) Blue Angels. As luck would have it, the contest involved two unbeaten teams, the Angels and a very rough bunch of kids from Morristown. The coach of the Morristown Colonials, the home team, called for volunteers. Anybody ever do any officiating? One parent stepped forward. Anyone else? No. Anyone with any football background at all? No response. Were we really going to have to cancel a game of that magnitude? I raised my hand and found myself in a strange world that was familiar in form but not execution.

What was the toughest thing? Amazingly enough, it was something I never would have thought of. Spotting the ball. Making sure it was lined up absolutely correctly. After that was done, I found myself actually enjoying the experience … well, not really *enjoying* it, more like surviving it. Until the end of the game. Then a bad thing happened. We had taken a lead, basically on reverses by Andy Bartek, the star, the fastest kid on the team. Trick plays, dick'em football that the Morristown boys did not appreciate at all. The Colonials stormed back, on power and good solid football. They were the better team. They scored and were down by a point. They lined up to run in the conversion. Kids didn't kick points at that level. I was to the left of the line of scrimmage, peering down the line, checking the offsides. A yellow helmet and shoulder pad came across, just barely. I blew my whistle and dropped the flag. Offsides, offense. The stands went crazy. Fans were trying to come out onto the field. The five yards pushed them back into very difficult range for running in the extra point. They tried anyway and were stopped just short. Game's over.

Their coach was a really nice guy, a gentleman. "I want to thank you two for working the game," he said, "but if I were you, I wouldn't stick around here. Get your boy and get home." Which we did.

I had fun with officials when I was a coach. How could I have been a coach, you ask, when I hated authority? Well, I was actually coaching my classmates, among others. This was in my senior year at Columbia. The Ivy League Presidents Committee nailed me on its five-year rule and declared me ineligible early in the season. The league, not the NCAA but the Ivies, had this ruling that said that a player's career had to be wrapped up within five years, the army being the only exception allowed, and this was a year before my tour of duty began. I had started Stanford in 1949, been there for three seasons, left after the fall of '51, dropped out, worked on a ship, did, uh, other things, finally re-enrolling, this time at Columbia with its legendary coach, Lou Little, for whom I should have played in the first place. Ineligible as a transfer in '53, I was counting on one solid 1954 senior season, but the five years had elapsed.

I found out from the director of athletics, Ralph Furey, who told me, with a wide smile ... and that's what I will never forget, that smiling face of his ... "Hey, you're ineligible." I never knew about that five-year thing. I cursed myself, dumb, stupid, idiot moron. Had I known, I just would have lied about my original Stanford date, but where's the sign that says that when you're young you have to be smart, too?

Coach Little called me in. "You want to keep your training table, don't you?" Yes, I most certainly did. "You'll coach the lightweight team, the 150-pounders, with John Wagner. You coach the line, he'll coach the backs."

Coach? Coach? Wow! Well, we went 2-3 that year. Most successful season in the history of the Columbia lightweights. You could look it up. I enjoyed putting in the line drills. Most of all I enjoyed tackling practice when I would volunteer as the ball carrier, and they'd have to tackle me. I felt like Bronko Nagurski, running through those 150-pounders. I might not have been a great coach, but I was a terrific recruiter. My most fertile territory was drinking buddies who had been bounced out of Columbia a year or two before and were just kind of hanging around. One guy, Carson Scheidemann, had been out of Columbia at least two, maybe three years. He was working in a warehouse.

Top allowable weight was 155, which presented no problem because we were on the honor system. It was our duty to weigh our own lightweights. What we had were the type of guys who once were known, if you went back to old boxing circles, as "Philadelphia Lightweights," in other words, overweights. We had guys 170 and 180 pounds. I'll bet Carson was pushing 190.

I remember, when we played Rutgers in our final game, we were lining up for the kickoff, and all of a sudden, the assistant director of athletics,

Les Thompson, appeared alongside me. A nasty, skinny redhead with a pervasive squint, he was squinting at our kick team, especially at L2, a wedge-busting position, manned by Carson Scheidemann.

"Is that Scheidemann out there?" he said, and I mumbled a "No, sir," and moved away from him, down the sidelines, trying to attract Scheidemann's attention in a combination stage whisper and shout ... "Carson! Carson!" Finally he noticed me. I pointed to the assistant D of A. Carson took one look and made his exit, holding one hand over his face, like a Mafioso on his way to arraignment. The kickoff was delayed because the guys on the unit were laughing so hard.

Oh we had fun, all right. That's what it's all about, isn't it? At one point, Jack Lauterborn, one of our tackles, whom I happened to be drinking beer with at the West End the night before, showed signs of fatigue, and I pulled him out of the game.

"Put me back in," he said. "There's a prick I gotta get even with."

"Be my guest," I said and sent him back in for the next play. And I watched him as he wound up and delivered a huge, bolo right hand punch to the guy opposite him. Tweet! Whistles everywhere. A blizzard of flags. The ref started marking off the 15 yards. But he hadn't announced the penalty to our bench, and I liked to put on a sideline show for the kids anyway, so I started yelling, "The penalty, ref! What's the call?"

He was one of those old-time ECAC officials. He kept walking, never turned to the bench but announced in an authoritative Boston accent, "Fifteen yards. Intent to main and disfigyah!" Sure, we all broke up again, myself included. We had a hell of a time that year.

My own dealings with officials have been interesting. The NFL likes to wrap them in cellophane. You can interview the president or the pope but not an NFL official. I have been arguing for more than 40 years, ever since I started covering pro football, to make them available to the press. Maybe Roger Goodell will change the protocol ... he's young and seemingly forward-thinking ... but so far it hasn't happened. And I'm not as revolutionary about it as I used to be.

The system that was put in by Pete Rozelle involved one designated pool reporter to forward the press questions to the referee or the official involved and then forward it back to the press. The weakness of the system, from our standpoint, is that the pool reporter is a writer who's working the game, and he has to worry about his own story and quotes, in addition to getting to the officials. Delay is deadly in the postgame hurly-burly, which, of course, is known to the officials and acted upon accordingly.

Well, in 1973, I was covering a Jets-Bills game in Shea Stadium. The game hinged on a key pass interference penalty on Burgess Owens, a rookie defensive back for the Jets. It was an awful penalty, actually a blown call on a foul that never had taken place. Dick Creed, a first-year back judge, made the call. Our pool reporter was Bob Kurland from *The Bergen (N.J.) Evening Record*, a nice little guy, kind of mousy, but a decent person. We pumped him full of fire and brimstone. "Talk to the guy who made the call," we told him. "Find out whether he was in position to see the play," etc.

Pat Haggerty, a nasty, overbearing old warhorse, was the referee. He approached Kurland outside the officials' room and turned on a tape recorder. Val Pinchbeck from the league office was on Kurland's other side, running a tape machine of his own.

"The official ruled that the defender had made contact with the receiver in such a manner as to prohibit him from ..." blah blah blah, Haggerty intoned into his recorder.

"Can I talk to the official?" Kurland asked him.

"You've got your statement, now get the hell out of here!" Haggerty yelled at him. A few years ago Haggerty's name came up for possible Hall of Fame induction. It never got very far. I told the Hall of Fame people that the only way he'd ever get in would be if I were dead or fired as a selector.

Kurland reported his information to us as we were writing our stories. Everyone jumped him. "Waddya mean, you didn't talk to the official?" etc. Poor guy, he got hammered from both ends. I was still fuming hours later, when I drove down to the *Post* to write my game piece. We were an evening paper, which meant practically unlimited deadlines. Damn lying sons of bitches. They knew they blew it.

I turned to the officials page in the NFL yearbook. Richard Creed, back judge, first year, Poland, Ohio. I looked at my watch. Would he have had time to fly home already? Maybe. I dialed Ohio information. His number was listed. I called it. He had just gotten home.

"Dick," I said, "this is Dick Maxwell from the league office."

"Yeah, Dick, what is it?" His voice sounded shaky.

"There's gonna be a lot of flak about the interference call," I said. "You'd better tell me what happened."

"Hell, I was screened from the play, but it was my call," he said. "I didn't really see it. I looked around for help. It was a veteran crew, Pat Haggerty, Tony Veteri, that bunch. They all looked the other way. I had dropped the flag. I had to call something ..."

"OK, look," I said. "If anyone else calls you ... any writer or someone like that, just refer it to the league office, OK?" He said OK and hung up.

I called Art McNally, the supervisor of officials, who lived outside Pennsylvania, a good guy who happened to be working within a system, a person I could talk to. I related the previous conversation.

"You did WHAT?" he said.

"Look," I told him, "if I wanted to be a prick, I could have the whole back page of the *Post*, with a nice red, banner headline, I DIDN'T SEE IT — NFL OFFICIAL. That's how easy it is. Why the hell don't you guys loosen it up and let us talk to these officials?"

Well, I never used the Creed stuff, obviously. And the league people never changed their system. The change they did make, however, was to remove the officials' home addresses from their guide.

Last year someone sent me this question for my *SI.com* mailbag column: "What's the worst call you ever saw on the football field?" I couldn't answer it, not exactly, but I mentioned the worst call you saw on *any* field. Our rugby club, the Columbia RFC, was playing at West Point for first place in our division. I had enjoyed visiting there, particularly when my best friend, Paul Lansky, was a cadet, the tradition, the beauty of the place. But what I learned through the years was that if you were up there for any kind of athletic competition, be ready for a royal screwing. No site was as bad. After a while the whole traditional legacy ... the Corps, the Long Grey Line, Benny Havens O, paled in comparison to what they did to you.

It was a hot day for the rugby game. We trailed by a couple of points. The game was almost over. Then Pat Moran, our fullback, kicked ahead, and the ball hit one of the uprights, boink! And bounced straight back and Tommy Haggerty, our open side winger who had been an all-Ivy halfback and a rookie in the Giants camp, caught it in full flight and ran it in for the score. Tweet! Whistle. Game's over. We cheered and hoisted Haggy onto our shoulders. The West Point guys hung their heads and slouched off the field. It was up to the referee, a big fat guy in white pantaloon type things, or knickers like old-time golfers wore ... I'll never forget him ... he still haunts my dreams ... to announce the score. He was studying his sheet, and I was getting a real queasy feeling in my stomach.

"Final score," he announced. "Columbia 25, West Point 27." What? No waaaait just one minute, podnah. I was on him like a flash. I mean, I'd been in college, off and on, for almost seven years. One thing I knew how to do was add.

"Excuse me, sir, your honor, your worship, can we just go over the scoring for a minute?"

He turned his back on me. "I've announced the score," he said and began to walk off.

"Take it easy, Zim," said our captain, Dick Donelli. "Take it easy? Take it easy! You dumbshits! He's stealing the game from us." Past tense it, please. *Stole* the game from us.

Later in our party, the other team, a rugby tradition, in a woodland spot called The Grove, a couple of the cadets I was drinking with just shook their heads. "I've seen some bad ones up here," one of them said, "but this was the worst."

I had been through with serious rugby for a few years, into my 40s I would guess, when I got a call from Billy Campbell, Ballsie we called him, who'd been my Columbia and Old Blue RFC teammate for many years. Ballsie later would go out to Silicon Valley and make a fortune, starting his own computer company called Claris, but those days he was Columbia's head football coach. He said the college was trying to drum up interest in the rugby program, and they thought it would be a rather catchy idea to bring back alumni who might be known in the sporting world as guest competitors for one of their games.

"I'll do it if you will," Billy told me. Oh yeah, fine for him. He was still an avid jogger, and I just knew he did a full workout program with weights and things. As for me, I wouldn't lift anything heavier than a fork, but what the hell? Yeah, I'll do it.

The college was playing the Cornell Medical School at Baker Field. As I was warming up, my graying hair and ample belly drew odd looks from the kids I would be playing alongside. I mean, was this a freak show, or what? I thought it through. What can I do to impress these kids? There must be something. I could think of only one thing. Start a fight.

So the game started, and I began checking the opposition for likely candidates. Early in the contest, I'd found my man, a short stocky roughneck who would cruise the edge of the loose scrums, the loose rucks, dart in and pop someone and then beat it. A sneak, in other words. Perfect. So I waited, and as he was breaking out of the next melee, I delivered my cobblestone right. Unfortunately, he'd been over the course before and he saw it coming and ducked his head. All I'd done was create an awareness in him that he was not liked and bruised my hand severely, bouncing it off the top of his rock head.

He came up swinging, naturally, and people jumped in and broke it up, and the referee shouted,

"You! You're off the field!" And who was he shouting at and throwing out of the game? Why, the Cornell guy, of course. And out went sluggo, protesting mightily, which just ruined things beautifully for his sweet patootie date, who'd driven all the way down from Ithaca for the game.

Just to show him we were all God's children, I offered him my hand afterward. "Hey, no hard feelings, OK?" To his credit, he turned his back and walked away. He should have spit in my lying, hypocritical face. Ah, Fra Diavolo!

I've known some boxing referees, colorful characters for the most part. Jimmy Devlin had been a promising lightweight in Ireland. When he retired he came to New York and worked at first as an equipment man at George Brown's Gym on 57th St., the place where Ernest Hemingway worked out. Once in a while, Jimmy would spar with the customers, just exercise. I got to know him pretty well. Eventually he became a well-known ref, working the fights in the clubs around New York. A good storyteller, but not as good as Arthur Mercante was.

I had the pleasure of sitting next to Mercante, who was considered at the time the dean of boxing referees, having worked more than 120 title fights, including the first Ali-Frazier. This was at a New York University swim team dinner, of all places. Don't ask me what I was doing there because I don't remember, but Mercante was present because he was a distinguished alumnus and former swimmer for the Violets. He showed up a bit late, huffing and puffing a little. I asked him what was up.

"I've just seen the greatest fight I've ever seen in my life," he said. I figured he'd worked something in St. Nick's or Sunnyside Gardens in Queens or some other place. I asked him where it was and he said, "Driving east on 59th St., heading for the monument across the street from the Plaza.

"There's a cab going side by side with a panel truck, and the cabbie and the guys in the truck are yelling at each other. And then they stop for the light at 5th Ave., and three guys jump out of the panel truck and run over to the cab driver's side. They're in sweatshirts, kind of rough looking, you know, street fighter types.

"So they open the door and start pulling the cabbie out, and he just keeps coming out, and coming out, and it's the biggest, blackest guy I've ever seen in my life. Before he's even all the way out, he pops one of them and put him on the ground. He rolls a few feet, and his head gets stuck under the front wheel of a Cadillac waiting for the light, and then the light changes, and a few people who are watching yell, 'No! Don't go! There's a guy under there!' So the Caddy driver gets out, and they pull the guy free, and by now the cabbie has decked the second one.

"The third one runs away. Both the cab and the truck are unattended and blocking traffic, and there's this big honking thing going on, but a crowd has formed, and they're watching the cabbie chase this guy around the monument. And then he catches him. The guy covers up his head with his elbows, and the cabbie is flailing away ... he's a little tired by now ... and then the police arrive.

"They grab the cabbie, and the crowd yells, 'No! Not him! The others started it!' This one cop looks kind of puzzled. 'Do you want to press charges?' he asks the cab driver.

"'No,' says the cabbie. "I've had my pleasures.'

"How's that for a story?" Arthur asks me. "Sensational," I tell him. The speeches have started, but neither of us is paying attention. Our stuff is much more interesting.

"What's the best fight you've ever seen?" Mercante asks me. I had to think it through, but then a real gem popped into my head. I told him I didn't know if it was the best, but it was the most interesting. "Let's hear it?" Mercante says.

I was working in Sacramento, my first newspaper job. My father had come out to San Francisco and I was meeting him for dinner. I had to walk through the financial district to get to the restaurant and somewhere near Montgomery Street I saw a small crowd gathered. Naturally, I stopped to look. A man and a woman were giving a loud, ugly argument. She seemed drunk and very noisy. He was well dressed in a dark business suit, good looking in a bland sort of way, mid to late-30s maybe, average height and weight.

"Will you come on? Can we go? People are looking at us," he was saying, quietly but firmly.

"I don't give a damn! I'm not going anywhere!" she was yelling. This went on for a short time, and finally someone stepped out of the crowd, a big guy, a Man-Around-the-House type.

"Why don't you leave the lady alone?" he said.

"Why don't you mind your own business?" he was told.

"Look, pal," the intruder said and put his hand on the man's shoulder. I swear, it happened so fast that, literally, I didn't see it. Once I read a description of a piranha striking at a piece of meat, and the writer said it moved so fast that he only saw it in its original place and then gone, never in the process of getting there. That's what the punch must have been like. I saw the hand on the shoulder, then the guy on the ground, little in between.

The crowd backed off a little at this. "Look what you've done, just look what you've done!" the woman was yelling drunkenly. His eyes were gleaming now. "Let's just get out of here, let's just go," he said through clenched teeth. He took her arm.

"Let go of her," said a new arrival, stepping forward, and this time I saw the punch, or at least the end of it, because I was expecting it. It was pure lightning and it landed somewhere around the throat, and the guy went right down, just as quickly as the first one had. And that did it. Something had broken, and now the fighting spirit of that bland looking guy in the business suit was aroused, his blood lust, and he turned on the crowd savagely, and yelled, "OK, who's next? Come on, who's next?" Only once in my life had I seen a crowd part that fast, and that was in the Bronx Zoo when a lion let go this long, steaming piss into the crowd outside his cage. It was the same parting of the Red Sea.

He turned to the woman. "Let's go," he said.

"OK," she said, calmly, and away they walked. I turned to the guy next to me. "Did I really see this or was it a dream?" I said. "I'm wondering, myself," he said.

Well, it started as a chapter on officials, on authority figures, and it ended up with Greatest Fights of the Century. Sorry, but sometimes a twisted path gets you to the most interesting places.

Chapter 14

National Anthem

SINGING THE BLUES
This column appeared on SI.com *on Feb. 26, 2004.*

Whilst, snug in their clubroom,
They jovially twine
The Myrtle of Venus
With Bachus' Vine.

Does it mean anything to you, this verse? Well, it's obviously about a clubby set indulging, if you cut through the classical references, in the combined pleasures of fornicating and drinking.

This was the chorus of one of six verses of the club's song, the club being the Anacreon Society, which flourished among young Londoners toward the end of the 18th Century. The melody might be familiar to you if you substitute for the words above, the following:

Oh Say does that Star-Spangled
Banner yet wave
Oer the land of the free,
And the home of the brave.

That's right, the song is "To Anacreon in Heaven," a paean to indulgence, and the chaps singing it were just the young Britons who, if the mood seized them, would buy a commission and venture across the seas to command a brigade or a battalion against General Washington's Colonial Army in revolt. And that is the tune that is the basis for our national anthem. Ironic, huh? Our most cherished song a clubroom ditty for young blades from a nation at war with us.

I think I've mentioned before that I time the national anthem before every football game. And every other sporting event. Actually, I time it every time I hear it. If you ask me why, then you'll be like some other people in the press box who have annoyed me through the years with that question. It's so obvious that I don't feel compelled to give them any answer at all, much less a sensible one.

"Say, why do you do that?"

"I do it because I do it; that's why I do it."

"What are you, nuts or something?" a fellow reporter remarked not too long ago. That's right, "Or something." That sums me up perfectly. I'm an Or Something. Which might explain why not too many people want to sit next to me in the press box. Which is fine with me. But I'm getting carried away.

The tempo of "To Anacreon in Heaven" is not geared to the rhythm of marching feet. It's in waltz time, actually 6/4, which is like a speeded-up version of the old one-two-three, one-two-three, 3/4 waltz time. The melody is slightly different from our national anthem, as well. The first three notes, "O-ohh say," instead of being in G-E-C descending order, remain in place at C-C-C, giving it a kind rapid fire launching into the song.

Which adds a kind of rakish charm to the thing. I like this tune better than the way the "Star Spangled Banner" begins. I searched for the song on the Web and when I finally found the original version, it came on in a kind of hokey, root-a-toot fashion. I put a stopwatch on it, and it timed out in 43.4 seconds. In 50 years of timing the national anthem at sporting events, I have *never* clocked one anywhere near that speed.

But that's the way the song was designed to be sung. It was a ditty, for goodness sake, not the two-minute drill they've turned it into now.

Well, actually I have to take back that claim about never catching one that fast. Remember in the movie, *Tora! Tora! Tora!* about the bombing of Pearl Harbor, when a shipboard ceremony is taking place, and the bombers are approaching, and the band members blitz the national anthem so they can get the hell off the deck in a hurry? I clocked that one at 38 seconds, but it gets an asterisk, and it also took place at a non-sporting event.

Slow, slow, slooooowwwww national anthems are not correct national anthems. They are personal statements, insults to the song, which, let's face it, is not the greatest thing, musically ("Battle Hymn of the Republic," for instance, puts it away) but is all we've got. I make it a point to try to congratulate fast singers of the song, or fast instrumentalists.

How fast can it be sung? Well, my daughter, when she was 12, bet me that she could sing it in under 30 seconds, and I'd still be able to understand all the words. I took the bet, not so much to win but to hear her do it. She came in at 22 seconds, every word clear as a bell. See, it can be done. Try it yourself.

For years the fastest rendition I regularly clocked was that of the Princeton band. Always around 53 seconds. Then in 1977 I covered a Yankees-Red Sox series at Fenway. The organist was an older man named John Kiley who'd been playing the anthem at Red Sox games for years. The first night he hit the turn ("And the rocket's red glare") in 23 seconds. "Oh my God," I said to myself. "He's on a record pace."

When he reached Heartbreak Hill ("Oh say does that Star Spangled banner yet wave ...") he looked like he was going to break five-oh, but the Hill got him, as it does all of them. He staggered in and held the last note for a couple of counts, but the watch still read 55 seconds. Gosh, if he picked it up at the Hill and got off the last note ... well, I had to talk to him about it.

So I entered the booth, and he was a nice old guy, and when I told him what was possible, he said he'd have to think it over. "Some people complain that I do it too fast anyway," he said.

Next night the press box was poised. Everyone who owned a stopwatch had it out. John came through. He took the Hill at a gallop and gunned it at the end and, when he cut off the last note, the readout was 51.0. A big cheer went up among the writers, and I dashed into the organist's booth to congratulate him.

"Mr. Kiley," I said, so choked with emotion I could barely speak. "This is a very big moment for me."

"Well, son," he said, "I must admit I was thinking of you."

No instrumental nor band rendition ever has beaten Kiley's time. Vocals are another matter because ego figures in here. I'm still waiting for my first sub-one-minute vocal. I guarantee that if someone posted one, it would generate plenty of cheers because the song would gain immeasurable power. I used to love to cover Canadiens games up in Montreal if only to hear Roger Doucet, that legendary little barrel-chested Frenchman with the white hair, belt out "O Canada" in French. Brought the house down. I mean, people would cry when he finished that song. And it never ran longer than 47 or 48 seconds. Right, I know, different anthem and all that, but the punch is gone when you have to listen to anything too long.

The fastest singer I've ever heard was an operatic chap named Sam Hagen (I think he was a basso, but I'm not sure) who turned in a 1:03.4 before a 1977 Rams-Falcons game in Atlanta's Fulton County Stadium. And he hit the turn in 27.5 seconds, which had me dreaming of a sub-one-minute job, but he died on the Hill.

A few years later, I was at a Bears game in Soldier Field and I got to the press box around three hours before kickoff. Some woman was rehearsing the national anthem on the field. No, I don't remember her name offhand and I'm not going to go look it up because this is a depressing story. She was doing 1:05 practice runs without breaking a sweat. I got down to the field in a hurry.

"Look," I told her, "just pick it up a little at the turn and don't hold any notes at the end and you can break one minute. It would be a record. I've never seen it done." Foolish idiot that I was, I didn't see Bears owner Mike McCaskey lurking nearby. He heard everything.

"Never mind about any records," he told her. "You sing the national anthem the way it's supposed to be sung." So she came in at 1:05. In the press box, I smacked myself in the head so hard that people jumped at the sound.

New York Metropolitan Opera baritone Robert Merrill has been a fixture at Yankee games in the stadium for years. He regularly clocked in at 1:10-1:12, nothing exciting either way. It would be exceedingly quick for a rock star, since they drag the song out to ungodly lengths, but about average for an operatic voice since the serious singers are more concerned with musical correctness than ego. Then I covered a World Series game in 1981, and on opening night he came in at 1:17.8.

I saw him after the game in the press lounge, having a drink.

"Going Hollywood because it's the World Series, huh?" I said in my tactful way.

"Waddya mean?"

"Well, you came in almost at 1:18 and you're a regular 1:10-1:12." The guy went bonkers on me.

"Like you really know about singing, right? Like you really know anything about music?" And on and on. I just shrugged, but next night, once again, the guys had their watches out in the press box. He clocked 1:07 flat.

Five minutes later he came into the press box. "What was I?" he asked me. I told him 1:07.

"Awriiiight!" he yelled, pumping his fist in the air.

The longest one I ever clocked was Leola Giles — 2:34.8 at an Oakland Raiders game. People were groaning. I think some fans passed out while the song was going on. It was an awful, awful thing to listen to.

Once, in a New York Knicks locker room, I heard Walt Frazier telling someone about the great national anthem he heard Aretha Franklin sing. He said it lasted four minutes. I immediately jumped into the conversation.

"No national anthem in history ever lasted four minutes," I told him. "The fans wouldn't let it happen. It would be so weird that they'd hoot it off the stage before it was finished."

"Four minutes, man," he said. "I heard it."

"Yeah, but you didn't time it," I said, realizing how ridiculous that sounded, but so did his four-minute thing sound ridiculous, at least to me. Just try dragging it out for four minutes and see what you've got.

The famous Whitney Houston national anthem at the Giants-Bills Super Bowl in Tampa — the one everybody talked about because it was so stirring — clocked out at 1:41.4, a little long for a popular entertainer but nothing exciting. In this last Super Bowl, I got Beyonce Knowles at 2:01.7. That was at the game, live.

But when I shut down my stopwatch, one guy sitting behind me said, "Look, her mouth is still open." Damned if he wasn't right. She was holding the final note. And holding it. And I blew it.

When I got home, I prayed that I'd set my tape machine early, to catch the national anthem. I had, thank God. Her real time was 2:09.7, a long, long Super Bowl national anthem. She had held the last note for a full eight seconds. Some people think this kind of stuff is just great. Personally, I can't stand it. Give me that nice 43-second "To Anacreon in Heaven" without all that mooing and hooing and "Oh-oh-oh-oh say-ay-ay-ay?"

But I guess most people don't agree with me, at least the ones who think I'm nuts. "Or something."

Acknowledgments

I wish there were a clever way for Paul and me to say thanks to so many friends and family who have helped us through this unnerving ordeal ... some way to truly express our gratitude ... but words fail.

We are left with only a continued heartfelt thanks to:

Peter King — without Peter's tenacity and support Paul's memoirs would never have made it to print. Peter and his remarkable wife Ann, were the first to arrive at the hospital ... their welcoming arms were a haven and they continue to provide us strength.

Arthur Frank ... Artie, as Paul has called him since meeting him at Columbia in 1954. Arthur has guided us through all the turmoil and has continuously been there for every question that needed answering. He is the brother that Paul has always wanted!

Art Rooney Jr., you have showered Paul with postcards, candy and Florida sunshine citrus for the last eight years. You bring light into Paul's life.

Kim Wood, you quietly send the world to Paul in your sports-studded packages ... you are a gem.

Coach Vermeil's generous supply of his fabulous wines.

Ken Rogers of NFL Films ... thanks for the incredible gift of including Paul in your Emmy Award. You are brightly carrying Steve Sabol's torch.

Sarah, Heather, Nathan and Michael ... our four children who greatly miss Paul's large presence.

My sister Gail ... I could never make it through without your constant love and support.

Barbara Neibart ... the Friday night martinis are a must.

Susie and Mary ... my other two musketeers, you are the link to my santity.

We are also extremely grateful to all the NFL owners, coaches, staff ... fans ... friends and foes who have donated to Paul's rehabilitation and care. You will never know how much it has eased our daily burden!

Thanks Triumph Books ... You have put a crowning touch on Dr. Z's career.

— Linda Bailey Zimmerman